PRAISE FOR *The 13th Disciple*

"Deepak Chopra is such a treasure. Once again he illuminates, opening our imaginations to possibilities beyond any we have visited before. *The 13th Disciple* is a riveting tapestry of ideas, woven by one of the great voices of our time."

—Marianne Williamson

"Deepak Chopra never ceases to amaze me. If you know him for his wise advice on health, wellness, and spirituality, let him also astound you with his vivid imagination and skillful narrative."

—Maria Shriver

"Deepak is both my medical doctor and my spiritual mentor. There is no one whose advice I prize more highly. Over the years, he has been a source of immense happiness for me, and . . . he can be one for you as well."

—Wayne Dyer

"A renowned physician and author, Deepak Chopra is undoubtedly one of the most lucid and inspired philosophers of our times."

—Mikhail Gorbachev

"Deepak Chopra is among the influential scholars, authors, and thinkers—like Arthur Schopenhauer, Carl Jung, and Aldous Huxley—who have found truth in the Perennial Philosophy and developed ways to help people apply that truth to their daily lives."

—Huston Smith

DEEPAK CHOPRA

THE *13th* DISCIPLE

A SPIRITUAL ADVENTURE

HarperOne
An Imprint of HarperCollinsPublishers

HarperOne

HarperCollins books may be purchased for educational, business, or sales promotional use. For information please e-mail the Special Markets Department at SPsales@harpercollins.com.

HarperCollins website: http://www.harpercollins.com

FIRST HARPERCOLLINS PAPERBACK EDITION PUBLISHED IN 2016

Designed by Ralph Fowler

Library of Congress Cataloging-in-Publication Data is available upon request.

ISBN 978–0–06–224142–9

16 17 18 19 20   RRD(H)   10 9 8 7 6 5 4 3 2 1

CONTENTS

part one

THE
MYSTERY
SCHOOL

CHAPTER 1

It was a morning without sunrise, frigid and overcast, during the weeks leading up to Christmas. Mare was just heading out to work when her cell phone jingled. Her mother was calling.

"Sister Margaret Thomas just died."

"Who?" The question came out as a garbled mumble. Mare was washing down the last bite of a raspberry Pop-Tart with the dregs of her instant coffee. The last few crystals left dark smears at the bottom of the cup.

Her mother replied impatiently, "Your Aunt Meg, the nun. I'm very upset."

There was silence on the line for a moment. Mare's aunt had been out of the picture for a long time.

"Mare, are you there?" Not waiting for an answer, her mother went on. "The convent won't tell me how she died. They just said she's gone. Gone? Meg was barely fifty. I need you to go out there for me."

"Why can't you go?"

Mare resented her mother for various reasons. One was the fact that she never ran out of demands, most of them trivial and meaningless. Making a demand was like tugging an invisible apron string.

The voice on the phone turned wheedling. "You know I'm afraid of nuns."

"Meg was your sister."

"Don't be silly. It's the other nuns I'm afraid of. They're like scary penguins. Sign something so they can release the body. We're all she has—had." Her mother started crying softly. "Bring my dear sister home. Can you do that?"

Because no one had spoken of Aunt Meg in years, "dear sister" sounded a little insincere. But the job Mare was heading for was temp work, easy to call in sick for.

"I'll do what I can," she said.

Soon she was driving west on the turnpike, half listening to a James Taylor album that came out twenty years ago, about the time her rattling Honda Civic was born. The Great Recession had stalled a career that Mare hadn't actually chosen yet. Like others in her generation, she was drifting, worrying from month to month that she might have to move back in with her parents. That would mean choosing between them. Her mother stayed in the old house after the divorce. Her father relocated to Pittsburgh with his new wife and remembered to call on Christmas and birthdays, usually.

She glanced at herself in the rearview mirror, noticing a scarlet smudge where she'd been careless with her lipstick. *Why did she think nuns would want her to wear makeup?*

Before she ran off to the convent, Aunt Meg used to wear the most stunning shade of lipstick, a dark burgundy red; it contrasted with her pale Irish skin like a drop of wine on a linen tablecloth. There was no question Meg was a looker. She had high cheekbones and that elegant McGeary nose, their proudest feature. She hadn't turned into an old maid for any particular reason. (Meg liked the term "old maid," because it was so outdated and politically incorrect.) Men had vaguely drifted in and out of her life. "I've had my chances, don't you worry," she said tartly.

She even frequented singles bars in the day. "Nasty places," Meg said. "Soul killing."

Nobody remembered her as being especially religious, so it had come as a surprise, and not the pleasant kind, when Aunt Meg suddenly announced, at the ripe age of forty, that she was becoming a nun. She had had enough of her family role as the oldest unmarried sister, being on call to babysit, expected to shop and tend house whenever somebody fell sick, listening to nieces gossiping about their boyfriends before suddenly drawing up short and saying, with embarrassment, "I'm sorry, Aunt Meg. We can talk about something else."

It made the family feel guilty when she announced that she had asked to train as a novice. There was a nagging sense of *What did we do wrong?* Mare's grandmother had died of stomach cancer two years before. If her grandmother had ever held strong religious convictions, months of excruciating pain wiped them away. She didn't ask for Father Riley at the end, but she didn't resist when he showed up at her sickroom. Doped up on morphine, she was barely aware of the wafer and the wine as he lifted her head off the pillow for the Eucharist. Nobody knew whether to be glad that Gran hadn't lived to see the day a McGeary girl took the veil.

Mare's grandfather was adrift in lonely grief after his wife died, retreating into his house and keeping the lights off well past sunset. He mowed the front lawn every Saturday, but the weeds in the backyard grew rank and tall, like a cursed woods guarding a castle of sorrows. When Meg knocked at the door and told him she was entering the convent, he became more animated than he had been in months.

"Don't give yourself away. You're still good-looking, Meg. Lots of men would be proud to have you."

"Don't be such a fool," Meg retorted, blushing. She kissed him on the top of the head. "But thank you."

In the end, she shocked everyone by simply disappearing one night to join a strict Carmelite order that was completely cloistered. She wasn't going to be one of those modern nuns who wore street clothes and picked up some arugula at the supermarket. Once the doors of the convent shut behind her, Meg was never seen again. She left her apartment untouched, the furniture all in place, waiting patiently for a return that would never occur. Her dresses hung neatly in the closet, giving off the forlorn air of things turned useless.

Mare was eighteen when her aunt pulled this vanishing act. "The flight into Egypt," her mother called it, sounding bitter and neglected. "Not one real good-bye."

Being a big family didn't protect them from feeling the hole where Meg once had been. It seemed vaguely sinister that she never wrote or called for ten years. They hadn't heard anything until Mare's mother received the news that Sister Margaret Thomas, the ghost of someone they had known, was gone.

The convent was remote and not listed in the phone book, but GPS knew where to find it. "Turn left in three hundred yards," the voice advised. Mare took the turnoff; after another half mile through some overgrown woodland of pine and birch she slowed down. The convent grounds were protected by a high wrought-iron fence. The road ended at a gate flanked by a deserted sentry box. There was a rusty squawk box for visitors to announce themselves on.

Mare felt the awkwardness of her situation. How do you say you're here for a body? She raised her voice, as if the squawk box might be deaf.

"I'm here for Sister Margaret Thomas. I'm her niece."

No one answered; the box didn't even crackle. A moment passed, and Mare began to think she'd have to turn back. Then with a click the iron gate slowly swung open. She drove through.

In the distance sat a redbrick mansion, drearily Victorian under the gray sky. The old Honda's tires crunched on the gravel. Mare felt increasingly nervous, her mind flashing on Dickens and orphans without enough gruel to eat. The mansion was the real orphan, rescued by the church after it became a stately wreck.

Going up the long driveway to the convent, Mare brought her mind back to what she had to do. The woodland along the way was overgrown, but the grounds skirting the mansion were threadbare, stripped of the fountains and shrubbery that once adorned them. The place was probably built by a ruthless tycoon at a time when such immense piles were "summer cottages," serviced by their own private railway spur.

She parked her car at the end of the driveway and approached the front door. A stern hand-lettered sign hung next to the doorbell: "Silence is observed between vespers and terce. Do not disturb."

Terce? Mare couldn't remember what frighteningly early hour of the morning this meant—it made her shiver to imagine the nuns' bare penitent feet hitting cold stone floors before dawn. She rang the bell. After a reluctant moment she was buzzed in, just as anonymously as at the front gate. Cautiously she entered, allowing her eyes to adjust to the sudden drop in light. She found herself in a grand foyer. On one wall was a niche with a statue of the Virgin. Straight ahead a stout metal grill, divided into four-inch squares, blocked the way. The openings let visitors peer at the inhabitants without getting too close. The effect was a cross between a zoo and a jail.

In this case there was nobody to peer at. Mare took a seat on a rickety visitor's chair with a sagging cane bottom and waited. She began to worry that a nun would swoop down to scold her for dropping out of parochial school after the fifth grade, as if every sister in the area had gotten the guilty news. She gazed at the sweeping staircase on the other side of the grill. When the place was a rich man's country retreat, those stairs had felt the pumps of satin-gowned debutantes skipping down to meet their beaus, she thought idly.

More time passed. The silence felt eerie and alien. The Carmelite order is unworldly, devoted solely to the rule of "prayer and toil." Mare had found a YouTube video about it. The nuns in the video smiled a lot. They greeted the interviewer from behind a metal screen like the one Mare was sitting at. The brash interviewer asked, "How long have you been behind bars?" The nuns laughed. As far as they were concerned, they were living on the right side of the bars.

Mare glanced at her watch. She had been there less than five minutes. *Let's get this over with,* she thought. It was sad, but trying to recapture Meg as she once was seemed pointless.

At last there was a soft tapping sound as a nun came downstairs—slowly, not swooping—and moved toward the visitor across a wide expanse of marble floor. She couldn't have been more than twenty. Mare had read that convents were having a hard time finding new members and were steadily growing older. Death was thinning the ranks.

"Sorry to keep you waiting," the young nun apologized with a shy smile. She didn't seem like the scolding type. She smelled faintly of laundry soap and Clorox. Her small hands were scrubbed red and raw; she hid them inside the sleeves of her habit when Mare noticed them. Mare resisted the impulse to cross herself.

"I've come about Sister Margaret Thomas," she said. Her nerves made her speak too loudly, creating an echo in the big empty space.

"Ah," said the young nun, who looked Hispanic and spoke with an accent. She had stopped smiling.

"I'm her niece," Mare added.

"I see."

The sister averted her eyes. Her face, encircled by a brown and white cowl, remained friendly, but it was giving nothing away.

Mare cleared her throat. "I don't know your procedures when somebody dies. It was very sudden, a shock."

"What do you mean?" The sister looked genuinely confused.

"You don't know? We got a phone message that Sister Margaret Thomas, my aunt, was gone. I'm here to claim the body. So if there are papers for me to sign, and if you have the number of a local funeral home . . ." Mare's voice trailed off.

Now the sister became alarmed. The faint roses in her soft cheeks suddenly turned pale. "That's not possible. You see—"

Mare cut her off. "You can't keep her and not notify the authorities."

"What? If you'll let me finish." The young nun raised both hands, asking for patience.

But Mare was getting suspicious. "She's not yours to just stick in the ground. How did she die anyway?" Mare tried to sound irate, but a doubt crossed her mind. Maybe the convent had legal possession of anyone who died in the order.

The sister wrung her hands. "Please, stop. Your aunt's not here anymore. She's gone. The whole thing's a misunderstanding."

A light came on in Mare's brain. "My mother assumed that 'gone' meant 'dead.'"

"No. Yesterday Sister Margaret Thomas didn't appear for terce, and her room was empty. We were very worried. We left a message at the only contact number on file. Our interaction with the outside world is minimal. That's the rule we live by. Are you Catholic?"

Mare nodded. She felt ridiculous and started to mumble an apology, but the young nun went on, her accent getting stronger. It took an effort for her not to get emotional.

"Margaret Thomas was our sister. She belonged to Christ, not to her family. But when a sister suddenly doesn't appear for prayers and her room is deserted, *Dios mio,* we felt obliged to tell someone."

"So she simply left, and you don't know where she went?"

"Exactly. Forgive us. We didn't intend to hurt your heart."

"All right. There's nothing to forgive." Mare wanted to ease the distress of the sister, who seemed very vulnerable in her homespun brown habit and with her raw, red hands. But she was also curious.

"Just one thing. Can I see her room?"

"Oh dear. I'm afraid that won't be possible." Unable to hide her agitation, the sister suddenly turned to leave. She felt bad, but rules are rules. No one was getting past the screen.

Mare called after her. "What about her personal things? If she left any, I want to claim them. You said you didn't want to hurt my heart."

It felt manipulative to throw the young woman's words back at her, but Mare knew her mother wouldn't settle for "She's gone." One vanishing act from Aunt Meg was the limit.

The retreating sister didn't turn around. "Wait here," she muttered.

She scurried upstairs, and the grand foyer returned to silence. After a moment a new nun appeared on the sweeping staircase, which was beginning to look in Mare's eyes like a Hollywood prop fabricated solely for grand entrances. The new nun was older, perhaps seventy, and the habit that concealed her from head to toe like a brown cocoon couldn't disguise her arthritic gait. She looked unsteady as she dealt with the heavy cardboard box she was carrying in her hands. Padding across the marble floor toward the screen, the old nun nodded at an opening off to one side. It was just large enough to allow the cardboard box to slide through.

"That's all there is, I'm afraid," said the old nun. She was panting slightly, her upper lip moist from exertion. Like the young sister, she didn't introduce herself. Her eyes had remained downcast when Mare tried to look into them. Unlike the young sister, she gave off no waves of sympathy.

Mare mumbled a thank-you, but the old nun had already turned away.

It was time to vacate the eeriness. Mare lifted the box, which was bound in layers of packing tape. Although less than a foot square, the parcel felt as if it contained lead weights. There was a white envelope taped to the top in place of a label.

After she returned to the gray light outside and drew a breath of sharp winter air, Mare's head started to clear. Each step she took toward her car made her feel a little less hazy, as if she was waking up from a narcotic medieval spell. Her hand was on the handle of the car door, now frosted with flakes of snow, before she realized all the questions she had failed to ask.

She'd learned nothing about her aunt's last days in the convent. Had she left the cloister sick or well? Was she disgruntled? Were there signs of mental disturbance? Mare had read about old monks breaking decades of silence, only to reveal that they were insane, driven into hopeless psychosis by their fixation on God.

Suddenly she felt an ache in her wrists from toting the heavy parcel. Getting in the car, she dumped it beside her on the passenger seat. Snow was falling thick enough to blanket the windshield, turning the interior into a twilit cave. She turned on the windshield wipers and checked the radio for weather warnings. The morning forecast said a blizzard would arrive late in the day. Now it was barely two o'clock. The storm had swept in early.

Bald snow tires gave Mare a reason to rush back to the turnpike, but she sat there, gazing blankly at the hypnotic swipe of the windshield wipers. Then the parcel caught her eye, like an object of wonder. The right to open it really belonged to her grandfather, since Meg was his daughter and he was next of kin. But

Mare now saw that the envelope taped to the top wasn't blank. A message was scrawled in a fine spidery hand.

For You

Who was "you"? None of the sisters thought it meant them, or they would have opened the package. If Mare hadn't shown up, the box might have remained sealed and silent forever. Did Aunt Meg anticipate that "you" was certain to arrive? Mare reached over and tore away the envelope, which was affixed to the parcel with a scrap of Scotch tape. There was no one to tell her not to snoop.

There was a crisply folded note inside. Carefully she opened it, reading what was written in the same spidery hand.

Hello, Mare,

This is from the thirteenth disciple. Follow where it leads.

Yours in Christ,
Meg

CHAPTER 2

Of all the ways to change the world, Frank Weston would never have picked bringing back miracles. First, he wasn't superstitious, and in his mind a miracle was just a superstition that enough gullible people believed in. Second, and more important, he was a reporter, and journalism is a career dependent on facts. (There's an old saying in journalism: "If your mother tells you she loves you, get a second source.") A miracle was the opposite of a fact.

But then the possibility of miracles entered his life through a side door: death.

One day a woman stood in front of Frank's desk.

"Excuse me," she asked. "Are you the obituaries man?"

Frank spoke without looking up from the copy he was editing.

"Down the hallway, second door on the right. Only he's not in. He's out on a story."

His lean, rangy body was sprawled in the battered lounge chair he'd dragged into the newsroom from his shambolic bachelor apartment. His face was hidden under the scooped visor of a baseball cap.

The woman wasn't to be put off. "Can you help me then? It's urgent."

Frank was on a tight deadline, so he had no intention of help-
ing her, or anyone. But he knew he should at least look up before
blowing the woman off.

"Mare?" he said, suddenly surprised.

He almost hadn't recognize her. She was swaddled up for
winter. She'd pulled a woolen cap down over her forehead against
the cold and wrapped a gray muffler high on her chin. Her eyes
were hidden behind oversized sunglasses. But Frank remembered
those eyes. He could still picture them—it didn't matter how
many years had passed.

"You look like a double agent in all that gear, but it has to
be you."

Mare took off the sunglasses, confused. Her eyes blinked in the
harsh newsroom lighting. She clearly didn't remember him.

"This is awkward," said Frank, taking off the baseball cap so
she could get a better look. "It's Frank, from college. Brendan's
roommate?"

He had stirred a memory. "Oh, God. Brendan. We were
freshmen. I only looked him up because our parish priest told me
I should."

"Really? You made quite an impression. He talked about you
all the time. And now I know why."

Being tall and self-confident, Frank had gotten into the habit
of saying whatever he thought. He tried to ignore Mare's slight
flinch.

"Sorry, I meant it as a compliment."

When she didn't respond, he thought about apologizing again,
but decided against it. Instead he said, "What's this about an
obituary?"

Her eyes, which were large and brown, betrayed anxiety. "I
shouldn't be bothering you."

"No, it's okay. We're just short-staffed at the moment."

A nasty flu had taken out two reporters, and Malcolm, the regular obituaries writer, had rushed out to follow up a lead on a breaking story.

Frank straightened up in his chair. "Do you want to submit an obit? I can pass it on. Malcolm will get to it once he's back in the office. I can't promise it will be today." As he said all this, he kept wishing that Mare would remember him.

She shook her head. "I don't want to put in an obituary. I want to take one out."

"I'm sorry. Someone died by mistake?" He meant to be funny, but she didn't smile.

"No. I just don't think anybody needs to know about my aunt's death."

Frank flipped to a new screen on the iPad he used for writing stories. "If it was a private death notice . . ."

"It was. My mother submitted it this morning." Mare bit her lip nervously. "You have to cancel it."

"Like I said, all I can do is pass on the message."

Mare's face fell, and the corners of her mouth started to tremble. He saw how important this was to her.

"Wait, let me call down," he said.

He got hold of the head typographer, who wasn't thrilled. The obits page was already set. Frank did a little arm twisting. "I owe you one," he said and hung up. He directed a triumphant smile at Mare. "Done."

Her eyes lit up, and Frank watched the tension melt from her body, even though she was wearing a puffy down coat.

"Now maybe you can sit down?" he said.

She wavered, her eyes glancing at the door, but she took a seat on the other battered chair in the cubicle, unwrapping the gray muffler. She removed the stocking cap, and her light brunette hair fell close to her shoulders. "I think I'd better have some water," she said.

He fetched a paper cup of water from the office cooler, surprised at how quick he was to please her. *What did it mean?* He didn't know, but he wanted to find out.

Mare sipped the water and went quiet. Frank figured he had about thirty seconds before she took off again.

"I almost didn't remember your name," he said. "I've never known anyone named Mare." He had to start somewhere besides dying relatives.

"I get that a lot. It's short for Ann Marie," she replied absently, glancing at her watch.

Unless Frank called on his renowned powers of invention, she'd be out of his life again. "I'd like to see you," he blurted out. "When nobody's dead. Or not dead."

She sat back and crumpled the empty paper cup in her hand. She was pondering the situation, the way a hitchhiker wonders whether it's safe to get in a car. She made a calculation in her mind, and it must have come out in his favor.

"I have a secret, and I need to tell somebody. Not a complete stranger, I mean."

So she did remember him, however vaguely. When his roommate had aroused Frank's curiosity, he had wangled a seat behind her in a psych class. There were two hundred students in the room, but Frank must have made an impression.

"You can't trust a stranger," Frank said.

Mare nodded nervously. "But I have to talk to somebody. My family wouldn't understand. They'd probably call the police."

"Sounds ominous."

"No, it's not like a crime or anything."

She looked ready to take back her decision to trust him. Frank kept quiet. He had been a reporter long enough to know he couldn't press her.

She took a deep breath. "My aunt left a cardboard box behind when she died. It was sealed with packing tape and addressed to me. What I found inside is disturbing."

Her pale hands fiddled with the dangling ends of her muffler. She bit her lip again, an unconscious tic, he figured.

"I'm pretty sure it must be stolen. That's why I don't want to announce her death. Not until I find out."

"What is it?"

"A church. Or maybe a cathedral. I can't tell which."

Mare saw the look on his face and caught herself. "A miniature church, I mean." Her hands made a shape in the air about nine inches around. "It looks old, and it seems to be made of gold."

"Wow."

"It's quite lovely, actually." Mare leaned forward, lowering her voice. "My aunt had no money. But in a way, I wasn't surprised. She was a nun."

"An order of nuns is into stealing?" Frank smiled indulgently.

Mare didn't smile back. "No, she was a Carmelite, but rebellious. She left the order very suddenly, probably under a cloud—at least I think so. We weren't close."

She was on the verge of telling him more, but something stopped her. "Why am I saying this to a reporter?"

"Because I'm the first person you actually know. Sort of know," said Frank.

"Maybe." But Mare wasn't reassured. Just the opposite. Her mental image of Frank was vague, a face in a crowded classroom that only stood out because he wore bright red suspenders. It took cockiness to do that. The last thing she needed right now was a cocky boy pretending to be a responsible adult.

She stood up, holding out a gloved hand. "Never mind. It's not your problem."

Frank didn't take her hand. "You have to go?" It was obvious the scales had swung against his favor.

"I'm late already. Thanks for keeping the death notice out of the paper."

Frank frowned. "I might be out of line, but you could be in real trouble. I don't have to be a reporter, you know. I can just be somebody who's ready to help. And I can keep a secret," he added.

"Really?" A smile crept into Mare's voice, despite her anxiety. The way Frank looked at her wasn't subtle. "Is this about wanting to see me again?"

"Is that so bad?" He made as if to straighten the necktie he wasn't wearing. "I'm presentable."

She took a moment to think about this. "Maybe we could go out for coffee. Now, if you can take a break. I'd be more comfortable someplace else."

Frank followed her eyes across the surrounding cubicles. There were about five reporters in the newsroom, where once there had been twice as many. The firing squad hadn't picked Frank off yet, but anyone could be next. After five-thirty, he and a few coworkers would grab a drink and complain about how they hadn't gotten a raise in two years, even though none of them dared to ask for one.

Frank snapped the cover on his iPad. "Now is perfect," he said, mentally kissing his deadline good-bye.

After throwing on his peacoat and leading Mare outside, Frank saw that it was snowing hard. The city was no stranger to the Arctic vortex, even before it became famous. The wind howled from the northeast, and the new snowfall added a layer of white frosting to the brown old snow piled up at the curb. He took Mare's arm, and they crossed the slippery street to the diner where Frank ate half his meals. For the first time that day, he felt good.

A minute later they were settled in a booth at the back of the diner. Mare scanned the menu silently, and then ordered a Greek yogurt with fruit salad. Frank ordered coffee, black.

When the waitress was gone, Mare smiled, looking directly at Frank. Confessing seemed to have calmed her nerves. Her eyes were like still pools no longer ruffled by the wind. *They are the most beautiful thing about her,* Frank thought, distracted for a moment.

"I'll tell you the whole story," Mare said, "and then I can show you what my aunt gave me. I tucked it in the laundry hamper in my closet. I really hope it's not stolen, but it must be."

"Maybe she was just guarding it," Frank suggested. "The Catholic Church has a lot of treasures."

"Maybe."

Mare lost her smile. But she didn't object when Frank took out a spiral notebook and began taking notes. Her story was as strange as promised. He ordered two refills of coffee before she finished telling it. Halfway through, he had already decided that her aunt was either a saint or a nut who needed to be put on stronger meds. Either way, Frank was pretty certain he could rule out archcriminal.

CHAPTER *3*

Mare's eyes took in her cramped studio apartment. "Sorry for how it looks," she said.

A dangling naked lightbulb was covered with a Japanese paper lantern to soften its glare. The room held a few sticks of Ikea furniture, a tired mustard yellow sofa handed down from better decades, and a framed poster of a scared kitty dangling from a branch (the ubiquitous one that says, "Hang in There"). On the far wall was a closed door. Frank suspected a Murphy bed was lurking behind it, since there was no bed in sight.

Mare followed Frank's glance to the poster. "Not mine. I'd take it down, but it was a gift."

She kept the place tidy, what there was of it. All she could afford was a converted basement in an old triple-decker that started life as an Irish boarding house. Mare's apologies had started at the curb before she and Frank even entered the yard enclosed by a chain-link fence. Withered junipers did nothing to beautify the sagging wreck of a building. Self-consciously, she led the way down a set of creaky stairs off the side of the house. Their shoes punched through the crusted old snow that no one had shoveled from the walk.

She shouldn't have bothered with her apologies. At the moment the only thing on Frank's mind was seeing the miniature church she had hidden in a laundry hamper. Somebody had gone to the expense of gilding it, or even making it out of solid gold. Frank suspected there might be something locked inside that was even more precious to a believer. What do you call the receptacle that holds a saint's bones? A reliquary. It would border on blasphemy, but he wanted to hold the little church up to his ear and shake it. The sacred bones inside, if that's what was hiding there, would rattle, unless they had already crumbled to dust.

As long as he was speculating, what about the incidental mysteries that swirled around Mare? Why had her mother put a death notice in the paper? She had no real evidence her sister was dead, just a cryptic phone message from the convent.

Frank had put this question to Mare on the ride across town. All she did was shake her head and say, "You don't know what she's like. My mother always assumes the worst."

"But your aunt is out there somewhere. You told her that, right?"

"Yes. I told her everything I told you, except about the box."

At every red light, Mare's car had skidded on the icy streets. Frank was a bad passenger; he held a tight grip on the door handle to keep from grabbing the wheel.

"Maybe the wish is father of the deed," he suggested.

Mare gave him a puzzled glance. "What's that supposed to mean?"

Another skid zone was coming up at the next corner, where a big furniture truck was sliding halfway through the yellow light.

"Just keep us alive, okay?" Frank said. "I meant that if your mother resented her sister vanishing like that ten years ago, she might not be thrilled to have her back."

"So she makes her dead?"

"I'm just thinking out loud. Where do you suppose your aunt would go? You should have pumped the nuns for information."

"Says the man who has so much experience pumping nuns for information. Have you ever tried?"

"Point taken."

Other questions were on the tip of Frank's tongue, until he remembered his promise not to act like a reporter. He kept quiet the rest of the way, and so did Mare. He noticed that her knuckles were turning white seizing the steering wheel. One step at a time, he told himself.

Inside her apartment, Mare tossed some shoes aside in the bottom of her closet and brought out a laundry hamper. A dirty sheet was on top, ready to be pulled back like a stage curtain.

"Once you see it, you're kind of complicit, aren't you?" Mare asked.

"In a way, I guess. Assuming we don't turn it over to the police."

"Yes, assuming that."

Frank caught a new note in her voice. She had sounded guilty and furtive, but this was something different. Greed, was it? But that would be understandable. The fantasy of finding buried gold was part of growing up, and now it had pretty much come true for her. How far would she go to keep it? Before revealing the treasure to him, she could still change her mind, and the gold's secret would be safe.

Mare hadn't turned back, though. She stood over the laundry hamper, and with a whisk she lifted the sheet, revealing the reliquary. It looked exactly like a miniature church. If the naked lightbulb hadn't had a paper lantern on it, the gleam of pure gold would have hurt their eyes. The object was the size of a loaf of bread. Even hollow, it would be heavy.

"Who's going to lift it out?" Frank asked.

"I'll let you, if that's okay."

Frank wrapped his hands around the miniature church, and as the object emerged from its hiding place, he could see how beautiful it was, carefully wrought on all sides with etched flourishes, tiny flowers, and a border of summer grass fringing the bottom. The conceit was of a chapel sitting in a meadow. The peaked roof was adorned with gothic steeples at the corners, each one topped with a cross. Delicate enamel medallions were embedded on the four walls, painted with scenes from the life of Jesus.

Frank was too astonished to do anything but make light of it. "As the world's leading art experts would say, 'Wow.'"

They gazed at the treasure. Frank had been raised as a Christmas-Easter churchgoer by his lax Methodist parents (in the vernacular, their kind are called "Chreasters" by the regular congregation), but at that moment he felt what a devout believer must feel: reverence, wonder, awe. *That's the trick of great art,* he thought, and he hadn't the slightest doubt that they were in the presence of great art.

"It must have a home somewhere. Somebody knows it's missing," he murmured, finding it hard not to whisper, as if they were in church. "They would have reported it stolen to the local authorities or the FBI."

He'd read about the thousands of paintings stolen from museums every year and the special agencies that track them down. Not to mention the Nazis and their wholesale looting. They had boosted millions of dollars' worth of artworks from all over Europe to haul back to Hitler's Berlin.

Heavy as it was, the miniature chapel didn't have the weight of a solid object. But Frank was too spellbound to rattle it, even though he still suspected that something precious was locked inside. To true believers, that was the whole point. The gold exterior was just a distraction to dazzle the eyes.

For pilgrims in the Middle Ages, traveling immense distances across Europe in search of relics was a costly and dangerous business. After all the trials and dangers of their journey, when they reached a shrine, they expected to be awed before a holy relic— a piece of the True Cross, the jawbone of John the Baptist, the spear that pierced Jesus's side. There had to be a payoff, and if there weren't enough true relics to go around, well, what better way to convince pilgrims that a dubious relic was authentic than to strike awe with shining gold?

Frank's own sense of awe was quickly yielding to more practical thoughts. "I don't think it's empty," he said. "Did you shake it?"

"No, I couldn't."

"Because it's sacrilege?"

"Isn't it?"

"We need to get inside," Frank declared firmly.

But how? It would draw heavy suspicion to try and get the object X-rayed at a museum laboratory, not to mention the expense. There couldn't be many machines that can see through gold. And what would the faint ghostly image of some old bones really tell them? Frank's impatience grew. He was about to shake the reliquary without her permission when Mare touched his hand.

"I suddenly had the strangest feeling. There's someone sleeping inside it. I can feel it."

"And you don't think we should wake them up?"

"Something like that."

Frank shook his head. "Let's assume for the moment that your idea isn't crazy. We don't know if waking them up is good or bad."

"It wouldn't matter. Not if they are meant to sleep."

Before he could respond, the gate in the chain-link fence clinked, and a shadow passed across the room's only window, which was small and high up, letting in a feeble light from the outside. Someone was approaching. If they burst in, the first thing they'd see would be a man kneeling on the floor surrounded by five pairs of women's shoes and a woman turning red, her hand clapped over her mouth with embarrassment. It wasn't the time to wake the sleeping or the dead.

"Hurry!" Mare exclaimed.

Frank dropped the reliquary back into the hamper, and she threw the sheet back over it. Was she about to be arrested for having it in her possession?

"Wait, don't talk. Listen," said Frank.

Click, click, click. A woman's light, tapping step. It was unmistakable. The police wouldn't be storming the place in high heels. Frank had no time to wonder what kind of woman wears stilettos in the snow.

A very irritated woman, it turned out. There was a sharp rap at the door. Mare opened it nervously. The intruder on their privacy was tall and in her sixties, her graying hair pulled back tightly from her face, which at that moment wore an impatient grimace.

"I won't ask if you have come into possession of a package," she said. "You'd probably just lie." Her voice was clipped and efficient, the kind of voice that meant business.

Mare couldn't hide her nerves. "Who are you?"

"Miss Marple. Perhaps you've heard of me."

"What?"

"My name is Lilith. That's enough for now. I'd advise you to let me in."

Mare gave a weak nod and stepped aside. Lilith looked around the modest apartment with a critical eye.

"You never know where you'll wind up, do you?" she murmured, addressing no one in particular. For the moment she ignored Frank, who stood in front of the open closet.

"Your Aunt Meg is alive," she said. "But you've probably figured that out already, haven't you?"

"What do you have to do with her?" asked Mare.

Lilith thought for a moment. "I'm a connection, just as she is. That's one way to put it." She plopped herself down on the mustard yellow couch, which gave a tired groan. "When your aunt disappeared from the convent, something precious disappeared with her."

"Then you'd have to ask her about that," Mare replied.

"Don't play coy. The trail leads here and nowhere else."

Mare lowered her head, and Lilith's eyes narrowed.

"That's what I thought," she said before turning her attention to Frank.

"And you are who? The boyfriend?"

"Imagine what you like," he replied.

She shrugged. "No. You're not the boyfriend. She's clearly nervous, but you didn't rush in to help her or even put your arm around her. A boyfriend would have."

"No comment."

"Why can't he just be a friend?" Mare asked.

Lilith smiled knowingly. "Because you did something rash. You invited a strange man into your house. For what reason?"

"None of your business," Frank snapped.

Lilith fixed him with a hard stare. "I'm more likely to figure out your game before this young woman does."

Frank bristled. "There is no game."

"Really? You plan to get the goods and the girl at the same time, or will you have to choose?"

Frank turned red, but before he could deny the accusation, Lilith held up her hand.

"You're right. It's none of my business what you're up to. I'm here about the gold shrine. It holds the key to everything."

Mare had been moving toward the closet, either to guard the treasure or show it to Lilith. Frank couldn't be sure. He shot her a warning glance. If Lilith noticed, she chose to ignore it.

She said, "The trouble is, whoever has the shrine *is* meant to have it. That's the first of the secrets I can tell you." She gave Mare a smile that was almost friendly. "You're the rightful owner, I promise you."

Mare looked so relieved that she would have blurted out everything that had happened since the phone call from the convent, but Frank stopped her. "We're not giving this shrine or whatever it is, just because you deliver a load of mumbo jumbo."

Lilith smirked. "There, that's more like a boyfriend."

Frank changed tack. As a reporter, he'd learned to handle all kinds of difficult people, and his first rule was, you catch more flies with honey than with vinegar.

"Maybe we can work something out," he said.

"We? Who gave you the right to say 'we'?" Mare cried. "I don't really know either of you."

She spoke in a loud, anxious voice, and the other two stared at her. Up to this point she'd played the part of the quiet observer, a shaky fawn caught in a room with two bulls.

"I didn't mean anything," Frank stammered.

"No?" said Mare. She took a deep breath, trying to regain her composure. But her heart was racing. Her body couldn't deny the threat it was feeling.

"You pushed too hard," Lilith said smoothly. "That's what insensitive people do."

She turned to Mare. "And you need to calm down. I'm only here to help."

Lilith brushed stray bits of snow sticking to her high heels. "I appreciate your wariness. We all have to be as sharp-witted as possible from now on. There are invisible forces at work. Do you imagine the gold shrine came to you, or to your Aunt Meg, by accident?"

The atmosphere in the room was still tense, but a subtle shift had taken place. It was now the tenseness of a mystery more than the tenseness of a threat. Lilith took advantage of this. To Frank she said, "You noticed my shoes when I came in. What do they tell you?"

"They tell me that you were doing something else—maybe eating at a fancy restaurant—before you suddenly got the news that brought you here. No time to change."

"So you're a rationalist," Lilith said approvingly. "You reached for a logical explanation. Someone else might assume I was eccentric or out of touch with reality."

"Are you?" Mare asked. She had wandered over to the corner of the studio that served as a kitchen and was holding a battered teakettle under the faucet.

"That's right," said Lilith. "Make tea. It will calm your nerves." Her tone had become less confrontational. "Your mother is still frantic. I apologize, but we can't let her in on any of this. I hope you understand."

"Outside attention would be unwelcome," said Frank.

"Exactly."

Mare turned on the tap, talking over the knocking sound of old plumbing. "But I don't understand. Do you know where my aunt is?"

"She's here in the city."

"Can I see her?"

"Not yet. After all, you haven't wanted to see her for a long time. No need to rush."

Mare went silent, considering what to say next, when her cell phone rang. She went to her purse, pulled it out, and examined the caller ID.

"My sister Charlotte," she said doubtfully.

"Answer it," Lilith advised. "She'll be suspicious if you avoid her."

Mare took the call, and from across the room Frank could hear the angry buzz of her sister's voice. Questions were being jabbed at Mare, which she fended off with short replies. But it wasn't the words that mattered. Frank sensed that they were closing in. He had no idea who "they" were, but his antennae were out, picking up signals. Mare was the innocent; that part wasn't in doubt. Lilith was a wild card, and behind her seemed to loom hidden figures, hinted at but invisible so far.

Mare closed her outdated cell phone with a click, cutting short the conversation. She looked worried.

"You won't be able to keep your nosey sister away for long," Lilith warned.

"But that doesn't mean we should trust you, does it?" Frank snapped.

Mare let the "we" slip past without comment this time. Her bewilderment outweighed her doubts about Frank.

He crossed the room and held her hand. "Don't be scared. We're in the strong position here, just remember that," he said quietly.

"Touching," Lilith remarked. "But you're not allies yet, not by a long shot. The only ally anyone has is tucked away in there." She pointed toward the closet, which had so obviously been the place Mare was anxious to conceal. "One of you is dazzled by the gold, because that person has a crass mind. But one of you is sensitive, and that person will pierce to the heart of the mystery."

She saw the dark expression on Frank's face. "We'll get nowhere fighting. I propose we get down to business instead. Are we agreed?" she asked.

Lilith sat back, waiting while tea bags were put into chipped blue-and-white china cups and water poured in. When the tea was brewed, she began talking.

"This all goes back ten years ago. Your Aunt Meg woke up one morning from a bad dream. It was an unusually cold winter, like this one. Her sleep had been restless. She crawled out of bed, trying to shake off her dream, but she couldn't. It wouldn't let her go. You see, it wasn't a dream at all. It was a vision. She hadn't asked for one. It seems rude of God to interrupt a person's nice, comfortable life with something so inconvenient. But what can you do?"

Frank gave her a disgusted look. "Nobody you can trust hauls in God."

"You sound very bitter," said Lilith calmly. "Did someone hurt you, to make you lose your faith? Or is that something you'd rather keep hidden?"

"None of your damn business!"

Frank threw down his teacup, which missed the table and clattered on the floor. "I don't know who you are. But Mare doesn't deserve to be played by a manipulative bitch."

He turned to Mare for support, but she surprised him.

"I want to hear this out." she said quietly.

"Why? It's garbage."

Mare was firm. "You've gotten yourself worked up. Maybe you should go."

"And leave you with her?" Frank was incredulous. "She'll be on you like a cheap suit."

Mare didn't reply, but got up and walked to the door. Frank grabbed his peacoat and followed, fuming.

"I'll call you tomorrow," Mare said, trying to sound reassuring.

Frank shook his head. "You're going to be sorry. That's all I can say."

He trudged up the rickety stairs, and a moment later his shadow went across the grimy window as he tramped through the snow.

Mare closed the door and returned to where Lilith sat, waiting.

"I need to hear the rest of this," she said. "For my peace of mind."

Lilith shook her head. "No, you need to hear it because God wants the story to come out."

CHAPTER 4

Elsewhere in the city, a man was plotting a supreme act of revenge. To look at him, you'd never credit Galen Blake with violence in his heart. It's true that he wore an outdated badge of the revolution—his round, wire-rimmed glasses, which were known as Trotsky glasses in the Seventies, when Galen went to college.

Little round glasses are associated with Harry Potter now. Galen had vaguely heard of Harry Potter. He preferred fact to fiction, with the exception of science fiction, which Galen consumed in binges, the technical kind of sci-fi where computers and robots rebel against their foolish human masters. He was fifty-six, short, and unassuming. He was a loner, retreating from social contact as predictably as his hairline had retreated after he turned forty.

Loners plan acts of violence for various reasons. Delayed revenge for being bullied on the playground at school. Inner desperation that can't find an outlet. Fantasies of grandiosity. But Galen suffered from none of these. His motive was not clearly formulated in the logical part of his brain. It was swallowed up in the hurt and hate that swirled inside him.

However, the main contenders for Galen's hatred were God and love, the two biggest hoaxes in the world. For a long time he had mistrusted love. He knew early on that this was necessary if he wanted to survive. Young Galen came home from school one day to find his mother standing in the kitchen surrounded by sheets of chocolate chip cookies, warm and fragrant. She sat him down and silently watched him eat as many cookies as he wanted. She offered no warning that gobbling down so much sugar would make him sick. She waited until he could eat no more before telling him the bad news. They were alone; from now on, there would be no more Daddy, because Galen's father had walked out, abandoning them.

Even at ten Galen knew it wasn't healthy to be the only person in his mother's life. She worried about this too, but worry didn't help. She clung to him until she died; Galen was in his thirties. He came home from the funeral, ripping off his black tie and opening his collar so he could breathe. It was a hot July day. He went into the bathroom to splash cold water on his sweaty face.

He caught a glimpse of himself in the mirror over the sink. *You're lucky,* a voice in his head told him. *No more mother. Father gone. You're free.*

The face in the mirror—pale, pudgy, with circles under the eyes—brightened up. *Free!* Galen loved his mother, but she fretted constantly about his being unmarried. "My son's a confirmed bachelor," she told her friends, who took this as code for "gay." Galen wasn't gay. He was just born to be alone, which other people, including his mother, couldn't comprehend. So losing her was like losing one more person who didn't understand.

These sketchy facts might have helped the police after Galen committed his act of revenge. But what do they really say? His worst secret was that he had no secrets.

No one observed his silent plotting. The plan he had in mind was simple, if extreme. It unfolded on a Wednesday, the day the city art museum was open to the public for free. Galen wandered in, mingling with the crowd, staring blankly at the gallery walls as if they were empty. His mind was solely fixed on the task at hand.

He headed upstairs, turning right, then left, before reaching a small, dimly lit gallery on the second floor. It was filled with people craning to see the old masters, but Galen was interested in only one work, a priceless *Madonna and Child* from fifteenth-century Florence.

He paused to take in the painting, loathing what most viewers adored—the rosy, glowing faces of mother and child, those ideal emblems of love. Galen snarled with disgust. The guard standing in the doorway turned her back for a moment. With a small inconspicuous motion Galen reached into his overcoat and pulled out a can of red spray paint. He stepped forward.

"Hey!" somebody yelled.

Galen sped up until he was directly in front of the masterwork, aiming the nozzle at the smiling, chubby baby Jesus. The visitor who yelled out took a dive for him. Galen only finished spraying a single letter, *L,* before he was tackled and pinned to the floor.

"Crazy bastard," muttered the man who had knocked Galen down. He was a middle-aged tourist from Michigan, burly enough to have probably played college football. At that second it wasn't clear if he swore because he loved art or because the red paint had hit his jacket, which now had a large *L* on it. Galen had missed the canvas entirely.

A loud racket broke out, of running feet, shouting voices, an angry alarm bell. Galen lay quietly in the middle of the erupting chaos, staring at the ceiling. He put up no resistance when the police arrived. At the precinct he was given a form to fill out—name, age, current address, phone number—like waiting at the dentist's office. When offered his legally allowed phone call, Galen said he wanted to talk to a reporter from the local paper.

"I want to report a lie," he said calmly, reciting the word beginning with *L* that he had tried to spray across baby Jesus. "There is no mercy. There is no God. Love is a fiction. People have to wake up."

The desk sergeant was indifferent. "Reporters will be crawling all over this. You don't need to phone them. Call your lawyer," he advised. "Unless you have a shrink."

But Galen insisted. Using the desk phone and the yellow pages, he dialed a number but only reached an answering machine.

"No one's picking up," he told the desk sergeant.

"Too bad. Off you go."

Galen paced his cell, practicing the speech he intended to deliver when he got his moment. An hour passed, then two. He was slumped on the floor in the corner when a guard came by and unlocked the steel door.

"It's your lucky day. No one's pressing charges."

Galen slowly got to his feet. So the whole thing had been a waste, a joke to pile on top of God's other jokes. Behind the scenes, the museum officials had worked it all out. They couldn't afford the bad publicity from prosecuting him. The museum's fortunes depended on big traveling exhibitions. If word got out that their collection was this vulnerable, it would become twice as hard to borrow precious masterworks from other museums. Their insurance would skyrocket. Anyway, the *Madonna and Child* had come through unscathed.

As he was being discharged, Galen caught a young man in jeans and a T-shirt staring at him.

"Are you the guy?" the young man asked. He looked about nineteen.

"Leave me alone," Galen grumbled, scooping up his things, the small change, wallet, and belt collected by the police. The kid grabbed up his parka from the waiting bench and followed him outside.

"I'm sorry you couldn't carry out your mission," he said. "Well, not sorry, exactly. Listen, there's still a story here."

"About what, a loony or a laughingstock?" Galen looked up

and down the street, but there were no cabs. He'd left his car at home that morning.

The kid stuck out his hand. "Name's Malcolm. I'm a reporter. I just want to hear your side of the story."

Galen stared blankly at the proffered hand. He turned up the street, heading for the nearest bus stop, which was two blocks north. Malcolm trailed after him. Galen didn't brush him off. As much as he felt humiliated, he still wanted to talk to someone who'd listen.

"Are you on the crime beat?" he asked.

"No crimes so far. I do obituaries, only your story got priority. We have two guys out with the flu."

Great, Galen thought mockingly. *I'm a notch more interesting than the dead.*

He had been stoked on adrenaline all morning, and he realized that he was starving.

Under his parka the kid reporter looked underfed.

"I'll buy you a burger," Galen offered. He couldn't bear the idea of crawling back home yet.

They crossed over to a fast-food franchise, put in their order, and sat down at a plastic table and chairs away from the freezing draft that blew in every time a customer entered. Galen felt a compulsion to wipe the tabletop clean, but restrained himself.

Malcolm pulled out a mini tape recorder. "You mind?"

Galen shrugged.

The reporter wore a smile, but he wasn't thrilled when he first set eyes on the suspect, who looked like a rumpled English professor, completely harmless. The terrorist angle would have been great for Malcolm's career, but it was quickly fading. He clicked on the machine. The tape whirred quietly between them on the table.

"One, two, three. Okay, we're recording now. So why did you do it?"

"Because everything is a lie," Galen said firmly, using the same tone of voice he'd use to return an overcooked steak: matter of fact and displeased.

"Um, can you be more specific?" Malcolm asked. "Do you belong to a movement or something?"

"No. I belong to the mass of humanity who have been swindled for centuries by the biggest lie ever perpetrated." Galen suddenly felt his rage boiling up. "Belief in God has killed more people in history than all genocides put together. Where is mercy, where is love? It's all a monstrous lie." His eyes were glistening now with the fervor of his words.

A nut job, Malcolm thought to himself. But a hint of the terrorist angle was still breathing, on life support.

"Is there a version of God you think needs defending?"

"No. Weren't you listening? I said it's all a lie. Religion is mass hypnosis, and countless people fall victim to it every day."

"Including you? Something must have happened to you. How did God hurt you personally?"

Galen hesitated. He wasn't all that sure how God had hurt him. The whole thing was a jumble. Iris's mad love, the angel paintings, her certainty that she was on some kind of spiritual mission. It had all glommed together in Galen's mind, a festering mass.

"I don't matter," he said insistently. He searched for words. "If God is love, then all love is tainted. That's the gist. That's the thing nobody sees."

"So your message is 'Down with God'? You weren't trying to improve the painting with a little squirt of red?"

"Don't mock me."

"I guess what I'm saying is, a lot of people hate religion or whatever. Not a lot of people vandalize art."

Galen sat back in the flimsy plastic chair. "You don't give a damn, do you?"

"How I feel isn't the point."

"Right."

They were interrupted by hearing their number called. When Galen started to stand up, Malcolm preempted him. "Let me get this." He trotted off and soon returned with a tray of burgers and drinks. "A bit of goodwill," he said brightly.

But Galen's mood was dark. He felt as if he was slowly deflating inside with a faint whoosh, shrinking into a curled-up ball. For a few minutes the two didn't speak, distracted by their food.

In the silence Malcolm reassessed the story, if there was a story. It wouldn't have legs as a feature, not without charges being pressed. He clicked off the mini recorder and put it away in his pocket.

"Wait. You haven't let me finish," Galen complained.

"I've got enough for now."

Malcolm felt sorry for the nut job slumped in his chair knowing he had botched everything. "Frankly, you'd be better off if this whole thing dies down quickly. Put it behind you," he said.

Wadding up the napkin from his burger, Malcom took a shot at a trash bin in the corner, sinking the paper ball in one clean motion, and then stood up.

"No harm, no foul. Okay?"

When Galen looked away, a pained expression on his face, the reporter shrugged. At least he'd have an anecdote for his buddy Frank back at the paper.

"Can I offer you a lift?"

Galen was too upset to do anything but shake his head. His eyes followed the kid out the door. Any chance to get justice went out into the cold with him.

CHAPTER 5

For every strange event that had unfolded so far, Meg McGeary was the absent element. Was she pulling invisible strings? What gave her the right to? Ten years ago Meg didn't stand out for any reason. She could easily have blended into the bustling holiday shoppers at the local outdoor mall. She was forty then, dressed in suburban style: gray parka with fake-fur trim around the hood, baggy jogging pants, and running shoes. Society was changing, so the absence of a wedding ring wouldn't have made her stick out. One thing did, though. On a particular day in November, she was standing stock-still, her eyes fixed on the distance, as if mesmerized by the front of a Subway sandwich shop and the Nike store next door.

The sun was shining feebly through a patchwork of clouds. Shoppers were feeling flush—the Great Recession hadn't yet burst the bubble—and nobody took notice as they walked around Meg. An alert passerby might have suspected that something was very wrong with a woman glued in place. Maybe she was having some kind of psychotic break that made her go catatonic. For now, though, the crowd parted and swirled around Meg like the sea swirling around a rock jutting out from the beach.

Meg wasn't psychotic, but she wasn't normal either. She was suffering from extreme disorientation—and with good reason. In her mind she was on her way to be crucified. Literally. Before noon, she would be hanging from a tall wooden cross. Roman soldiers were going to drive long iron nails through her hands. She could see the angry mob thirsty for her blood.

The "thing," as she called it, started that morning. Her cat had woken her up from a bad dream by clawing at her chest through the coverlet. Outside, winter darkness had cleared. Meg's bare feet hit the cold floor, searching for a pair of fuzzy slippers. She padded down a hallway to the bathroom and stared at herself in the medicine-cabinet mirror.

A puffy face with frowzy bed hair stared back. Yet she also saw an ancient biblical city in the mirror, as if two films were superimposed in a projector. Suddenly the ancient city came to life. People in robes lined the street, eager for a vicious spectacle. Like actors in a silent movie, they jeered at her without making a sound.

Meg was dimly aware that this was the same dream that had kept her awake all night. She splashed cold water on her face to make it go away, but it didn't. Whether she looked in the mirror, out the bathroom window, or at the white-tiled walls, this other scene played—a hot day, the sun burning down from a clear sky, bystanders straight out of Sunday school illustrations. Meg's feet were snug in her slippers, but the man's feet wore sandals and felt hot. She was certain now, with waking clarity, that it was a man. His breathing was heavy as he gazed around at the mob, fighting against his fear. Meg could feel the pressure in his lungs. Was he carrying something heavy on his back? She suddenly felt an enormous weight.

Meg decided to call Clare, the closest of her two sisters. Back to the bedroom she walked, with nervous steps. The cat lay curled up by the radiator, opening one eye to watch Meg dig around in her purse for her cell phone. Yet the minute she pushed the button for Clare's work number, she thought, *Bad idea. She's a worrier. This will ruin her day.*

Before Meg could hang up, however, Clare answered. "Hey you," she said, expectantly.

"Hey," Meg mumbled mechanically.

"You sound sleepy."

"I'm not sleepy."

"Well, it's nice to hear your voice. It's been a madhouse with the kids out of school and me working." Clare, who had moved to another city after she got married, was always in motion, building her realty business.

"If anyone can cope, it's you," said Meg. She was stalling, disoriented. The movie became twice as vivid now. The man stumbled to his knees under his crushing burden, then struggled to regain his footing. Meg could feel his back muscles cry out in pain. This wasn't a movie. She was inside him.

Clare's worry radar kicked in. "Sweetie, is something wrong? Why are you really calling?"

Luckily, a flickering gap appeared in the movie just then, which gave Meg an opening to think straight. "I was feeling a little lonely. We never connect the way we used to."

"I know. It's been weeks. I'm sorry."

Her sister's voice, which had anxiously risen a few notes, came back down. Clare was usually good about not losing touch. She was good about a lot of things.

"So maybe you should come for a visit?"

"I'd like that," said Meg.

"You won't mind the kids being underfoot?"

"No, it's all great." Meg desperately wanted the call to end.

"All right, sweetie. Love you."

It was a relief to stop pretending, and the call hadn't been a disaster. But as soon as she hung up, Meg was in pain again, gasping and bent over. She tried taking deep breaths, but it didn't help. The movie in her head relentlessly unspooled. The man had regained his footing and was stumbling forward again, sweating heavily now.

Who else could she call? It was a depressingly short list. Nancy Ann, her other sister, would freak out. She rarely left the house without thinking that she had forgotten to lock the front door or left the gas on. Her mother was totally preoccupied with whatever her husband wanted. Some girlfriends came to mind, coworkers at the bank where Meg was assistant manager, but they'd probably laugh and hang up on her.

Meg began to panic. The four walls were closing in, suffocating her. She had to get back in control. A dose of reality might be the best medicine—inhaling the cold winter air, mixing with people. This idea sounded sane. She hastily threw on some clothes and rushed downstairs, squeezing past a bicycle and some moving boxes piled in the foyer. The smell of bacon frying in one of the apartments made her feel faintly sick, but the sensation of nausea distracted her from the movie. *That must be a good sign, right?* On her way out, Meg remembered to call her assistant and tell her she was taking a sick day.

It wasn't far to the outdoor mall. Meg had gotten into the habit of wandering there after work. She didn't do this out of loneliness. At forty, being single had settled in. It felt like something between a comfortable armchair and a stain on the wallpaper you can't be bothered to fix.

She set a brisk pace. It was hard to keep her balance, though, trying to rush when he was struggling just to put one foot in front of the other. He looked up. A hill loomed in the distance. Two dangling silhouettes were outlined against the sun, already hanging from crosses. Meg shuddered, trying to get back into present time, and quickened her pace.

Five minutes later she was standing in the central square of the mall. Despite her parka, she was freezing. The wind cut through her, biting with wintry fangs.

Something new was happening in the movie. She could feel the ground sloping upward. He was climbing the hill. Behind him a soldier gave a hard shove. The centurion was anxious to return to barracks and get drunk. A third cross was outlined against the sun. The condemned man searched the waiting mob for a friendly face. One young girl was crying, and when he set eyes on her, she shifted her head scarf to hide her tears. He barely caught a glimpse of her, but all at once Meg felt a wave of relief wash over him. More than relief. A deep sense of peace entered him. It erased his fear, and he stopped struggling against what was to come.

The chants of the mob grew obscene, but the man's sense of peace only deepened. The world and its terrifying images faded like a candle flickering invisibly in the noonday sun.

The procession arrived at its destination. He had only an instant to look back at the girl who felt pity for him. He wanted her to see that he was at peace, but she was gone. He didn't think about the crushing finale of his drama. He only wondered what would become of her.

This is where the movie in Meg's head jammed. The images stopped unspooling. The crosses on the hill vanished. Suddenly she was just herself, standing motionless in a crowd, with no idea of how long she had been frozen in place. Tilting her head back, she no longer saw two suns, only the feeble November sun of the present. There was no lingering fear. It was almost as if nothing had happened. But it had, undeniably. Meg noticed a few peculiar looks from people as they walked around her. Time to move on.

So she did. A few minutes longer, and they'd be calling security to take her away.

Two weeks passed. Meg would have forgotten her road to Calvary if she could have. She did her best. Others noticed no blips in her daily routine at work. She still arrived every morning at seven thirty to open the bank. She still took her place at her big desk near the front and smiled reassuringly when young couples nervously approached her about taking out their first home loan. She was genuinely comfortable in her work, never a boss hater or a cause for the assistants she supervised to even remotely hate her.

If a surveillance camera had tracked her every movement, it would have recorded only one odd occurrence, a minor deviation from her normal routine. One night, after leaving the bank, she stopped at a pharmacy near her apartment building, where she asked for the strongest sleeping aid she could buy without a prescription. When she got home, she watched old reruns of *Friends,* ate a Lean Cuisine Chicken Parmesan, and took two of the pills before going to bed. Better to be in a faint chemical haze in the morning, Meg figured, than to revisit the terrible images of her hallucination.

But the echoes still sounded. She couldn't ignore the faint cries of woe that came from inside her. They almost went away if she distracted herself with work and TV or if she turned up the car radio. But there are only so many ways to escape your inner world. The horrifying images in her vision were actually easier to bear. Meg had seen them every day on the walls of her old Catholic school during the Bible class run by the Sisters of St. Joseph. The problem was that now she had lived those images. Who did that? Only saints and psychotics, so far as Meg knew, and she didn't fit into either category. She struggled to imagine a third possibility.

Anxiety comes equipped with a volume control, and the more Meg ignored the wailing voice inside her, the louder it became, little by little. By the third week, the volume of her anxiety was so loud, she could barely hear anything else. It was hard to keep her composure when she went to her parents' house for Sunday dinner.

"You're unusually quiet," her mother commented at the table. "You've liked my corned beef and cabbage since the day you were born."

Meg managed to smile, because this was only a slight exaggeration. Her mother said the smell of the dish brought back the green hills of Galway, although she hadn't literally come from Ireland or even visited it. She came from near the railroad tracks in Pittsburgh. Still, corned beef and cabbage was like a light in the window, attracting the McGeary sisters home, no matter where they happened to be. This wasn't really true anymore, ever since Clare had gone off to raise a family and Nancy Ann had gotten married to that handsome Tom Donovan. Nancy Ann was barely eighteen, the same age as her daughter Mare. Time was a thief.

It was just Meg and her parents at the table now. Since she never mentioned a man, her mother had to be content with how well her single daughter was doing at the bank. Her father kept her mother's prying impulses in check, usually with a sharp glance if she strayed anywhere near the word "marriage."

"I think I like your cooking more as I get older," Meg offered. "You haven't lost your touch."

"What kind of touch do spuds take?"

Her mother smiled indulgently at the compliment and passed the potatoes. But really Meg was attempting a mild diversion, in case her inner state looked too obvious. It took all her strength not to tell her parents how worried and disoriented she felt. At any moment she could have a relapse. Worse, the movie in her head could pick up from where it had stalled. This was a possibility she didn't dare think about.

After dinner, Meg walked to the bus stop. Her car was in the shop. She felt relieved nothing had gone amiss. The sky over the city was unusually clear, the stars giving a bright winter show. Meg glanced up, thinking that stars somehow become sharper when it was cold. This observation would have given her pleasure, but the stars suddenly seemed like the points of a million nails. She felt a wave of panic. The animal contentment of having a full stomach wasn't calming her at all. A liquor store on the corner was still open—impulsively she rushed in.

Cheap vodka would be the fastest anesthesia, she figured, running her eye over the shelves. She wasn't a drinker, but the need was urgent.

At the counter a bored clerk was watching a basketball game in overtime on a small TV. When Meg took off her mittens to count out the money, he glanced at her palms.

"I'd have that looked at if I was you, lady," he said, cautiously taking the bills from her hand.

Meg looked down. Her palms were marked by two spots the size of a nickel, bright red and moist. She was sure they hadn't been there at dinner. Her panic escalated, and she started swaying in place. She had to grip the counter to stay upright.

"Hey, are you okay?"

Unable to reply, she stared ahead with wide, frightened eyes. The clerk started to reach for the phone. Meg shook her head violently.

"Please, no," she managed to whisper.

The clerk was no humanitarian; he was glad to get her out of his store with her bottle and eighty-nine cents change. Meg wouldn't have stuck around for the 911 call anyway. She blindly headed for the bus stop, running to catch the bus waiting there. The driver paid no attention to her as she collapsed onto a seat near the front. Except for two older black ladies at the back, the bus was empty.

Her mind wasn't working. Holding on tight was her only tactic now. Meg looked out the window at the passing dinginess of the city while the bus's fluorescent lights flickered every time the driver pumped the brakes.

Once she got home, she stopped at the small table by the door where she kept her gloves and keys. If she took her gloves off slowly enough and wished hard enough, the round red spots would be gone. Magical thinking, the last resort, the final rung the mind clings to as it gazes into the black abyss. No magic this time. Meg gazed at the spots, which seemed redder than before, the moistness forming into a rivulet of blood.

But her mind didn't let go of the last rung, and she didn't plunge into blackness. She felt unusually calm, in fact, like a surgeon clinically examining a clean incision made by a scalpel. Once the blade slices open the skin, there's no turning back, and with Meg it was the same. This was the point of no return. She knew what the spots meant. She knew about the stigmata. As a girl—ten, maybe eleven—she had gone through a brief period of religious devotion. She took to reading the lives of the saints in books with glossy, colored illustrations. Already an advanced reader, the suffering of saints mesmerized her.

Now, though, it was happening to her. The things that she couldn't bear to see in her movie were now appearing on her body. Holy wounds. First the oozing blood where nails were driven into the hands. If the wounds kept going, there would be a wreath of bloody points around her forehead, a gash in her side, more blood from her feet. But even this didn't disturb her calmness. Instead, she undressed for bed and looked at herself in the full-length mirror on her closet door. Nothing else had manifested, only the two red spots on her palms. Without bandaging them, she fell into bed, skipping the pills, ignoring the vodka. Instantly, she descended into a deep, dreamless sleep.

CHAPTER *6*

Lilith's visit was more than strange. As soon as she was gone, Mare couldn't settle down again. She ran to the window, watching the intruder make her way in high heels back through the snow. It felt as if any chance of seeing her aunt again was slipping away. Mare had to do something.

She rushed to the door, grabbing her coat on the way, and flung it open, only to find Frank standing there.

"I've been waiting in the car. What's going on? You're not running after her, are you?"

"I have to," Mare said, peering over his shoulder to see if she could still catch a glimpse of Lilith.

"Whoa. I don't think that's such a good idea."

"Why not? She's figured out everything, and we know nothing."

Mare was biting her lip hard; the tic had returned. But at the sight of Frank she began to calm down.

He came in, shutting the door behind him. "I couldn't just leave like that. God knows what she's capable of."

"Please, don't freak me out any more than I already am."

Mare began pacing the small open patch in her cramped apartment, running her hands through her hair.

"I'm so stupid. I didn't get her number. I don't even know her last name."

"It's okay. We're both wound up right now," Frank said.

"My mouth feels like cotton." Mare opened the battered fridge in the corner and grabbed some bottled water off the shelf, knocking over the two bottles next to it, which she ignored. "I shouldn't have let her in the door. Now she's filled my head with such strange ideas."

"She was spouting nonsense," Frank said firmly. "You know that, right?"

Mare was walking in circles now, taking big gulps of water. Suddenly the phone rang, and she jumped. It had to be her family again. They weren't about to let this die down.

She looked at Frank. "I'm not going to answer it. What could I tell them?"

They both understood her predicament. Even if you subtracted the Lilith quotient, the mystery of Aunt Meg was squarely on Mare's shoulders.

Frank felt a momentary paralysis. There are moments when one step forward or backward makes all the difference. He wasn't going to sweep Mare into his arms and murmur, "It's all right. I'm here. I have your back." He couldn't promise that. So taking a backward step was the smart choice. He could extricate himself now and return to the newsroom. Thompson, the crusty city editor, would scorch him for blowing off his deadline, but he wouldn't fire him. Mare could get through this on her own, somehow. Having worked it all out, Frank stepped forward anyway.

"Let's sit down and think this through," he said, touching Mare's arm.

She took a deep breath and did what he said, draining the last of the water in one gulp.

He began thinking out loud. "Lilith had her suspicions before she came here, and now she's sure we have the object. But think back. She said it belongs here."

Mare was bewildered. "What does that mean?"

"I don't know. Maybe we'll find out from your aunt. You really have no idea where she might be?"

Mare shook her head.

"Okay, then it's like the news business. If you lose your best source, you fall back to the next best. I hate to say it, but that means Lilith."

"She might not talk to you, not after what you said."

"Right, but if anybody knows the whole story, she does. That's why she was doling it out bit by bit."

Mare was rolling the crumpled plastic water bottle between her hands. Her panic had passed. She could think as logically as Frank now.

"So Lilith doesn't want to get the shrine for herself."

"No, otherwise she'd have tried to scare you—more than she already did, I mean."

He won a faint smile. Then Mare said, "I get the strongest feeling that the shrine isn't stolen, which means somebody gave it to Aunt Meg. Why? And if she's not dead, why pass it on to me?"

"To draw you in."

Frank was stating the obvious, but only now did it hit them. They stared silently at each other. He racked his brain for what to do next.

"You said there was a note. Let me take a look at it."

She fetched it, and for such a short message, Frank realized, it said a great deal.

Hello, Mare,

This is from the thirteenth disciple. Follow where it leads.

Yours in Christ,
Meg

He began to decipher it. "You see how it begins, so casually? She starts talking as if you two are close, as if she's sure you're the one who will read the note first."

"I see that."

"Then she plants a tease. Who is this thirteenth disciple? Your aunt knows already, but she wants you to find out for yourself. The shrine holds the answer."

"That's brilliant!" Mare exclaimed.

"It's all between the lines. When you get to the end, she says 'Yours in Christ,' which means that leaving the convent had nothing to do with losing her faith. She's reminding you that religion is the focus, not how much the treasure is worth. But she signs off with her old name. She could have used her nun's name, but she wanted you to know that she's family again."

He turned the note over before handing it back to Mare, who was looking at him with admiring eyes.

"That's all I can see," he said.

Mare was thoughtful now. "So Aunt Meg is drawing me in. What happened to her in the convent? Why did she decide to vanish a second time after all these years?"

"I don't know. But Lilith isn't acting on her own. Let's say the two know each other, and maybe Meg is orchestrating everything. She must have a reason for staying in the shadows like that. Your aunt could have just phoned. She could walk in the door right now and tell you what's going on without sending somebody else. Either she's toying with you, which leaves us where we started, or this is a test. 'Follow where it leads.'"

Suddenly Mare became animated. "I have an idea." She went to the closet and brought the golden church out from its hiding place.

"Maybe there's some writing on it we didn't notice before. It could be the clue we're supposed to follow."

She started examining every surface minutely. But except for the etched grass and flowers, the outside surface was perfectly smooth. A dead end.

"We need to get inside," said Frank, following his first hunch. "At least let's shake it."

Mare nodded in agreement. She didn't bring up her premonition that someone, not something, was hidden in the church. If she still thought so, she kept it to herself.

Frank lifted the heavy golden object next to his ear and shook it hard. There was no sound from inside, no rattle of bone, no whisper of ashes.

"Damn it. There has to be something." He was quickly growing frustrated.

Mare's face changed, and she took a deep breath. "Please don't laugh. Maybe we should pray for the answer."

He did laugh, abruptly and sarcastically. "Come on."

Mare didn't back down. "There are only two ways to look at the treasure. Either it's a precious artwork or it's sacred. Aunt Meg didn't leave it to me as my inheritance. It's not the gold that matters to her. I mean, isn't that obvious?"

"All right," said Frank reluctantly. "But you do the praying. I'll sit back and watch."

This wasn't good enough for Mare. "Are we in this together or not?"

"I didn't say I was pulling out." Nor did he say that he had never prayed in his life, unless you count "Now I lay me down to sleep" when he was five.

"Okay. You hold one end, and I'll hold the other. Is that asking too much?"

It would have been under other circumstances. The golden church hadn't lost its spell, however, and something about it was irresistible to Frank. He slipped his fingers under one end while

Mare took hold of the other. They grew quiet; she shut her eyes. He was sure that praying would lead nowhere. It was all on her.

So what was on him? Had he committed to anything? Frank felt a guilty twinge. Mare's face had taken on a childlike innocence. Who was going to rescue her before she was pulled farther down the rabbit hole? Not him. He wasn't gallant enough to rescue anyone, if it came to that. His motives ran more the other way. He was nosey enough to pry deeper into the ongoing weirdness. He'd probably wind up writing a helluva story. All kinds of people would read it and start prying into Mare's business. In the end, she'd hate him.

This gloomy line of thought went nowhere, because the room suddenly turned black. Not dark, but as black as a starless night. Frank looked in Mare's direction. He couldn't see her, but he could sense that she was still there, breathing but invisible. A strong gust of wind ruffled his hair, which was impossible. The wind was cold enough to prick his skin, raising goose bumps. He heard Mare gasp, and Frank reached out into the surrounding darkness, catching her arm. There was no golden church between them, no cramped apartment even. They were standing outside on a chilly night.

"What's happening?" he asked, but the words made no sound, the way words in a dream don't make a sound.

Even if Mare had heard him though, there was no time for her to answer. From behind them Frank caught voices. He whipped around, his right shoulder hitting up against a rough plastered wall. The voices continued, quiet and close by. There were two people, a man and a woman. They spoke in a foreign language. No sense came through, but the woman sounded bewildered and scared. The man sounded older, and his voice was calm, as if he was trying to reassure her.

The blackness obscured everything. Frank jumped when Mare's hand found his and clutched it tight. If he was delusional, she was right there with him.

He tried talking again. "Where are we?"

Mare gave no sign of hearing him, but the impenetrable darkness cleared a bit. The plastered wall that Frank had banged his shoulder against belonged to a house; there were windows high up that cast a faint glimmer of flickering candles or oil lamps. He realized that he wasn't afraid. His heart didn't pound in his chest; his legs weren't rubbery. The whole thing was more trancelike than frightening.

The two people who were talking came closer, then stopped. He could hear the woman breathing raggedly; she was quite agitated. The man said only a few words more, and then he turned to walk away. He was headed in their direction. Frank pulled Mare beside him and pressed his back to the wall. The man's approaching steps were measured, and when he got nearer, Frank could make out the silhouette of someone shorter than himself. He wore sandals that flopped against the cobblestones, and each step made a swishing sound, as if he was dressed in robes. If he was armed, the dim light didn't catch the glint of steel. A minute later, he was right on top of them, two figures pressed against the wall.

Now Frank was afraid. His pulse thudded in his ears, and it took all his willpower to stand there. The man must be used to moving around in the dark. He had to see them. But he gave no sign, not turning his head or changing his gait as he passed in the narrow alley. The flop of sandals began to fade away.

Suddenly the woman ran after him, crying out. She rushed by so close that her skirt brushed Frank's leg; in the dark he made out that she was quite tiny. Her cry was that of a girl, not a woman. The man didn't stop. She cried out again, and a shutter swung open overhead. Someone leaned out, waving an oil lamp to see what the commotion was.

Almost with a click, Frank was back in Mare's apartment, holding on to his end of the golden church. The other end was trembling.

"You saw it too?" he mumbled. Mare could barely hold on to her end, and they lowered the church together to the floor. Mare sank down beside it.

"Oh, my God," she mumbled.

He sat down next to her, taking her hand. It felt very cold and small. Frank wasn't so dazed that his mind wasn't working. He could feel a crack in his skepticism.

"It was your prayer. What else could have triggered something like that? I wouldn't believe it if I hadn't been there."

"Where is there?" Mare asked weakly.

He was at a loss. Between them sat the golden shrine, glowing by the light of the dangling bulb in its paper lantern. The scene was more or less the same as when Frank first walked in. The only thing that had changed was a small sign, white with red lettering, hanging right in front of him. It didn't matter that the sign was invisible, because the lettering was unmistakable: "No Exit." Frank could bet on that.

CHAPTER  7

After the kid reporter left, Galen couldn't finish his burger. The whole place reeked of charred grease and cinders, like a crematorium. All he wanted to do was go home and collapse into bed. He trailed out to the street, where a taxi cab was idling at the curb. The driver nodded, and Galen got in, telling him the address.

They headed over to the other side of town. On the way, Galen rebuked himself. He had lied to the kid. He hadn't told him the real story behind his attack on the *Madonna and Child*. How could he? It was the cause of his rage, but love was tangled into the story like gold thread in a martyr's hair shirt.

Two years before, he had decided to spend a rainy afternoon in the art museum. This wasn't a predictable choice. Museums didn't figure into Galen's short menu of possibilities for a rainy afternoon, which usually included catching up on work, reading back issues from a dusty pile of *Scientific American*s, or rearranging the newest samples in his mineral collection—he specialized in rare earths. Nowhere on the menu was visiting the art museum, because he didn't really like art.

What he liked was strolling through places where he could feel alone in a crowd. He went to shopping malls on Black Friday for the same reason. Being part of a mob scene—an invisible integer—made him feel armored, protected. It reinforced his splendid isolation. It also happened to be a Wednesday, and the art museum was packed because admission was free. If Galen had known that picking up girls was the goal of a good percentage of the day's male art lovers, he would have stayed at home.

A young woman was standing beside Galen as he gazed at a prized *Madonna and Child* from the Italian Renaissance. The serene expression on the Madonna's face was a depiction of timeless peace.

"Mmm," the woman murmured in appreciation.

Galen paid no notice. He was only staring at the painting to figure out which mineral might have produced a peculiar shade of green. Malachite? It was a good guess, unless the lush grass beneath the Blessed Virgin's feet was tinted with a vegetable dye. He decided this was unlikely. A vegetable dye would have long ago faded to gray.

The young woman's glance darted sideways, although Galen had no idea she was taking him in.

"Lovely," she murmured.

This constituted too much communication. Galen sidled away. Without warning, she plucked at his sleeve.

"I could tell you were enjoying it." She gestured at the painting, but her eyes remained on him. "Tell me what you see."

"Why?"

She smiled. "Because I'm interested."

Galen couldn't help but notice how young and attractive she was. His immediate instinct was to retreat, but he took another look at the painting.

"The mother looks hypnotized. The baby's face looks shriveled, like an old man's."

"Fascinating. Go on."

The young woman fixed him with an adoring smile. This was even more unnerving than plucking at his sleeve.

Galen continued. "There's a disease that shrivels children's faces," he pointed out. "Progeria. It's quite horrible. That baby probably had progeria."

His clinical remark didn't repel her. Quite the opposite—her eyes lit up, and with a laugh she exclaimed, "Brilliant! I knew I should talk to you. My name is Iris, by the way."

Galen stared. An attractive woman no more than thirty, with loosely gathered blonde hair that fell to her shoulders, the kind of hair once referred to as tresses, was admiring him. He peered over his shoulder to see if she had an accomplice—chatting up a middle-aged nonentity like Galen might be their way of having a cruel laugh.

His discomfort made Iris laugh again. "Let's get a drink," she suggested. "We'll take one last look at this marvelous painting that we both love, and then I know the most amazing place where the mixologist is divine."

He'd never met anyone so vibrant. If Galen had been imaginative, he could have compared her tinkling laughter to sleigh bells attached to a troika in a romantic Russian novel. If he had been versed in abnormal psychology, on the other hand, he would have frowned at Iris's unquenchable exuberance. Who assails strangers in public with outbursts of emotion? Borderline personalities? Normal people don't act this way.

Caution should have stopped him. Instead, he allowed Iris to drag him, half-dazed, to a bar. Galen didn't drink, so the allure of exotic cocktails was nil. He sat there with a glass of soda water while Iris did all the work of seducing him. She flattered and cooed. His every remark invited a peal of laughter.

Being a virgin and nervous, he didn't ask Iris back to his place that first night, but she got his number. She had to be the one who called; he never would have. A real date followed, then two. He learned, with awkward, embarrassed slowness, how to kiss. An omission in his adolescence, petting with a girl at the movies, was remedied. Within a span of two months Iris became his wife. An oyster dies when its shell is cracked open, but Galen was reborn as a flood of love entered his being. His initial fear changed to intoxication. He lay awake at night with Iris cradled on his shoulder, and he never complained that the pressure made pins and needles shoot down his arm.

The way that love turned to violence was just as unexpected as their courtship. Iris's passion began to shift. She didn't grow tired of Galen, but suddenly her exuberance demanded a creative outlet. He came home from work one day to find a pile of art supplies stacked up in the living room.

"What's this?" he asked.

There was a large easel with mechanisms to adapt it to any size canvas, along with myriad jars of acrylics in every possible color, and blank canvases ranging in size from miniature to epic.

"I'm a painter!" Iris exclaimed.

"I didn't know," Galen said cautiously. "You didn't tell me."

"Oh, not before. I just realized it. I'm a painter. I always have been, but my talent was hidden."

As much as he loved her, some part of Galen looked upon his wife as an alien being, beginning with her passion for him. He began to worry that this was her first delusion. Being a painter might be her second. Yet his fears proved unfounded. Iris spread a plastic drop cloth in the middle of the living room and set up a makeshift studio. She threw herself into her first painting, and by the time Galen was ready for bed, she rushed in with a wet canvas.

"Done! What do you think? Isn't it beautiful?" she enthused.

He was afraid to look. But instead of being a garish daub, she had produced a semi-abstract landscape in harmonized colors, which, to his eyes, was amazingly good. It didn't matter that the sky was yellow and the grass blue. The colors worked. They expressed the same vibrant joy that Iris could find in anything, like life bubbling up from an endless spring.

She pointed to a streak of light that crossed the canvas from a source far in the distance. "That's an angel. Angels are pure light."

"Oh," Galen said. Angels were a nontopic for him.

Iris began to paint furiously, barely leaving time for sleep. Galen would wake up after midnight to find that his wife had quietly gotten out of bed to return to her latest canvas. Not that her love for him waned. If anything, it grew warmer. She greeted him when he came home from work wearing a dress, complete with matching pearl necklace and earrings.

When he suggested that she needed to slow down, tears welled up in the corners of her eyes. "I just want to show you my soul," she said. The soul was another nonsubject for Galen. He was mystified as he witnessed her paintings grow more religious. Not conventionally religious, though. She produced shimmering organic shapes—they reminded him of intricate snowflakes under the microscope, only in iridescent colors.

"That's what souls really look like," Iris said, as certain as when she told him what angels looked like.

Galen couldn't tell anyone what was happening at home. It was too dreamlike. Not that he had any colleagues to tell. His days were spent at the university library collecting references for scientific articles. He cobbled together a livelihood as a technical writer and researcher for professors at the university; his nights, however, were spent at a love feast. He had married a force of nature, not merely a lover and artist. What did he have to complain about, and who would believe him if he did?

Inevitably the day arrived when the outer world intruded. Iris wanted him to meet her parents, who lived in Milwaukee. There had been no formal wedding, just a civil ceremony at the registrar's office.

"Don't worry," Iris promised. "They'll love you as much as I do."

Galen knew otherwise. Intruders would break the enchantment that protected their crazy bliss. He was sensible enough to know that they were gripped in a *folie à deux* and, like any mad folly, outside eyes would expose it. Iris went to the airport, while Galen waited at home, sitting forlornly in his armchair. He felt naked and vulnerable.

That his in-laws were nice, pleasant people didn't relieve his anxiety. They stayed two days, and no one commented on the wide age difference between Iris and her husband. The chat was civil, if not warm. Her father, a doctor with a prosperous practice, assumed the role of alpha male. He paid for dinner at an expensive restaurant and told hunting stories.

"We've got pheasant and quail in the freezer back home. I'll send you a batch. It's too much for us."

Galen was content to submit. He tried not to look too hard into the mother's eyes. He expected to find worry there, and his own mother's constant worry still cast a shadow, all these years later.

"What's wrong?" Iris asked after her parents had left in a taxi for the airport. Her father had insisted on a cab, which would cost sixty dollars, his last show of dominance.

"Nothing. They're nice," Galen muttered.

He looked around, but could see no shards of wrecked enchantment littering the floor. Maybe they were protected after all. Iris went back to painting—her parents had been astonished at her hidden talents—and, if anything, her output increased. She was shy about approaching a gallery, so Galen set up a website to show off her work.

"Call it *Divine Messenger,*" she said. Within days it got dozens of hits, which turned to hundreds very soon. Her paintings clicked with people with spiritual stirrings.

One day an e-mail arrived in his inbox from Arthur Winstone, M.D. It took a moment for Galen to realize that this was his father-in-law.

Mr. Blake,

I've taken the liberty of writing to you privately. I hope you don't mind that I did a web search to find this address.

During our recent visit, I thought I spied a tremor in my daughter's left hand. It was faint, but I noticed that the shaking increased when Iris became emotional. I must add that her heightened exuberance felt unnatural to me. The Iris her mother and I know doesn't act this way.

I'm not a neurologist, and I don't mean to alarm you. But I strongly urge you to take her to a brain specialist. If my fears are unwarranted, I profoundly apologize. You must believe that I write out of a father's love.

One last thing—please don't share our communication with my daughter. In a good marriage, husband and wife tell each other everything, but at least consider keeping this e-mail a secret.

Respectfully,
Arthur Winstone

Galen was stunned. He read the e-mail twice more. His chest began to ache. This couldn't be happening.

The year that followed was a nightmare that ended only when Iris went into hospice and died. As he was leaving the room where Iris lay, unplugged from the medical monitors, pale and cold as a wax effigy, a voice in Galen's head spoke, having waited like a spoiled child holding its breath until it turns blue. *Fool! Wake up. You knew it couldn't be real.*

Now, sitting in the back of the cab on the way home from the burger joint, Galen shuddered. He was too exhausted to feel enraged anymore. He had been humiliated by God. He had been deceived in love by the very cruelest deception, that he could ever be loved in the first place. Now the last hope was gone. There would be no revenge to wipe the slate clean.

He suddenly noticed the cabbie's eyes in the rearview mirror.

"You okay back there?"

"What?"

"Sorry. You just looked a little upset."

Galen opened his mouth to tell the driver to mind his own business, but he was suddenly overwhelmed by a sense of complete futility.

He sank back into himself, oblivious of the time until the cab driver said, "We're here."

Galen reached for his wallet.

"That's okay," the cabbie said. "No charge."

Galen was confused. "Why not?"

The driver hadn't stopped looking at him in the rear-view mirror. "Because you've been chosen."

For no reason, this meaningless remark sent a wave of panic through Galen. He grabbed for the door handle, but it was stuck. Or had the cabbie locked him in? Galen wrenched the handle as hard as he could, and the door flew open so fast he almost tumbled into the street.

The cabbie jumped out of the front seat and ran around to help him.

"Leave me alone," Galen gasped.

"I can't do that."

The cabbie was short and dark, with stubbled cheeks, the very image of someone Galen feared. Hysterically, he wondered if the man had a bomb strapped to his chest.

Without looking back, Galen lurched from the icy street to the curb. His house, a wooden row house with peeling white paint and a sagging stoop, offered refuge. He stumbled as he went, kicking up sprays of snow like a rabbit fleeing a fox.

The cabbie followed a few feet behind. Feeling his shadow, Galen became terrified. He could barely extract his keys from his pants pocket, and when he tried to get a key in the door, the bunch flew out of his hand.

"Let me," the cabbie said, picking them up. He inserted the house key and turned the doorknob. "I'm Jimmy, by the way."

Galen's heart thumped in his chest. "If you want money, here," he exclaimed, thrusting his wallet at the man.

"I just want to talk."

Galen's eyes widened helplessly. The cab driver was blocking the door with his body.

"We've been watching you for a while," he said, smiling. "You're kind of my assignment. Look, it's freezing out here. I can explain everything better inside."

Galen was agitated, but he knew one thing for certain. Jimmy was the last person he'd ever let inside his house.

"I'm going past you," he exclaimed, "and if you lay a finger on me, I'll scream for the police."

Jimmy's smile broadened to a grin. "No offense, but I think the cops have had enough of you for one day."

Galen had his head turned away, so he never saw how Jimmy knocked him out, with a truncheon or the butt of a gun. There was no pain. A veil of darkness gently came down over his eyes; his knees crumpled. There was the sensation of cold as his cheek hit the packed snow on the stoop and a vague sense of Jimmy talking into a cell phone.

"I've got him, but he's so scared, he fainted. He's in no shape to plug in. Please advise."

CHAPTER *8*

Only half of Frank's suspicions about Lilith were correct. She was acting on orders, and Meg, who issued them, was hiding in the shadows. But the reason for her secrecy went much deeper than he could have imagined. In his world, sane people don't have visions of the Crucifixion, and if their hands bleed where the nails were driven into Jesus's hands, deception is being practiced.

Meg held the same beliefs ten years ago. When her palms suddenly oozed blood, she turned her back on the phenomenon. As soon as she got off the bus, she rushed inside and went to bed without turning on the lights. She didn't want to see what was happening to her. She wanted no part of it.

But it was a mistake not to bandage her hands before she crawled under the covers. When Meg woke up the next morning, the sheets were lightly smeared red. The stains were bright and fresh. She must have been bleeding all night.

She became very frightened seeing the two round spots on her palms, sticky and shiny in the morning sun. She faced herself in the bedroom mirror and said, "I have the stigmata," testing the word out. It sounded unreal.

After scrubbing the spots with soap, they disappeared, but within minutes the film of blood came back. And it was starting to drip again. She rummaged for a first-aid kit tucked at the back of the linen closet. Inside the kit was a roll of gauze bandages. Perching on the edge of the bathtub, she thoroughly wrapped up her hands. As far as anyone at the bank would know, she had carelessly burned herself taking a hot pan out of the oven.

The story was accepted without question. Meg's assistant winced and offered sympathy; she was careful to insulate a hot cup of coffee in three paper napkins before handing it to her. Otherwise no one took notice of her bandages. A week passed. Meg hung fire, applying a new dressing every morning. She felt a dull pain that didn't get better or worse.

Morbid curiosity sent her online, which was probably a mistake, because all she found were scary photos of people whose stigmata were worse than hers, much worse. Some had a row of ragged punctures across the forehead or a mark on the side of the body that looked like a gash, an open wound. Some stigmatics didn't bleed, some did. Some had recurrences every year, usually at Easter. Meg quickly turned away.

Two weeks later, without warning, a voice in her head said, *I will send you a blessing.* A gentle, unmistakable voice spoke these words. It was a female voice, yet not hers. The exact moment was etched in Meg's memory. She was alone in her office replacing a batch of documents in the filing cabinet. The sky outside was bright and clear. In the park across the street, work crews were stringing the bare trees with fairy lights for Christmas, and the frozen ground was feathered with snow like eiderdown.

After a short pause, the message in her head was repeated: *I will send you a blessing.*

Meg closed her eyes, willing the voice to explain what it meant. It didn't. So she went back to work, pretending that everything was normal. She moved cautiously, like a tightrope walker without a net. The worst thing would be to tip over.

If there was going to be a blessing, it didn't come that day. When evening fell, Meg started to wonder if she needed to do penance. She fumbled with the fingertips of bandaged hands and pulled out her rosary, tucked in the bottom drawer of her bureau.

How desperate am I? she thought. Maybe she would be praying to the God that sent this affliction in the first place. It was a disturbing possibility. She'd never had a reason to doubt her faith or even examine it. When she was just a speck in her mother's womb, her genes were already marked at the factory: female, green eyes, light brown hair, Irish Catholic. She was made this way before birth. God was a given. God was taken care of.

Reflecting on this, Meg felt a burst of anger. Who was God to force her hand? Who said he could point a cosmic finger and say, "You. You're it." Nobody had the right to play God. Which posed a problem, because no matter how hard she wrestled with it, God had a right to play God. He had just waited a long time before deciding to. She put the rosary back in the drawer, defeated.

Then one day a woman passed a sheaf of papers across her desk. A car loan application. Meg stared at it dully and picked up a pen.

"Your first name is Lilith?" she asked. "I don't see a last name."

"You won't need it."

Meg looked up, eying the customer, a tall woman in her late forties, perhaps fifty, with touches of gray at the temples.

"A last name is mandatory," Meg said, wondering why this was even an issue.

"Not this time. I like my old car. I don't need a new one." The woman had a decisive way of speaking that kept Meg from interrupting. "This is all about you—and that." The woman pointed to Meg's bandaged hands. "You've received a blessing."

Meg drew her hands out of sight under the desk.

"I don't know what you're talking about. I burned myself in the kitchen."

Lilith smiled. "Just unwrap them. You'll see."

Meg glanced down. A minute ago the gauze was beginning to show a slight discoloration from the seeping blood, but now it was snow-white.

"The blessing has been sent," said Lilith. "Don't be frightened. You're not crazy. Go ahead."

Meg looked around the office. A line of customers snaked toward the tellers, and her coworker was sitting with another loan applicant at the desk next to hers.

"Here?" she asked, mortified.

Lilith shrugged. "What do you have to lose? It's not like you're having a good day."

Gingerly Meg unwrapped her right hand. There was no stiffness from dried blood on the gauze. The bandage came off as smooth as a ribbon, and underneath her palm was unblemished. Rapidly she undid the other hand, and it was the same.

"What does this mean?" she stammered.

"It means you have a road to travel. Everyone does, but yours is different. You will walk a blessed path."

Without knowing why, Meg felt tears filling her eyes, blurring her view of her visitor.

"The soul is usually silent," Lilith continued. "It watches and waits. But your soul has called you out." She had showed little expression as she said this, but now she smiled wryly. "The good news is, you've been chosen. The bad news is, you've been chosen."

"I've heard better jokes," Meg mumbled. She wiped her eyes, and her strange visitor came back into focus. "Please excuse me. This is pretty overwhelming."

"That's what I'm here for. To make it easier. No one is ever prepared. But we mustn't let our emotions run away with us, must we?"

Meg started to laugh. Lilith seemed like a tart headmistress, right down to the tight bun she wore her hair in and the vaguely British accent. It was faintly outlandish, but effective. Meg's attention was totally focused; her panic was held in check. Fear was a great ocean wave ready to crash over her if Lilith wasn't holding it back.

Meg's laughter must have had a tinge of hysteria in it, because Lilith reached for her hand across the desk. "Do you need some water? Perhaps you should lie down."

"I'll be all right," Meg said, not at all certain. "I've got employees to look after."

She glanced out the window at the bright winter sky. A wave of calmness came over her, the first she'd felt in weeks. It was like a benediction.

"I'll be all right," she repeated.

Lilith watched her closely; she seemed satisfied.

"Then I'll take my leave." She stood up wearing an ambiguous smile, halfway between amused and knowing. She took back the car loan application, folded it neatly, and stuck it into her purse.

"Will I see you again?" Meg asked, feeling anxiety begin to creep back in.

"I'll be at your door when you get home tonight. We've made a beginning. Good."

"How do you know where I live?" asked Meg.

"How do I know anything?" Lilith replied. "It just comes to me."

After she departed, Meg played at finishing the work day normally. The tightrope walker didn't tip over. She balled up the gauze bandages and threw them into the waste bin in the ladies' room. Her reflection in the mirror was trying hard not to look elated.

She drove home at five, and every block deepened her sense of wonder. *Do things like this really happen?* Meg had read the New

Testament when she was sixteen, to please a boyfriend, a Protestant who was going through some kind of phase. The boyfriend dropped away, and Meg thought the Bible had too. Except that now, driving home, an obscure verse came back to her: "I bear on my body the marks of Jesus." A saint said it, and if Meg wasn't a saint, what was she?

Lilith was waiting on the stoop when she pulled into the driveway. She wore a thick tweed coat against the cold and held her handbag in front of her with both hands, as stiff as a palace guard on watch. Meg approached to unlock the front door. Neither spoke.

Once inside, Meg waited for Lilith's next move. The nearest room was the dining room. Lilith went in and seated herself at the head of the table. She patted the chair closest to her, which Meg obediently took.

"Have you reflected on what I told you?"

"I'm not sure. I can't remember anything except relief."

"Understandable."

Suddenly Meg wondered if the voice that had spoken in her head belonged to Lilith. "If I have you to thank . . ." she started to say.

"No. I'm not in such a position," Lilith said, waving off her gratitude. "I'm not a healer. But some people are. Maybe you, one day. In this instance, the soul spoke through your body. The flesh was willing, but the spirit was weak. I'm rather addicted to aphorisms, forgive me. I'll just keep talking until you're not dazed anymore."

Meg felt like she was breathing air from another world, but her mind had begun to clear already.

"Do you believe your experience was real?" Lilith asked.

"I have to, don't I?" Meg glanced at her hands, checking one more time to make sure they looked unblemished.

"You don't have to accept anything, actually. I didn't, not at first." Lilith paused. "You're going to meet some people. They'll also struggle with being chosen."

"When will I meet them?"

"That I don't know. I do know how many—seven, counting you and me."

Meg felt uneasy. She'd assumed all along, ever since the first morning of her ordeal, that she would face it alone.

"What if they don't want to meet me?"

"I won't let that happen."

Lilith was a cross between an oracle and a drill sergeant, but Meg wasn't afraid to stand up to her. "Who says it's your choice?"

"It has nothing to do with me. Reality is covered by a veil of mystery. You've penetrated the veil. It's a rare experience, and these seven people will have it, once you show them the way."

Meg was incredulous. "Me? I can't show anybody anything."

"That's going to change. When the whole group assembles, the person holding it together will be you."

Lilith saw the doubt lingering in Meg's eyes. She became more insistent. "You don't understand. I'm one of the seven. I need you, more than you can possibly know."

But the blessing Lilith had brought was already fading. Fear warned Meg to retreat into her shell.

Lilith read her mind. "The craving to be normal is powerful. It permits a moment of wonder, and then it drags us back, like an undertow we can't resist."

Meg gave an ironic smile. "As if normal is so great."

"Exactly. When all seven of us are gathered, a flame will spring up. If one member refuses to join, there will only be ashes."

Meg had a troubled cousin, Fran, who went to support groups for her addictions. They probably talked this way at the meetings. But she realized that she had to rethink who Lilith was—not a headmistress, more like a guide leading climbers up a treacherous peak. *Stay on the path. Don't stray. We're all in this together.*

Lilith veered abruptly in a new direction. "Do you think you can see to infinity?"

"I don't even know what that means."

"Then I'll tell you. Right now, your mind is fenced inside a walled courtyard, which keeps you safely enclosed. Anything that lies beyond the wall is frightening, including miracles."

"And you're saying I've had a miracle."

"Yes, and it scares you to death."

"Maybe that's a reason not to run after any more of them," Meg said.

"The chosen don't run after miracles. It's the other way around. The miracle found you. That's another thing that scares you."

Lilith was used to controlling the conversation. That much was clear to Meg. But was Lilith also trying to control her? *If I'm one of the chosen, what are we chosen for?* Meg wondered.

A string of visits followed. Lilith's appearances were punctual, right at ten after five when Meg came up the driveway from work. She always stood at attention with both hands clutching her purse, waiting for the front door to be opened. There was never anyone else with her, and the group of seven, whoever they were, wasn't mentioned again.

One day Meg had sunk into a dark depression. She was waking up every morning feeling exhausted. Nothing in her life was stable anymore. The bank was the worst. She felt like she was doing a bad impersonation of her old self, and every day it was getting harder to keep up the act.

Lilith tried to reassure her. "The beginning is always the worst. You're totally protected, but you can't see it yet. "

After a while their visits were silent for long stretches. Twilight felt gray and empty. Meg got sick of being encouraged. Her hands had healed completely. She would have tried harder to go back to her former life, but this was impossible. She kept remembering her own words: "What's so great about normal?"

One afternoon the house was desolately quiet, an echo chamber for the ticking clocks and rumbling refrigerator compressor.

Out of the blue Lilith said, "You resent me, don't you?"

Meg gave a silent shrug, unwilling to deny it.

"I'm just the messenger, you know," Lilith added.

There was no reply.

"Then what is it?"

Meg wanted to get up and walk away, but then she surprised herself by letting loose a wail of rage and self-pity. "I'm the one who had to suffer. I was bleeding! You don't know what it's like for me. You have it easy. You call yourself a messenger. Look around. You delivered a curse."

Like a dying siren, her anger trailed off into a whine. "Sorry," she mumbled.

"Don't apologize. Maybe you're right. But not about me."

Meg heaved a sigh. "I don't know anything about you."

"Maybe it's time you did."

The living room where they sat was being overtaken by the falling night, but Meg didn't reach for the lamp. She sat back, wondering what Lilith's story could possibly be.

When she was twenty, Lilith woke up from a bad dream, sweating and distraught. She was back from college on summer vacation. It was a time she loved, and besides, she almost never had bad dreams, nothing like this one, which was like being trapped in a hallucination.

She had landed far back in time, centuries and centuries ago. She was standing in front of a thick wooden door, the kind one might find in a medieval village. The door was nailed shut with rough oak boards. She realized that she wasn't alone. Several men, their faces tense and hard, stood around while two other men pried the boards loose.

The onlookers exchanged worried glances. When the last nail was pulled out, the boards clattered to the cobblestone pavement.

"What's wrong?" Lilith remembered asking in her dream. But the instant she asked, she knew the answer. Plague. She could smell death, a sickly rotten stench that became stronger when one of the men pushed open the door. Inside was darkness, because all the windows had been sealed too. The Black Death was merciless and swift. A boat carrying the plague might land in port, and within a week a quarter of the population in the town would be corpses littering the street.

The men looked at one another, hesitant about who should go inside to look. All eyes drifted to her. *What?* Lilith thought of herself as an unseen presence, but to them she was part of the scene. *You look. You are the one,* the men were speaking Italian, but Lilith understood every word. Around her, the crowd kept repeating the word *morte* excitedly.

With her first step through the door, she was repelled—the stench pushed her back like a hand over her face. The darkness wasn't absolute. Glimmers of sunlight came in through the boarded-up windows, and after a moment she saw something gleaming and gold.

Her eyes adjusted. The gleam took shape; she could see a small object sitting on the floor. At first it didn't register that the shape was a church or chapel, because her attention was frozen on the bodies. Six corpses lay around the object. They were arranged in a symmetrical pattern, extending outward like spokes of a wheel with the gold object as the hub.

The accursed sight caused the group of men—a search party looking for survivors—to disperse, screaming *Dio ci protegga! Dio ci protegga! God protect us! God protect us!* Below their confused shouting, Lilith could hear the sharp clatter of shoes scurrying over the cobblestones.

Her heart was beating fast. Whoever she was in the dream, the town's fear and dread had seized her completely. But she couldn't help staring at the wheel of bodies, wondering who had arranged them in a sealed and boarded house. Maybe no one. The logical answer was that they had lain down to die, deliberately forming the pattern. Knowing they were doomed, they wanted to send a message.

"And then I woke up," Lilith said when she got to this point in her story.

"Before you understood the message?" Meg asked.

"No. It was just a dream. I wasn't curious about it. I got out of bed, threw open the windows to cool off the room, and went for my morning swim. Our family always rented the same cabin by the lake every summer."

"And nothing happened?"

Lilith gave the first warm smile of their time together. "Everything happened. The golden shrine—that's the proper term—had found me. It always finds the chosen, one way or another.

"I came home from a date that night, a little woozy on wine. This boy and I had been teasing each other all evening, but he didn't get past second base. I remember wishing he had, when suddenly the same gleam I saw in my dream was in my bedroom. My hand had found the light switch, but I hadn't turned it on. But I instantly knew where the gleam came from."

"And it frightened you," Meg said.

"Just like you. I was frozen in place, and suddenly my mind was flooded with the truth. My dream was actually a prophecy. I had stumbled onto a mystery school. That's who the dead bodies belong to, a kind of secret society."

"I don't understand," said Meg.

"You will. The society is still around, and we're part of it, along with the others, once they answer the call."

"A mystery school," Meg said to herself, testing out the words. "Why?"

"Because mysteries need to be revealed, and at the same time they need protecting."

Meg was bewildered, but excited and intrigued too. "You saw six bodies in your dream. Why are there seven of us?"

"Because the seventh member of our mystery school is the teacher, and she is inside the shrine. She chooses us, and through her we come together, six complete strangers who share a path."

"Unless we die together. That was in your dream. Is it part of the prophecy?"

"I worried about that, until I realized that you can't be literal about these things," Lilith replied. "I think we will die unto death. Remember those words. You'll hear them in the convent when you get there."

Convent? Meg was speechless. If the McGeary family tree contained any nuns, she had never heard of it. A feeling of unreality returned, the same way Meg had felt when she was staring at her bleeding palms.

Lilith shook her head. "I know. This feels like someone else's life."

Meg nodded. It was good that Lilith understood, but it wasn't enough. The walls of the room began to close in, smothering her. Lilith had told her she was on a blessed path. Wherever that path was leading, Meg didn't care. She only wanted a way out.

CHAPTER 9

After returning from the dark alley, Frank was slow to get to his feet. His eyes told him that he was back in Mare's apartment, but his body wasn't so sure. The chilly air in the alley lingered on his skin. He was finding it hard to calm the racing thoughts in his head. The whole experience was overwhelming.

Mare looked up from where she sat on the floor, the golden shrine still between them.

"Are you okay?" asked Frank.

"I don't know." Mare's voice was shaky and distant. "I pulled you into this, away from work. But is there any way you can stay?"

"Sure, for a while. I just need to call in." Frank couldn't get a signal on his cell. "Let me step outside."

When his hand was on the doorknob, Mare said, "If I got you in trouble, just go."

"And leave you here? No way."

Suddenly Frank realized something. "You're not scared, are you?"

"No. It just took me a moment to get back. That's not why I want you to stay."

"Then what is it?"

"I want to go back," Mare said. "I have to."

Her eyes were steady, almost hard. He hadn't seen them like that before. He'd marked her down as a beautiful but timid girl, the kind who spent too much time feeling insecure.

"You're killing me here," he moaned. "You don't even know if we *can* go back."

"I'm not asking you to come with me. Unless you want to."

"You mean you'd go back without me? No way. It could be dangerous. What if you don't return this time?" Despite all his skepticism, Frank was talking as if they had traveled through some kind of portal.

"The note said, 'Follow where it leads,'" Mare reminded him. "That's what I'm doing. I can't stop now."

Frank couldn't deny that he was being lured in, first by the golden treasure, then Lilith, and now this. Mare was turning into a completely new woman before his eyes.

"I know what this thing is," she exclaimed, pointing at the shrine. "It's a truth-teller, or an oracle."

Frank balked. "You're stabbing in the dark. Where's the proof?"

"It's in the note. We're being led to the thirteenth disciple. He's at the center of everything that's happened. I know what you're thinking: that's not proof. But we saw him, there in the alley."

"That could have been anybody."

"Does it matter? The one who is sleeping inside the shrine. He trusts us. He's willing to give us these clues."

"Which is also why Lilith couldn't tell us the whole story," Frank chimed in. "It sounds too crazy."

"Until you go there. Now we have. We passed the test."

Frank was barely listening now. What mattered to him was the hope and excitement in Mare's eyes. More than anything, he didn't want her to be disappointed, but he had no control over these strange events.

"You can't believe how frustrated I am," he exclaimed. "We could be jumping off a cliff here." His voice became pleading. "We don't have to go back right this minute, do we?"

"I guess not," Mare replied reluctantly.

"Then let me clear my head first." Frank ran to the door and flung it open. "I've got six missed calls on my cell. Let me try and save my job. But I'm not leaving, I promise."

"I know."

He was bothered by the ambiguous smile she gave him, but what choice did he have except to trust her? They had to trust each other. His voice trailed "Sorry, sorry" behind him as he ran out into the cold. For the moment Mare was alone.

She felt woozy and exhilarated at the same time. A brilliant flash had revealed something totally unexpected. Her interior, she now realized, wasn't a dark domain littered with the debris of the past and the creeping footsteps of hidden demons. It was a chamber of secret magic. Whoever had transported her to another reality had only wanted to wake her up. The sleeper in the golden shrine knew her.

Now she was more eager than ever to go back again. Still sitting beside the miniature golden church, she bent over, putting her face close to it, as if she could peer through its windows. She was a giant Alice, and the little shrine was her looking glass.

Who are you? she silently asked. If there was a truth-teller inside, it would answer. She waited a long moment, her eyes closed. When no reply came, she tried what had worked before—praying. *God, if you're listening, guide me where I need to go.*

Her fingers brushed the gilded roof. It was the lightest of touches, and then she was gone.

The scene hadn't changed—the same dark alley, the same inquisitive neighbor leaning out of an upstairs window waving his oil lamp. The glimmering light revealed nothing, and he pulled his head back inside. Mare couldn't see anything either, but she caught a sound. The girl, the one who had run after the man in robe and sandals, was crying somewhere down the alley.

Mare followed the sound to a niche where the wall had crumbled. Even though the niche was shadowed in darkness, Mare could somehow see into it. The girl's head was covered; she wore a long clean shift, which was pinned with a silver brooch. This wasn't an impoverished waif.

"Why am I here? What do I have to do with you?" Mare whispered, forgetting that no one could hear her.

The girl stopped crying and looked up, staring straight at Mare. Could she see her standing there? The question was never answered, but a voice in Mare's head said something.

I am the sleeper. You have found me.

CHAPTER 10

When Galen passed out cold on his front stoop, the cab driver Jimmy had no choice but to call Lilith. She'd know what to do.

"Get him inside. We can't let him freeze to death." Lilith sounded impatient about this unexpected glitch in her plans. "He's part of the group, but he'll fight against it if you come right out and tell him. Just act friendly, and see if he warms up to you."

"I don't know," Jimmy said doubtfully. "I think we're way past that. He got really upset."

"What did you do to him?"

"Nothing. He's just strange."

"I know that. I've kept an eye on him for weeks. But everything has to come together now. It's what Meg wants. Do I have to remind you?" said Lilith sternly.

"No."

Jimmy hung up. The house key was already in the lock. Before turning it, he lightly shook Galen's shoulder.

"Come on, buddy," Jimmy coaxed, but Galen didn't respond. He had passed out as much from nervous exhaustion as fright, and now he was fast asleep.

Jimmy had a slim build, but was surprisingly strong. He managed to drag Galen into the house and lift him onto the futon sofa in the living room without much difficulty. As he softly snored, Jimmy removed Galen's shoes, then took a seat in a sagging La-Z-Boy across the room. The house was small; the musty odor of leftover pizza and dirty dishes piled up in the sink pervaded it. The furniture was old and worn, probably handed down from relatives, but the place was neatly kept. Jimmy's eye fell on the bookshelves that lined one wall. He considered whiling away the time by reading until his charge woke up, but when he examined the shelves, all the titles were scientific. They sounded very technical.

He'd have to sit and wait. Jimmy felt uneasy. He hadn't asked for this assignment; he wasn't even a cabbie. Lilith had devised the ruse to get Galen in a spot where he couldn't run away. As it happened, Jimmy had a cab-driver cousin who was willing to part with his car after his early shift ended.

Jimmy wasn't looking forward to Galen's reaction when he woke up. He'd probably make a racket and threaten to call the police again. Jimmy decided not to think about it. A year ago Lilith had told him that there was a group—she called it a mystery school—that was about to convene. The group was like a fraternal order, but even more secretive. Jimmy didn't see what it had to do with him.

"You're going to be part of it," Lilith told him.

"Not me."

But she sounded so certain, Jimmy became nervous. He asked questions, which Lilith kept avoiding. He only managed to coax some hazy details from her, something about the Middle Ages, when mystery schools were persecuted for heresy. If a pious citizen stumbled upon one, the culprits were rounded up, and the Church came down on them like a ton of bricks. A period of atonement was enforced. It began with torture and ended in death (unless you slipped a healthy bag of gold to the local bishop). But even the most extreme physical torture was insignificant compared with the fate of your soul. Back then, looking for God outside the church was like stepping into outer space, only instead of leaving the pull of gravity, you left everything that constitutes a normal life. Yet a few people dared to take this perilous step—mystics, misfits, freethinkers, and a sprinkling of crazies and spies. This was Lilith's unsavory sketch of the past.

"So why should I sign on?" Jimmy asked. In his mind's eye he could almost see those refugees from society huddled in a wine cellar or abandoned stone barn, dreading a knock at the door by the Inquisition.

"Because you've been chosen," Lilith replied.

"Like I said," Jimmy repeated, "not me."

But he knew in his heart that his protests sounded feeble. If a mystery school needed misfits, he qualified.

Jimmy's real job was as a hospital orderly. He and Lilith had been allies for a year now, a strange relationship that grew from an even stranger beginning. A young girl, not yet sixteen, was rushed to the hospital after a car struck her as she was walking alone on the side of the highway. She was brought to the ER in a coma; her chart said "Jane Doe," because the girl had no identification.

The damage to her brain was severe, and when she didn't regain consciousness in the first twenty-four hours, the doctors all but gave up on her. No family came forward, and after the second week medical care was minimal, not much more than turning her over to prevent bedsores and changing the IV drip.

Jimmy didn't know the medical details. He only knew that an older woman in a tweed suit appeared at the ICU every day. Lilith, he later learned. She showed up the minute visiting hours began and stayed by the girl's bedside until they were over. No one else came to see her.

Three weeks into her vigil, Jimmy approached the woman. "Is she your daughter?" he asked.

"My niece."

"I'm glad she has somebody. They couldn't locate her parents."

Lilith gave him a penetrating look, as if studying an X-ray. "Actually, she's not my niece. She's a total stranger."

Jimmy was taken aback. "Then you don't belong here."

"Why not? I'm not hurting anyone. Besides, you don't look like the kind to turn me in."

This was true enough. But why did she need to pretend?

"So no one will ask questions," was her answer.

Lilith gazed at the girl in the bed, who appeared to be sleeping. "She won't ever wake up."

Jimmy was startled. "You sound so certain. No one really knows."

"You can't say that unless you've met everyone, can you?"

Lilith didn't reveal her real motive for keeping a vigil, and Jimmy didn't pry. That wasn't his nature. But it was his nature to care. He made a point of regularly checking in on the girl, who lay motionless in her hospital bed like a forgotten mannequin, while beeping monitors signaled that the thread of life wasn't broken. If Lilith happened to be there, she'd acknowledge him with a silent nod. Jimmy, who hadn't graduated from high school and came from an immigrant family, was guarded in her presence. He was content, like the rest of his clan, the Noceras, to remember his place.

Then one day Lilith made a request in the form of an order. "When your shift is over, come directly here. Don't dawdle. You're needed."

"Why? I'm no doctor."

"We don't need a doctor." She shot him a stern look, one he would become very familiar with.

Jimmy felt uneasy. He wasn't prone to premonitions, yet the situation worried him. Was she planning to interfere? In the absence of any family, would she pull the plug on the girl's life support? He could easily have skipped out. At the end of his shift he had already changed into his street clothes and was halfway out the door, when he turned back and headed for the ICU.

Lilith was seated by the bed. She lifted a finger to her lips. "Don't speak. Watch."

Jimmy was spooked, but he did as he was told. He stood behind Lilith's chair; neither spoke for what seemed like an eternity. Suddenly the girl raised her head and opened her eyes. Her stare was glassy. *Dios mio,* Jimmy thought, repeating what his grandmother used to say whenever she felt in need of divine protection.

The comatose girl took no notice of her visitors; she only heaved a deep sigh before her head fell back on the pillow. Jimmy was certain that she had just died. He'd never been in a hospital room at the exact moment of death. The experience caused him to shiver. Lilith had anticipated this, he realized. That was why she had ordered him here. But how could she know?

Before he could ask, Lilith gave a loud "Ssh." It was unnecessary, though, since Jimmy was frozen in place. The dead girl emitted a faint glow around her head, a beautiful luminous vapor. The glow rose toward the ceiling, separating from her body. It formed into a blue-white shape roughly the size of the girl, vaguely outlining a head at one end and feet at the other. In a moment, it was gone. The glowing form had disappeared through the ceiling, or else it had evaporated. It happened too fast for Jimmy to tell.

"What just happened?" he whispered.

"Good, you saw. I had an intuition you would." Lilith got to her feet. "But if you really belong here, you know what just happened."

This last remark didn't sink in. Jimmy was too disconcerted. "How did you know she was going to die tonight?"

"I was directed, and I obeyed."

Lilith gathered up her things. She moved quickly out of the room in order to avoid the ICU nurses, who would appear in response to the monitors going flatline.

Jimmy followed her down the corridor. "Who gave you your orders?"

"It wasn't a who." Lilith looked impatient, annoyed that he was trailing her. "I don't expect you to understand."

She quickened her step, but Jimmy jumped ahead and blocked the way.

"You got me into this," he protested. "I deserve an explanation."

"'Deserve' is a little strong," she snapped. She didn't like it when the worm turned. But Jimmy refused to budge.

"Dying is pretty strong too, don't you think?" He was surprised by his own defiance. The first thing he'd learned as a child was to keep his head down. Remaining inconspicuous was the best defense for a spindly Hispanic kid whose relatives didn't want their papers to be inspected.

He couldn't guess at the thoughts running through Lilith's head at that moment. Events had been leading up to the mystery school for a decade. She was used to obeying her inner voice without question, which was how she had found Meg. The same voice told her to visit the anonymous runaway in the coma. Now she hesitated, waiting for some kind of signal. The human race can probably be divided into two camps, those who understand what it means to wait for a message from the soul and those who would scoff at the mere suggestion. Lilith had moved from one camp to the other. It had taken years, and she didn't want to recklessly expose herself.

"What you saw isn't so unusual," she began.

"So this isn't your first?" said Jimmy.

"No. Yours?" Lilith gave him another of her X-ray looks.

He stepped back. "Lady, I don't know who you think I am."

"You're someone with possibilities, only you don't realize it yet."

Her inner voice told Lilith that there was no turning back now. She began to unfold the whole story. Ever since entering the hospital, the girl in the coma hadn't moved, but her spirit was agitated. It had been badly shaken by the car crash. The coma sent it into a panic, knowing that death was around the corner, and so Lilith arrived to smooth the way. She knew she had to lay down a path of light for the spirit to follow, like a white line down the middle of the highway.

As he listened, Jimmy's face held an expression Lilith couldn't read. Was all of this foreign territory to him, or was he a natural? She only knew that he had been chosen as a witness for a reason.

"Let me pass," she said. "There's nothing more I can tell you."

"So you're just going to leave me hanging?" said Jimmy, unsatisfied.

"No. Keep your eyes open. If you see something like this again, I'll know, and I'll come back for you."

Jimmy was bewildered, but he stepped aside.

He suspected that what he'd seen wasn't accidental. In the world of his grandmother, a world filled with beeswax candles for the dead, roadside altars to the Virgin, and brightly colored *santos* painted on tin that were handed down from mother to daughter, there were spirits all around. As a boy, he couldn't envision what they looked like, so he thought of them as ghosts wearing white sheets.

He didn't have to use his imagination now. But he needed to know more. A week passed. Lilith didn't return, so Jimmy took the initiative. Nervously he began sneaking into hospital rooms where a patient was dying. An orderly was too lowly for doctors to notice, too harmless for anyone else to care.

Death keeps to its own timetable, and nothing ever happened. He tried standing outside a room during a code blue, but to no avail. The patients were brought back from the edge or resuscitated if they'd gone over it. And how could he explain his presence there in the first place? Out of desperation he drove to another hospital, claiming to be a dying patient's cousin. This backfired when some actual family members appeared. There were shrieks and pointed fingers. Jimmy mumbled excuses in broken English and was lucky not to get arrested.

Until then, his existence had been strangely content. He lived alone, surrounded by pictures of his many nieces and nephews, in a shoe-box apartment near a busy four-lane highway. His television was an old black-and-white portable, and he had never owned a microwave. Jimmy's family couldn't understand why he never got married or went back to their home country, Dominica, to find a good prospect among the many girls who would be happy to have him and a visa to America.

"That's for your generation," he'd say. "I was born here."

Behind his back, people saw him as an object of pity. The events of Jimmy's early life had unfolded in unfortunate ways, first by dropping out of school to go to work—a demand his father made because there were six younger children to feed. He lost touch with everyone his own age when he got a job as an orderly, where he put in so many hours of overtime that he came home exhausted and fell asleep watching *telenovelas* and Brazilian soccer. Seeing a spirit depart the body disturbed his strange contentment. For some reason, it also gave him new hope.

But as the weeks passed without a second sighting, his wonder at what he'd witnessed began to fade. Lilith didn't make any contact. Jimmy's mood darkened. Trying to catch someone's dying moment began to feel ghoulish. Then one night, as he was dragging himself from the living room after turning off the TV, Jimmy recalled Lilith's exact words when she summoned him: "Come directly here. Don't dawdle. You're needed."

This gave him a clue. Without quite knowing why, he sent a message to God: *Let me serve when I am needed.*

If he hadn't been so dog-tired, this prayer would have disturbed

Jimmy. It smelled too much of church talk and the humility of the priesthood. He wanted none of that—no amount of his mother's scolding drew him to the cathedral, except when his nieces, whom he loved dearly, were making their First Communion in white satin dresses.

Arriving at work the next morning, he was given no sign that anything unusual was going to happen. His pious words from the night before didn't spark any magic. On his lunch break he bought a bouquet of white carnations and took them upstairs to the children's ward. In one bed lay a ten-year-old girl, her body very thin and wasted. Jimmy had heard her family speaking Spanish in low voices; he felt a bond.

From the doorway he saw that she was asleep. He liked it better that way, actually, as he placed the carnations on the bedside table.

"Don't touch that!"

Jimmy whirled around. One of the interns had walked in; he looked very angry. "What are you doing in here?"

"Cleaning," Jimmy stammered.

"I don't see any cleaning materials. You were fiddling next to the patient. Did you touch her?"

Jimmy was too stunned to deny the accusation. The intern had red hair, and his face was turning florid to match it. Pointing to the ID Jimmy wore on his shirt, he said, "Give me your badge. We'll let security deal with this."

Jimmy unpinned the ID from his green uniform and held it out. He felt doomed. Hadn't his grandmother warned him? "*Mi querido,* listen to me. What you fear the most always comes true."

But the red-haired intern never took Jimmy's badge. Before he could, a strange look came over his face. He suddenly reached for his chest.

He croaked hoarsely, collapsing on the floor as heavily as a sack of flour. A passing nurse sounded the alarm; she told Jimmy to clear out and began running to the nurses' station.

Jimmy didn't clear out, but instead knelt beside the fallen man, lifting his head to help him breathe. The intern's eyes were open, and there was a glimmer of consciousness in them. Saliva bubbled in his mouth. The air in the room felt very still. In the moment before the cardiac crash cart appeared, the intern's eyes went dead, and Jimmy felt a slight stirring close by. There was no glow like before, only the faintest sense that an invisible breeze had brushed past Jimmy's cheek.

It can happen this way too, he thought.

The cardiac team rushed in, pushing Jimmy aside. Unlike everyone else hurrying about anxiously, Jimmy felt calmly detached. The little girl in the bed hadn't woken up, amazingly.

He left the room. Lilith was waiting for him at the end of the corridor.

"You kept your word," he said.

She gave an austere smile. "Welcome to God knows what."

After that they became allies. Lilith began to fill him in about the group he would belong to, the mystery school. She had been waiting ten years, and so had someone named Meg, although her name came up only once. Jimmy was baffled by most of what Lilith told him.

"It's better not to ask too many questions," she advised. "A mystery isn't something you figure out. It's something you disappear into."

"Like a ship vanishing in the fog?" Jimmy wondered.

"Exactly."

It wasn't a complete shock, then, when she told him to follow Galen. It meant that everything was finally coming to a head.

"You're excited, I can tell," Jimmy said.

"Just don't mess this up," she replied.

After half an hour, Galen stopped snoring and emitted a low groan. His eyes opened, adjusting to the dark room. Jimmy flicked on a lamp.

Galen gasped. "You! You knocked me out."

"No, you fainted, and I dragged you inside." Jimmy opened his jacket like a suspect ready to be frisked. "No weapon, see?" He braced himself for another outburst, but it didn't come.

Instead, Galen heaved a sigh of resignation. "Take what you want. I don't care. Just leave me alone."

"I'm afraid you've got this all wrong."

Jimmy stood up and approached the futon sofa. From his jacket pocket he pulled a folded sheet of paper. It was a watercolor that Lilith had told him to bring.

Galen mistook why Jimmy was standing over him. "Don't hit me," he pleaded feebly.

"No one's going to hit you."

Jimmy unfolded the picture and held it in the light, so that Galen could get a good look.

"You recognize this?" he asked. The watercolor was of a golden chapel with four steeples nestled in a flowery meadow.

Galen had no reply. He burst into tears and hung his head in shame.

CHAPTER 11

Lilith wasn't prone to self-doubt, and if it had been up to her, the mystery school would have been complete by now. On her instructions Jimmy had secured a meeting place at the hospital where he worked. When he showed it to Lilith, she didn't disguise her disappointment. The conference room was sterile and airless. It had no windows, only a long table with folding chairs around it and harsh fluorescent lighting.

"It's not exactly a palace," she said.

"But it's not a torture chamber either," Jimmy reminded her.

"True. There were too many of those."

Meg had set two weeks as the deadline, which left only three more days to go. The big question mark was Galen. Everyone else had been lured in, thanks to Lilith, with Meg guiding her over the rough spots.

"Leave Galen to someone else," Meg told her. They communicated twice a day by phone. For reasons of her own, Meg didn't want to meet in person. She preferred to be the invisible spider sitting out of sight away from the web.

"I can handle him," Lilith insisted.

"No, you can't. He's a delicate case. One misstep, and we'll lose him."

So when Jimmy called with the news that Galen had passed out, Lilith became worried. That was two hours ago, and still no word. She decided to go over there herself and was putting on her coat when the phone rang.

"Jimmy? Do we have him?"

But it was Meg instead. "You sound anxious. What's happening?"

"I was just about to go and find out."

"Don't." There was a short pause on the line. "Get everything ready. Act as if the pieces are going to fall into place."

If this was a statement of faith, it was wasted on Lilith. "We risk everything if we sit on our hands."

"It's okay."

"How can you say that?"

Another pause. "We're always being tested. It was hard for me to come back after all this time. You know that. It was even harder to let go of the shrine."

There was no more to say, and the call ended. But Lilith couldn't let go. Her frustration was killing her. Three days short of the goal, and the mystery school could collapse before it had even started. She should have been put in charge, not demoted to carrying out Meg's orders. The mystery school had grown out of her dream, hadn't it? The dream set in the plague years when Lilith saw the six bodies and the golden shrine?

But it was Meg who gave up her life. At first she totally rejected the idea of becoming a nun. Lilith was sent away with a flat refusal. Then two days later, Meg began to have symptoms of a strange heart malady. At first it manifested as a mild soreness in the middle of her chest. She applied ice, then a hot pad. But the soreness only grew worse. Meg didn't dare to see a doctor, not after all she'd gone through. *Another punishment,* she told herself, *that's what it has to be.*

Every night, she went to sleep with images of a bleeding heart in her head, stark visions that sent her back to her childhood. When she was seven, the nuns at school gave each child a picture of Jesus's heart. Meg was shocked. Why did Jesus wear his heart on the outside? Why was it wearing a crown of thorns, and above all why did blood drip from it? The very sight sent her running into a bathroom stall to hide. Her teacher, Sister Evangeline, found her and asked what was wrong.

"Jesus needs an operation," Meg said.

"It's a beautiful thing," Sister Evangeline corrected her. "If you love Jesus, you love his Sacred Heart."

Perhaps Meg wasn't suggestible, like people who are immune to being hypnotized. She didn't think a heart encircled with a crown of thorns could ever be beautiful. The dripping blood would always be horrible. Even at seven, though, she knew not to say such things aloud.

Within a few days, the soreness in Meg's chest grew so severe she started to wish for the stigmata to return. The bloody spots on her palms had caused only a dull ache. Some days she felt jealous of Lilith with her vision of a golden chapel; it sounded much nicer, more like what a loving God would send. Other days she looked on the whole thing as a bout of madness she had to escape. But there appeared to be only one way out, a route she dreaded the most: becoming a religious freak.

Just when the pain became intolerable, stabbing Meg's heart like nails, Lilith appeared in the driveway in her stiff tweeds with her hands crossed over her purse. Just like that, without any warning.

They didn't sit, as before, in the dining room. Meg had barely made it through the workday on heavy doses of aspirin and shots of vodka from a flask hidden in her desk. She collapsed on the living-room sofa while Lilith talked.

She showed no interest in Meg's suffering. "You're stuck on one idea, that what's happening is a curse. I told you it wasn't."

"Then what is it—a test, a penance?"

Lilith shook her head. "It's a message."

"Telling me what?"

"That it's better to suffer on your path than to be happy on no path at all."

Meg bolted upright despite the pain. "That's horrible!" she exclaimed. She was ready for an argument. "A loving God wants me to be in pain? Why, because I'm a sinner? No thanks. I've heard it all before."

"I can't read God's mind," Lilith retorted. "What I do know is that you have a path, once you submit to it."

"I hate that word 'submit,'" Meg grumbled.

"I don't blame you. But there's something beyond the pain. You just have to get there, and I can't help you. No one can."

Meg and Lilith sat in silence, wondering if they'd ever cross the gulf between them. Lilith, as stubborn as she could be, wasn't going to wear Meg down. If the pain couldn't, how could she?

"Just go," Meg said in an exhausted voice. When Lilith didn't move, she laughed bitterly. "Why are you so interested in me? It's abnormal."

"I have my own path. And I get messages I can't ignore. You're not the only one."

Silence followed. They had hit a wall, and there was no going around it. Lilith gathered herself and stood up. "If I leave now, I won't be back."

Meg hesitated. The prospect of Lilith leaving for good suddenly felt threatening.

But Lilith didn't wait for her to decide. "One way or another," she said, "God finds us where we are, and then he gets us where we need to be." She walked over to the mantel, where a pair of brass candlesticks stood. Drawing an imaginary line between them, she said, "You go from A to B. You do it every day, no matter how many days it takes. You put all your trust in the path that God lays out. It's simple."

Meg's resentment boiled over. "It's not simple! Not when you've got a thousand tiny knives sticking you in the heart." Collapsing back on the sofa, she began to cry.

The sight softened something in Lilith. "Don't abandon us. Don't abandon *me*."

Meg drew a ragged breath, trying to regain control. "You'll get along without me. We both know that."

Lilith shook her head. "I told you already, the whole thing falls apart without you."

Meg started to moan, her face in her hands. "It's not fair!"

"You can only know that if you see what God can't see." Lilith's stiffness had returned, but not harshly. "I regret that your path is so painful, but without you the rest of us will return to darkness."

Meg was speechless. The whole thing sounded so preposterous. A helpless feeling swept over her, and she flashed on how this all began, with a man walking to his crucifixion. His sense of helplessness dwarfed anything she had ever experienced.

From that moment, everything had spread out like ripples from a rock thrown into a pond. As most people do, she had accepted the small glimpses of meaning that came her way. All the big words—love, hope, compassion, grace—were minimized, placed into tiny compartments like pills in a pillbox. One compartment was for the few people she really loved and who loved her back. Another held her hopes, which had always been modest. Some compartments, like the ones that contained compassion and faith, she had barely peeked into. But there was no compartment for grace. Perhaps that was why she felt so afraid.

"You can't depend on me," she moaned. "I'm more in the dark than anyone."

Sensing Meg's despair, Lilith became more fervent. "There is another life, one you've barely dreamed about. You have been postponing it every day of your life. It's as close as breathing, but you don't see it yet. When you do, you'll lead the rest of us."

"The rest don't exist. The only one I know is you."

"The others will be just like me."

Meg forced a small laugh. "I hope that's not a promise."

She let Lilith stay until she regained control. Nothing had been settled, but afterwards Meg stopped fighting so hard, and the worst of her heart pains subsided.

She kept going to work. She still saw her parents every Sunday for dinner. She still wore her stunning shade of burgundy lipstick and listened to her nieces talk about their boyfriends. Never once, though, did she utter a word about what had happened. As far as her family was concerned, she was the same old Meg she'd been her entire life. Which is why her decision to enter the convent at forty took everyone by surprise.

"You can't," her bossy sister, Nancy Ann, protested. "I know a therapist."

"Don't bully her," said Clare, her sympathetic sister. But she was just as worried as everyone else in the family.

Meg refused to explain herself. The turning point had been with Lilith, who said, "You need to be away from everybody for a while. You have to ripen."

"I'm not a banana," Meg joked, but she knew what Lilith meant.

Lilith spelled it out anyway. "Your soul is ready, but you aren't. There's a mismatch, which is probably why you've been having so much pain. Your body is still protesting."

Meg couldn't deny it. The soreness in her heart, though lessened, kept reminding her of her dilemma.

"Walk away. Heal," Lilith urged. "And when you do, we'll be waiting for you. All of us."

Neither of them suspected that once Meg became a nun, there would be ten years of silence between them. Lilith visited a few times at first, waiting at the brass grate that separated the sisters from the world. Meg never appeared. On the third visit she sent down a note: "The patient is still in intensive care."

The nun who delivered it didn't know what the note meant.

"Is Meg all right?" Lilith demanded to know.

The nun gave her a starchy smile. "Sister Margaret Thomas belongs to God. There's no question she's all right."

Lilith almost cringed. The very thing she once told Meg was being thrown back at her. Years ago she had stopped visiting and simply waited. On an ordinary afternoon she was taking a nap when the phone rang. She answered reluctantly, in case one of the kids was in trouble.

"Hello?"

Drowsily she could hear a familiar voice on the other end. The first thing it said erased ten years in an instant.

"Have all of you waited for me?"

Lilith was instantly awake. "We have."

"Then it's time."

CHAPTER *12*

When Jimmy held up the watercolor of the golden shrine, he knew that everything depended on it. It was his ace in the hole if all other forms of persuasion failed. But he was shocked by Galen's sobbing reaction.

"Don't be upset," he said. It would be a disaster if Galen slipped out of reach.

"Thief!" Galen cried, his hands balled into fists.

The accusation was true. On Lilith's orders, Jimmy had snatched the picture from a room at the hospital. He felt guilty, but there was nowhere to go now but forward.

"I know your wife painted it," he said hesitantly. "Now I'm giving it back."

Galen lifted his head, wiping his damp cheeks with the back of a shirt sleeve. "You think that makes it better?"

"No, but I needed you to recognize the picture. It's important."

Galen had a flash of recognition. "I've seen you before, in her hospital room."

Jimmy nodded, holding his breath. No matter what, he couldn't let Galen throw him out of the house.

"So you're stalking me?" Galen said bitterly.

"Sort of, but it's for a good cause."

This brought a short, barking laugh. But at least Galen had stopped crying. The whole situation was grotesque, including the part he had played. Jimmy held the watercolor up again, but Galen couldn't look at it. It brought back memories of Iris, cancer, and death.

He had sleepwalked through the agonizing events as they unfolded. Iris showed a surprising lack of resistance to seeing a neurologist about her headaches. She had kept from Galen how severe they were, just as he kept from her the ominous e-mail her father had sent. A brain scan was taken, and the doctor described what it showed.

"See this shadow here? It's what we call a lesion on the prefrontal cortex."

"A tumor?" Galen said dully. Sitting beside him, Iris kept silent, gripping his hand tightly in hers.

The doctor nodded. "I'm very sorry. I have to tell you, it's aggressive, and it probably came on very suddenly, perhaps four or five months ago."

Just when she came up to me in the museum, Galen thought grimly. He winced. Iris's nails were digging into his palm like needles.

"There should have been early signs, though they're not predictable," the doctor went on. "A quiet person might suddenly become very outgoing and emotional." He pointed to the image illuminated on the wall beside him. "The lesion is on the right side, just here. The effects can be quite mysterious. In very rare cases, musical abilities appear out of the blue or a mania for painting that was never there before."

Iris didn't cry out, but tears started streaking down her cheeks. She hung her head as if ashamed.

"Can you make her better?" Galen asked, his face ashen.

There were no promises. Surgery followed, then radiation. Iris's parents rushed back, and their accepting mood had changed. They now looked upon Galen as an interloper, a stranger who had taken advantage of their sick little girl. Dr. Winstone as much as accused him of hiding Iris's symptoms.

Galen suffered through everything as numbly as he could. Iris moved to the spare room to sleep. They rarely talked, and when they did, it was an effort for her to show Galen any signs of affection. She pitied them both, as if a malicious magician had fooled them with his illusions, and now the spell was broken.

One morning she didn't appear for breakfast. Galen searched for her in her room, but it was empty. He lifted the phone to call 911 when he glanced out the window. Weak as she was, his wife had stacked up her paintings in the back yard and was setting them on fire. He rushed outside and, over her protests, pulled out all the canvases that hadn't been scorched yet.

"We have to save them. Forget the doctor. You're a genius."

A weird, squeezed laugh came from her. "I'm just sick. Art was my affliction."

Two weeks later, Iris died in hospice care. An orderly made up her empty bed as Galen rummaged through the bedside table for Iris's things. The orderly seemed to be eyeing him.

"Do you mind? I'm the husband," Galen said sharply. The vigilant orderly nodded and left. Now Galen knew it was Jimmy.

Iris's parents couldn't keep Galen from attending the funeral, but he stayed on the periphery, a silent incidental presence. As the first spade of earth was thrown on the coffin, the mocking voice in Galen's head said, *The comedy endeth.* The voice sounded very satisfied. Galen wasn't. He wanted to lash out at someone or something for the cruel trick that fate had played on him. Like a spindly sprout in a parched field, a plan for avenging a terrible wrong started to hatch in his numbed mind.

Galen pressed his head tightly between his hands, as if to squeeze these memories out.

Jimmy tried to say something that might bring him around. "This picture is very significant. Would you like to know why?"

"Absolutely not." Worn out as Galen was, he could still get angry.

Jimmy pressed on anyway. "It shows a precious object, a holy relic. Your wife must have seen it in a vision. You are our link to her."

Galen regarded him with disdain. "Whatever bullshit you're peddling, you've come to the wrong place. I don't have any money. I just want to . . ." He didn't know how to finish his thought.

"You just want to curl up into a little ball of misery? I can't let you do that, and you don't have to. You're a prisoner inside yourself. Iris saw it. That's why she was drawn to you. It's also why I was sent here."

Jimmy's strange response forced Galen to look at him more closely. The smile he wore, which Galen had initially despised, looked different now.

"I don't need your pity," he said.

"It would have to wait in line anyway, behind your self-pity."

Galen was about to drop the f-bomb, as his mother called it when he was a child, but Jimmy suddenly made a move. Getting to his feet, he took two steps toward Galen, who had no time for a defensive cringe. Before he knew it, Jimmy was lifting him up under the arms as if he were a cranky two-year-old scooped up by his mother.

"Good, we have you on your feet. Now take another look. If you know nothing about this picture, I'll leave you in peace. Not that you'll find any."

Was that last bit a taunt? Galen felt uneasy.

"Please, stop looking so afraid," Jimmy pleaded. "I'm bringing you hope."

Galen had been jerked to his feet too quickly. The blood was rushing from his head; he felt dizzy. He squeezed his eyes shut and willed himself not to faint twice in one day.

"We can talk," he whispered. "Just let me sit down again, please."

Jimmy stepped back, and Galen sank down on the couch, putting his head between his knees. After a moment, his dizziness cleared.

"Tell me what you remember," Jimmy coaxed.

Galen looked puzzled. "Nothing important. What she painted was just a symptom of being sick."

Jimmy shook his head. "Being sick was only a small part of it. When someone is dying, a part of them reaches out for the truth. As they go through the door into another world, they look back over their shoulder to give us a hint about the truth."

Galen felt helpless to argue back. "Whatever. You sound sincere. But I'm the one who got kicked in the teeth when she died."

"You're right. I apologize. You didn't ask for any of this."

Galen took the picture from Jimmy with a sigh, doing his best to recreate the scene weeks before Iris's death. He hadn't made much time to visit her in the hospital. The strain between them was part of the reason. The other part was that he had thrown himself into his work with ferocity. His days were spent at the research library with stacks of journals in front of him. He typed drafts of articles on the computer far into the night, too drained and distracted to face reality.

Galen took up smoking and threw back a shot of whiskey at sunset, the hour beloved by the demon of depression. Slowly he started to feel a shift inside. He was pulling away from Iris and everything she'd been to him. It was like standing at the rear door of a train as it crept away from the station. Before long, the station lights would recede into a faint dimness, and then nothing.

His escape plan wasn't perfect, though. Guilt made him drop in at the hospital, usually late in the afternoon, his arrival timed to Iris's dinner so he could excuse himself after a few minutes. At that point Iris was still eating a little, but the cancer wasted her ruthlessly, sucking out every bit of energy. Galen was relieved whenever he found her asleep, which was often.

On one particular afternoon, however, she was wide awake. Her motorized bed was propped up as far as it could go, and her hair was carefully pulled back and pinned, a few stray wisps framing her pale face. Galen tried to smile, but she had put on a drop of his favorite perfume, and the scent made him feel sick.

"You look nice," he mumbled evasively.

"Do I? I made sure I didn't bring a mirror from home." Iris's voice was clear, and her eyes glistened. Galen looked away. Her eyes had glistened like that when she was in her mania for painting.

"Please, don't be afraid of me," she whispered.

Galen's hand instinctively moved toward the cigarettes in his jacket pocket, until he remembered where he was. Before his mother died, she entered a spell of truth-telling. She held him captive by her bedside atoning for her mistakes, trying to make amends. *If we're into the truth,* he wanted to tell her, *I'm bored and fed up. Eat some Jell-O, watch TV. We can't change the past.* He never let the words out though, biding his time like a patient son.

But he wasn't about to play the same game twice. "The doctor wants you to rest," he mumbled. "I should go."

"In a minute," said Iris, not offended by his rudeness. She gestured toward the metal bedside table, which was just out of her reach. "Can you open that drawer, please? I want to show you something."

Galen opened it and retrieved a sheet of fine-grained paper with deckled edges

"I didn't know you brought any supplies with you," he said.

"I met a nice nurse. She fetched some paper and colors for me. You weren't answering the phone."

"You could have waited," Galen complained.

She read the guilt on his face. "I didn't want you to feel bad, seeing all the art stuff again. And I was in a hurry. I had the strongest desire to make this picture. Imagine that, after trying to burn everything."

She took the paper from his hands and turned it over, exposing the image hidden from sight in the drawer. "I wanted you to be the first to see it."

She wasn't being cruel. Galen knew this, but his heart began to ache. He dully gazed at the picture. It showed a steepled church in a meadow. There was a golden glow suffusing it. He scowled. The religious thing again. Her disease was showing no mercy.

In a sympathetic voice Iris said, "You don't have to like it. You don't even have to keep it. But somehow it's about you." Seeing that he wanted to protest, she rushed on. "The image came to me in a dream. I was happy in the dream, for once. Sleep is usually such a black hole."

She stopped. Galen showed no reaction. Against his will, he had been drawn into a round of deathbed truth-telling again.

Iris tried to keep up her bright mood, even though a tinge of defeat was creeping in. "This isn't something I can explain or help you through, Galen. I don't understand it myself. All I know from the dream is that you belong here." She pointed to the church, and then her hand fell.

She'd spent her energy; her body gave out, and the disease reclaimed her. The color drained from her face. Gray and empty-eyed, her head lolled on the pillow. The transformation was shockingly fast.

Galen couldn't spare any pity for her. He was too angered by what she'd said: "You belong here." The words made him want to rip the picture from her limp hands and tear it in two. Instead, he turned around and left. The ache in his heart had turned into the cold heaviness of stone.

Now, in his living room, Galen made a futile gesture. "That's all I know."

"I understand. It hurts to go back," Jimmy said.

Galen flared up. "Screw you."

Jimmy sighed. "We're going around in circles here."

Pulling out his cell phone, he walked into the nearby kitchen. Galen heard a mumbled exchange.

When he returned, Jimmy said, "We understand why you're resisting this whole thing. It's too much to take in, and you're exhausted. But you showed us what to do."

"Me?"

" 'You belong here.' If that's the message, a sign—whatever you call it—we're going to trust it." He pointed to the picture. "What your wife saw is real, a gift from God, and now it's in the right hands. I hope you get to see it. A lot of people are depending on you."

"I don't care. God is a lie, a huge criminal fraud. If anybody wants something from me, tell them that." Galen's voice trailed off. He didn't want to think about his failed revenge.

"What if you found out once and for all?" Jimmy asked.

"About what?"

"If Iris saw something real. If God is real. Here's your chance to find out."

"You're insane." But Galen's protest wasn't as angry as before. He could hear the compassion in Jimmy's voice.

"I'm just going on faith here," Jimmy said. "But there are people I trust, the way I'm asking you to trust me. They say that anyone who comes into contact with this object is never the same again."

Galen was poised with a torrent of objections, but Jimmy didn't give him the chance to release them.

"Here." He scribbled the number of the conference room on the back of the picture. "We're meeting at the hospital. You know where it is. The room's in the basement."

Galen stared suspiciously at what Jimmy had written. "Do I get paid?"

"That's not up to me. I'm just the messenger."

Jimmy didn't scold him for having selfish motives. He could see that Galen had to defend himself.

"Just think about it. I'll let myself out."

Without another word Jimmy stepped outside, closing the door behind him. He paused on the stoop to look up. It was snowing now, and by morning his footprints would be erased, as if he'd never been there. He headed back to the cab. The news wouldn't please Lilith; but it was her idea, when Jimmy phoned from the kitchen, to appeal to Galen's curiosity. Jimmy was about to report back when his cell phone rang.

"I think he listened." It was a woman's voice, but not Lilith's.

"Who is this?"

"We haven't met, but we will soon. I'm Meg."

Jimmy was confused. "I don't know any Meg."

"Just as well. I only wanted to thank you."

"Really? How do you know about any of this?"

"It's not easy to explain. But I'll try when we meet."

Before he could ask another question, the line went dead. Jimmy brushed the snowflakes from the driver's-side windshield with his glove. He climbed into the cab, not looking over his shoulder. Somehow he was sure that Galen had come to his front window and was gazing out to make sure he really left.

Jimmy tried not to feel disheartened. He had probably revealed more than he should have. Protecting the mystery of the golden shrine was the group's first priority, Lilith had warned. Galen might show up with the others just to snoop. He might extort money. Whatever happened, it was time to walk away. An invisible force was at work. If a miserable skeptic was destined to join, fate would find a way.

The cab left light tracks in the thin, new snow as it sped away. Galen waited at the window until it turned the corner and was out of sight. Seeing the intruder leave was a relief, but not enough to remove the tension in his body. He crumpled Iris's watercolor into a ball and threw it into the trash bin under the sink; then he hopped into the shower.

There was no reason to trust the intruder and his fantastic talk. What had talking done but stir up painful memories and play on Galen's emotions? Now he was left with nothing except nagging doubts. Iris believed in her vision. The intruder was right about that—she wanted to send Galen a message he couldn't ignore.

He turned up the hot water until it made red splotches on his shoulders as he stood under the steaming spray. It burned, but his muscles started to relax. Galen drank three beers before he went to bed, idly surfing the Internet to distract himself. Soon he was fit for nothing but crashing into stupefied sleep.

He didn't know the next morning how he happened to find the watercolor, rescued from the trash, lying open on the kitchen counter. Still less did he know why he got in his car on Saturday, three days later, headed for the hospital and the room number Jimmy had scrawled on the back of the picture. Galen's heart was racing as he got closer to his destination.

What am I doing? he thought to himself. Doubt, always his default position, began to tug at him.

But another force intervened. *You're going where you belong,* it said.

The words were meaningless. Galen almost turned back, but he had come this far. Besides, all he could think about was Iris, the love she'd shown to a lost soul, and how impossible it was to let go.

part two

THE INVISIBLE GOSPEL

CHAPTER *13*

So it befell that at seven o'clock on Saturday evening, they all arrived. First Mare, who brought Frank, who threatened in the car to walk out if anything weird started to happen.

"Weird would be an anticlimax after what we've gone through," said Mare. A grunt was his only reply. She smiled to herself, suspecting that Frank's resistance was merely token. He had a reporter's nose and couldn't wait to follow up this lead.

The rest of the group was already seated around the table when they walked in. Lilith hadn't placed herself at the head, where everyone expected her to be, but in the closest chair to the right.

"Don't introduce yourselves, and try not to stare," she ordered. "Someone's got the jitters."

She meant Galen, who had sunk into a sullen mood the moment he laid eyes on Lilith. Jimmy had switched work shifts with another orderly that day and only had to take the elevator to the basement.

When the five of them were seated, Lilith nodded, and Mare placed the closed cardboard box she'd walked in with on the table.

"Do you want me to open it?" she asked nervously. This was the first time the golden shrine had left her apartment.

"Not yet."

An awkward silence settled over the group. Galen shifted in his seat. Frank took hold of Mare's hand under the table. Lilith was stone-faced. The only person who looked pleased was Jimmy, because he had carried out his task of gathering the black sheep into the fold.

After fifteen minutes, Galen stood up. "Am I the only one who's choking in here? Is the AC broken or what?"

It was never discovered if he was about to bolt from the group at the last minute, because two critical things occurred simultaneously. From between the cracks in the loosely closed cardboard box a faint golden glow started to emanate, giving off a glimmer like the last live coals buried in the ashes of a winter fire. As if on cue the door opened, and a dignified woman entered the room. She wore a black suit and no makeup. She smelled faintly of lily-of-the-valley perfume. Her eyes went immediately to the box.

"Good," she said. "The sleeper is awake."

Mare was eighteen when she last saw her aunt, and the woman just entering didn't fit her memories. Her aunt's hair was more gray than the light brown Mare remembered. She was also smaller, as if shrunk into herself, with dainty hands. Her eyes had a faraway look in them. *The effect of ten years in the convent?* Mare wondered.

If Mare couldn't yet match her recollections with the woman in front of her, Meg immediately recognized her niece. She came over and whispered in her ear. "You've done very well. I'm proud of you."

Mare didn't know whether to feel reassured or to burst into tears—she had almost convinced herself that she would never see her aunt again. "Why is all this happening?" she whispered back.

But there was no time to talk. The room was in a commotion. Everyone's attention was fixed on the golden light peeking through the cardboard box, which was directly in front of Mare and Frank.

Trying to look unfazed, Frank pushed it toward Meg. "Welcome back, if that makes any sense. This belongs to you." He glanced around the table. "As you can see, it did the job."

"I'm sorry you were kept in the dark," Meg apologized. "I'll try my best to explain why we're here."

Lilith cut her short. "That can wait. Not everyone has seen what's inside. Time for the unveiling."

Meg gave a resigned nod. "I suppose you're right."

With visible uncertainty Mare opened the box and lifted out the shrine. At her touch, its glowing aura grew brighter, filling the room even under the harsh fluorescent lights. The reaction around the table was quiet awe, except from Galen. He shielded his face to keep the light out of his eyes.

"This thing could be radioactive. Have you thought about that?"

"Don't make trouble," said Lilith sharply. "There's nothing to be afraid of."

"And we're just supposed to believe you?" he asked.

Frank was getting annoyed. "You need to cool it. I'm as skeptical as anybody, but this"—he held his palms up to the light—"this isn't a cheap trick."

"Unless proven otherwise," Galen shot back.

Meg intervened. "It's our first meeting, and we have some important decisions to make. Let's not waste time arguing." She paused to let the golden light capture their attention again. "The one thing we can all agree on is that none of us, including me, ever imagined a phenomenon such as this. The only possible reaction is wonder."

"This is the mystery that makes us a mystery school," Lilith added.

Galen had to clamp his jaws tight, but no one contradicted her.

"Right," Lilith continued. "So we find ourselves in unknown territory. Each of us has been chosen, even though we don't know why."

"I have a suggestion," Jimmy interrupted, speaking for the first time. He was probably the most transfixed by the glowing light. "We better be careful what we say around this thing. It could be listening to us, you know."

Lilith's reaction was barely concealed pity.

"Really, I'm serious," he protested.

"I agree," said Meg. "We don't have to watch what we say, but it would be foolish to ignore a simple fact. There's something inside there. We have no idea where it came from or what it knows."

Lilith, after trying to seize control, fell back in her chair.

"You mean a ghost?" Jimmy asked, thinking of the dead spirits who surrounded his grandmother. She attributed good fortune to them when they were appeased. More often it was the reverse. If she couldn't find her prayer book or the roof leaked, his grandmother would get a knowing look on her face and mumble "Uncle Tito" or the name of some other deceased relative.

Meg shook her head. "I'd describe it as a presence. The shrine is hypnotic, but it only exists to get our attention."

"Like I said, it does the job. That still doesn't tell us why we're all here," countered Frank.

Now Mare entered in. "Perhaps the six of us are a test case. We've been given a sign to see what we do with it."

"We're being experimented on?" asked Frank, who looked uneasy at the prospect.

"Bingo," Galen said with a twisted smile. "God needs lab rats, and we're dumb enough to volunteer."

"I'm just trying to figure this out," snapped Frank. "If you've got a better idea, let's hear it. Or are you only here to shut us down?"

"I'm just not ready to swallow bogus miracles," Galen said with quiet defiance. "Let's put all our cards on the table, okay? The rest of you want this to be a miracle, don't you? Some of you in the worst way. If it turns out you were duped, laugh all you like. But you'll feel like fools."

Because you've been there, Jimmy wanted to say. He had a hard time restraining himself. He knew that Galen was churning inside. He had desperately wanted to believe in Iris's love, and he wouldn't be made a fool of twice.

"Why would anyone dupe us?" asked Frank. "Nobody here is rich, and besides, I work for the paper. I could blow the whistle on this in a heartbeat."

Before Galen could fire a new salvo, Lilith came back to life. "I was the first one who saw the object. It came to me in a dream. A nightmare, really. There was death all around, and somehow this glowing church appeared among the dying. Was it a symbol of life, a promise of heaven? I had no idea. A higher reality was reaching out, just like it's reaching out to us now. Will we welcome it or turn our backs and run? Believe me, I've spent anxious nights over this, but I'll never rest easy if I don't see it through."

She had spoken for everyone, but there was no murmur of agreement. The Lilith they all knew harbored no doubts, much less fear.

Galen stood his ground. "You think this is a test of faith? Then why was I chosen?"

"That may be unanswerable, and not just for you," Meg said. "Whatever is meant to happen, it starts now. This is a new moment. How many of those come along in our lives?"

Her words silenced the room, each person lost in private thoughts. They had spaced themselves widely around the table, like a collection of strangers and not a group. Galen had talked about God needing lab rats. He was being sarcastic, but God lurked in the back of everyone's mind. Was God toying with them? It was like one of those carnival machines where you insert a quarter and try to lift out a prize with a grappling hook. A cosmic player had dropped the hook and chosen them, six people out of all those on the whole planet, as his prize.

The cosmic player liked diversity. Mare and Frank were the only obvious couple. The youngest too, dressed in faded jeans and running shoes. Jimmy, just off his shift, was dressed in his uniform. Galen had thrown on the same khakis and white shirt he'd been wearing all week. Lilith and Meg, the two oldest, wore suits, which gave off an air of authority.

After a few moments, Frank began to speak. "You say the shrine is alive or has someone inside it, whatever. It isn't holding us here against our will. Let's talk to it and get some answers."

"You're right," said Meg. "Wonder isn't enough, and skepticism can't deny what's before us."

When no one protested, she was encouraged. The nervousness in the room, which had dominated everything so far, began to lessen.

"We must make contact," she continued. "The presence has no name. I think it's a she. The person who gave me the shrine said she was the thirteenth disciple of Jesus."

She spoke in a mild tone, but these words sent a shiver through the group.

"How could she still be alive?" Jimmy whispered, overwhelmed by this new piece of information.

"How could she be dead? That's what a believer would say," Lilith pointed out. "Death, where is thy sting? Grave, where is thy victory?" she quoted.

"At the risk of sounding obtuse," said Frank, "we're here with someone who knew Jesus. Is that what you're saying?"

"I think so," Meg said cautiously. "Lilith and I have been waiting a long time to find the rest of you. We were never sure what we were dealing with."

"I don't like the sound of that," Frank muttered. "You have to tell us what you know."

"All right, but it may not help."

Meg's indecision was genuine. She was at the center of the web that drew them together, but she had taken one leap of faith after another.

"Only recently has the golden shrine been given to me," she began, "and it happened as mysteriously as everything that's happened to you."

The delicate string of events went back to her first month as a nun. At vespers on the day she entered the cloister, she waited in a dark hallway. The double doors in front of her swung open, and she faced the entire company of nuns, their first novice in years. She was in her candidacy, they told her, which would last three months. In no uncertain terms, the nuns made it clear they would be keeping an eye on her. But they were mostly older and benign, and if not benign, lost in their private contemplation, with no inclination to bother her.

Her strategy was to blend in, but make no special friends. This wasn't difficult. Several other nuns ate alone and said little. A sister desiring complete contemplation was held up as a shining example for the rest to emulate. As the new arrival, Meg raised no eyebrows when she missed some prayers and worked in the kitchen without speaking to anyone. Outwardly she was accepted, but it still took her some time to be accepted on the inside. Bouts of absolute panic came and went. She would lie on her back staring at the small window of her claustrophobic cell, furnished with a metal-framed cot and a rickety dresser. She felt like a castaway at sea, lost from rescue.

After Meg's first three weeks, Mother Superior called her in to make sure Sister Margaret Thomas, as Meg was now known, was adjusting. Sitting in the hallway outside the old nun's office,

Meg had made up her mind to leave. It would be humiliating, but there was no alternative.

So when she was asked how she liked her new life, Meg was amazed to hear herself say, "It's everything I'd hoped for."

"You're not lonely?" Mother Superior asked. "It can be a shock. The new ones miss television, I believe. I arrived before television, you see."

"You must have been very young, Reverend Mother," Meg murmured. When the old nun looked puzzled, she repeated the words in a louder voice, suspecting deafness. The infirmity had made conversation with her grandparents practically impossible as they got older.

"Well, I came from a small farming town. Television took a long time to get there." Mother Superior was content to see the smile on Meg's face. If she was growing deaf or not, it cued her to end the interview quickly.

Walking away, Meg was mystified at her impulsive decision to stick it out. But what was done was done. In her second month, she stopped waiting for fingers to point at her accusing her of being a fraud. She felt a quiet awe around the Carmelite sisters and their dedication to a life of prayer. *They are married to God,* she thought, remembering the first time her mother had explained to her what a nun was.

It was a relief not to feel panicked and suffocated, but there was no inner light. The cloistered routine she once feared turned into something worse: a bore. The ripening that Lilith had promised hadn't yet shown signs of starting. Meg was stubborn, but how long could she hang from the tree like last year's withered crab apples?

I didn't come here with any guarantees, she reminded herself. *Wait and see.*

Twice a week, the church sent a priest, Father Aloysius, to perform Mass and hear confession as chaplain to the convent. Meg openly took Communion, but she dreaded going into the confessional. It couldn't be avoided, though, and she got through the ordeal by confessing to minor sins, which became harder and harder to dream up. How many times could she covet Sister Beatrice's diamond rosary, a present from a rich, devout grandmother? The visiting priest was old and crusty; he went through the motions without really listening.

Meg enjoyed working in the garden that summer, yet with the arrival of the first hard frost, her spirits matched the somber light outside. Spying the sliver of a new moon through her grated window, she fought off despair. At her next confession, Father Aloysius slid aside the panel that divided them. He smelled of strong soap and wheezed as he breathed.

Instead of saying, "Bless me, Father, for I have sinned," she blurted out, "I don't belong here."

The old priest hesitated. This deviation from the prescribed ritual caught him off guard.

Before he could find a reply, Meg went on, "I'm not here because I want to be a nun. I'm not even a good Catholic. I had to tell somebody. I need a friend who can keep my secret."

The old man's chronic wheezing grew worse. Was he horrified? Outraged? After a long pause he said, "God understands what it means to have doubts. Is there more?"

"Yes." Meg felt the courage of reaching the point of no return. "I've had some very disturbing experiences."

Behind the screen, Father Aloysius shifted. "What kind of experiences?"

"They felt spiritual, but who can really know?"

"Are they why you came to the convent, to escape?"

She had no choice but to describe her visions and the stigmata. "I felt trapped. I didn't belong with normal people anymore."

Father Aloysius murmured sympathetically. "I hear the distress in your voice."

"I think God found the wrong person."

Meg said these words with bitterness. There followed a longer silence. She wondered if she had just committed blasphemy.

"God never finds the wrong person," Father Aloysius replied finally. "Your secret is safe with me. Here's what you need to do. Don't come to confession next Sunday. Find an excuse to go outside. Meet me in the parking lot."

Before Meg could ask why, he slid the door back in place with a click, leaving her alone in the confessional, anxious thoughts swirling in her head. Outside the chapel, she could hear the other nuns begin to file into the refectory for Sunday dinner. Meg rushed out of the box, hoping that her expression didn't give away her agitation.

She spent the next week in suspense. The weather grew colder, and the walls of her freezing cell seemed to close in on her. In the creeping pace of days, Sunday eventually came. She went to Mass, but averted her eyes when Father Aloysius gave her Communion, afraid that his expression might show contempt for her unbelief.

After Mass, Meg found him in the parking lot leaning up against the old black Lincoln town car that the church had assigned him for the long trip to the convent. A sharp wind ruffled his thin white hair, and he was smoking a cigarette.

"You've gotten us into something, haven't you?"

"Have I?" asked Meg in bewilderment.

"More than you know."

The wind stung the old priest's face. He removed his spectacles and rubbed his rheumy eyes with bony knuckles.

Don't. They'll only get redder, Meg thought.

"I checked you out," he continued. "But before I say anything more, let's get one thing straight. You were right when you said you aren't a good Catholic."

Meg was alarmed. "But I have to stay here. Don't send me away."

"Let me finish." The old priest took a final drag on his cigarette before crushing it out under his shoe. "Nasty things."

He looked sharply at Meg, but he wasn't frowning. "Do you know why you're not a good Catholic?" He gave her a grave smile. "Because you've heard from God on his private line. He pushed the church out of the way. You probably have no idea how many teachings he violated to get through to you."

"It was all his fault," Meg blurted out.

"So to speak. Is God allowed to be a bad Catholic? The bishop's quite strict, you know."

They both laughed. Meg felt a wave of relief, and a deep sigh escaped from her lungs. Without realizing it, she hadn't been breathing.

"I believe in a living gospel," Father Aloysius said. "Which means that the truth is all around us, as alive as we are. For most believers, the gospel lies only on the page. And there it dies. The truth is in an invisible gospel, and whoever it touches, well, there's no predicting what happens then."

"You think it's touched me?" asked Meg.

Instead of answering, he said, "You didn't ask me who I checked you out with."

"I was afraid to. The bishop doesn't exactly approve of me."

"I went over his head. You're not alone. Others may be getting messages from God. They may be as troubled as you are, and it could last for many years. That's why I didn't report you."

"But you asked God about me. What did he say?"

Father Aloysius's thin lips tightened. "Have we gotten to the point where a priest can't keep the secrets of the confessional? I hope not."

He reached into his heavy black cassock, fumbling for his car keys. "Meet me here again next Sunday. Be extra careful. You won't get into trouble if someone saw you speaking with me, but Mother Superior is sharp. Don't let her deafness fool you."

Meg was anxious to learn more, but her new ally had turned away, walking around to the driver's side. His arthritic limbs made him groan as he got behind the wheel. The old Lincoln belched a plume of exhaust fumes as it lumbered down the long driveway. Meg watched until it disappeared around the bend. The wind penetrated her habit, but she wasn't shivering. Standing outside in the biting cold didn't feel like penance anymore.

When she finished this part of her story, Meg paused. "I know you all have reactions to what I've just told you, but we've reached a turning point. Look."

She pointed to the golden chapel. Its glow had grown dimmer, now almost masked under the brightness of the fluorescent lights. As soon as their eyes turned to it, the glow went out.

"Show's over," Galen remarked with thinly disguised relief.

They were all bewildered.

"Did it give up on us?" Jimmy asked.

"Not that. It means we don't need a beacon anymore," said Meg. "The lighthouse has served its purpose. So what's our next move?"

"Maybe there isn't one," said Galen. "Maybe we're just spectators."

"I'm not with our resident skeptic on this one," Frank said, pointing at Galen. "Walking away is not an option."

Mare spoke up. "I believe what Father Aloysius said. Once the truth touches you, no one knows what will happen next. I got here by following the truth. There wasn't any plan. It must be the same for the rest of you."

"Sure, but we can't proceed blindly," Frank protested. "What happened to getting answers?"

He stared glumly at the shrine, whose life was snuffed out. No answers were coming from it.

"Let's go around the table, then," Meg suggested. "Each person can ask one question if they have doubts. I'll do my best to answer. Maybe it will clear the way."

There was a murmur of agreement at this suggestion.

"I'll go first," Lilith volunteered. "How did you get the golden church?"

"Father Aloysius passed it to me just before he died."

"So he was part of a mystery school himself?" said Lilith.

Galen piped up. "That's two questions. Who's next?" He kept his arms folded across his chest, where they'd been from the moment he sat down.

Jimmy raised his hand. "I'll use Lilith's question."

"Yes, Father Aloysius belonged to a mystery school. He followed a very difficult path," said Meg. "As a young man he was tormented by doubts, even after he was ordained. Certain signs came to him, but he was afraid to trust them. He made light of being a bad Catholic when actually it was a great fear of his. Eventually, he was drawn into a mystery school, and by the time I met him, he was its only surviving member."

"Which means that it doesn't take the whole membership," Frank pointed out.

"Is that your question?" Meg asked.

Frank nodded.

"It takes the whole membership to be a school, even when it's down to one. The purpose is always the same, keeping the spark alive."

"I guess I'm next," said Mare. "He told you about an invisible gospel. What is that?"

"It's a body of knowledge that doesn't appear in the Bible," Meg replied. "The knowledge gets transmitted from generation to generation by those who are attuned to it. That's why mystery schools began, to see beyond the written word. In our case, the transmission comes from the purest source, the thirteenth disciple. Our school is named after her."

By now it was hard for the group to keep still. They wanted to question Meg for hours. But she hadn't forgotten Galen.

"What would you like to know?" she asked.

"Nothing. I don't need any answers, not the kind you're selling. When it's time to vote, I'll vote with my feet."

Jimmy couldn't contain himself any longer. "Shame on you, mister. God touched you the deepest. He brought you pure love."

Galen turned red; the others looked mystified.

Weakly Galen muttered, "I just want to get back to reality."

"I hear you," said Jimmy. "But you've already gotten there. This is it."

Galen had lost his defiance, but he still looked doubtful.

"Don't leave," Mare coaxed. "The rest of us will be stranded. The mystery school will collapse before it's even begun."

"Don't plead with him," Frank grumbled. "That's just what he wants."

"Pleading won't work. There is no mystery," Galen retorted. "That's what you people don't seem to get."

But Frank had gotten it right. Galen was enjoying being in the driver's seat. It was a very unfamiliar place, as timid and invisible as he had been all his life. He would push the privilege as far as it would take him. But inside he had a secret wish that would blow his cover. Whatever happened, he wanted to hear or see Iris again.

Meg was good at reading the situation. "It's been a long evening. Let's meet here at the same time next week."

Jimmy was startled. "Didn't you hear what he just said?"

"Yes, but I don't think we need a formal vote anymore. Is everyone willing to come back? If not, raise your hand."

The rest felt uncertain about Galen, but when no one raised a hand, neither did he.

Meg smiled with relief. "Then it's decided."

There was nothing more to say, so they began to file out. At the door, Lilith took Galen aside. "You're walking a fine line, mister. You've had a lot of pain. This could be your way out. Don't throw it away."

Trying not to look cowed, Galen stiffened his back and left without a reply.

Putting on his coat, Frank was apologetic to Mare. "Can we do this later? I have to catch up on the work I missed. There's a morning deadline."

She kissed his cheek. "You go. I'm fine."

"You're sure?" Frank sounded concerned, but it was a mask for guilt. He didn't want to lose Mare, and if they got into a deep discussion now, she'd realize how far apart they were about the mystery school.

"I told you, I'm fine."

Frank nodded and left.

Actually, Mare welcomed the chance to be alone with her aunt. When the room was empty, she said to her, "Should we tell the family you're back?"

"That depends," Meg replied. "Will they consider it good news or not? Don't worry about it right now. It's for me to take care of."

Mare was eager to hear more details of Meg's recent life, but Meg made a show of pushing in the chairs, turning off the lights, and rushing them both out. She made small talk on the way to the parking lot and ignored Mare's stare when she saw the silver Mercedes Meg unlocked.

"You're dissatisfied. I see it," Meg said kindly. By driving away, she'd be leaving Mare empty-handed, so she said, "Father Aloysius left me everything in his will—he came from a rich banking family and outlived all his siblings. I was set up to continue the mystery school where he'd left it."

"And the golden chapel, where did it come from?" Mare asked.

"I don't know. It was a deathbed bequest. He'd never even hinted at it." Meg became pensive. "I hope this is the right thing to do. It could all come crashing down around us."

Mare hesitated. Her aunt had become frail-looking in the convent, and she seemed slightly bewildered to be back in the world.

Her eyes, however, contained mystery. She had seen things few others have seen.

"You've sacrificed ten years of your life for this," said Mare. "I want to see it through for your sake."

Meg stepped into her expensive car with undisguised embarrassment. "It looks ridiculous, doesn't it?" she said. "His family believed in having only the best. But he wasn't like that. He was exceptional in a way the world will never know."

"Will we ever be known?" Mare said.

"I'm not the one to ask. Remember, I'm the expert at hiding my light under a bushel basket."

The remark was offhand, but true enough. After her aunt drove off, Mare walked to her car on the far side of the parking lot. The night was frigid, and she wondered why everything about this story seemed to happen in cold weather. She began to hum to herself, half unconsciously, a favorite Christmas carol.

In the bleak mid-winter
Frosty wind made moan.
Earth stood hard as iron,
Water like a stone.

She stopped there, and a shiver ran through her. The mystery school was reborn, but the world was still hard as iron. The tests that lay ahead would be just as hard. Something inside her was sure of it.

CHAPTER *14*

A week later, the second meeting convened like the first. Every-one except for Mare and Frank again sat spaced around the table like strangers. The golden shrine had been placed in the middle. No one paid it any attention, though, now that its spell was gone. Galen eyed it suspiciously. He hadn't abandoned the possibility that the thing might be radioactive.

"All of you were nervous last week. This week you're tense," Meg observed. "But no one stayed away."

"Curiosity wins over doubt," said Lilith, seated again in the lieutenant's chair to Meg's right.

"For the time being," Frank remarked curtly. "My week was a total waste, nothing but waiting. Aren't we supposed to do something?"

"I'm with him," Jimmy chimed in. "We're not going to sit around like in school, are we?" He dreaded school as much as he resented it when his father forced him to drop out.

Not that anyone cared. They had all gone through strange ex-periences they couldn't explain, but it didn't draw them closer, perhaps the opposite. They wanted to keep the strangeness private.

Frank and Mare had found excuses not to spend much time together. The first meeting had somehow made them shy around each other—shy or wary. Frank tried to charm her on the phone.

"I'm calling from God Anonymous. Does anyone in your family have a religious addiction? We can spray for that."

Mare wasn't in a joking mood. "Have you heard from anyone in the group?"

"Not a peep. You sound worried."

Mare moved on to another subject. Frank knew better than to try to be funny again. His own life wasn't going that well. He hadn't slept. It was hard to concentrate at work. He thought he was keeping it together fairly well until his buddy Malcolm, the kid reporter, stopped by Frank's cubicle.

"Want to see something hilarious? Like weird and hilarious?"

It was a jolt when Malcolm held up a photo of Galen, looking slumped and sullen in the police station.

Frank's stomach was tied in knots. "How do you know him?"

"I don't. Do you? You look kind of peculiar."

"He just looks like such a sad sack. Was he arrested?"

"Yep. It happened a while back. I forgot to tell you." Malcolm laughed. "This old dude tried to spray-paint a masterpiece. I bought him a burger, and he told me all about hating God. Something to do with his wife dying."

"And you find that funny?" asked Frank.

Frank's disapproval puzzled his friend. "I thought you'd want a laugh. This guy's a nut case. I'll show you my write-up."

"No rush."

Frank buried his head back in his work. Malcolm walked away with a look of, "What's gotten into you all of a sudden?"

When he picked Mare up for the meeting the following Saturday, Frank was right about her being worried.

"Aunt Meg's been out of touch all week," she said. "She told me she'd handle everything about the family, but then there was no word."

"Maybe she just needs time to adjust. She was in a convent for ten years. Be thankful she's not totally bats," he said.

Mare couldn't be talked out of her anxiety. Even when they entered the meeting room and saw that Meg was there, calm and faintly smiling, Mare was unsettled. When Frank reached for her hand, she drew it away.

Now everyone was venting their frustration. Galen said, "Whatever we do, no more Q and A about the ghost in the box. It's like a quiz show with imaginary answers and no prizes." He rocked back in his chair and waited.

Buddy, if you were five feet closer, I'd kick that chair out from under you, thought Frank. But he kept quiet. Last week's arguing had gotten them nowhere.

No one was happy with Galen, who was determined to keep stirring the pot. If Meg was annoyed, however, she didn't show it.

"I hear what you're saying, Mr. Blake."

"Use my first name. I'm not your boss," Galen growled.

"Indeed." Meg regarded him with an unperturbed smile.

The rest of the group exchanged puzzled looks. Why was Meg kowtowing to an obvious troublemaker? She and Lilith wore the same suits as the week before, but the air of authority had faded. *They could have dropped in from a knitting circle,* Frank thought. *Or a spinsters support group.* Lilith gave him a sharp sideways glance, and Frank suddenly recalled her unnerving ability to read minds when she wanted to.

Meg went on. "We went around in circles last week, but we agreed that the presence in the shrine knows we're here. What else does she know about us? Let's find out."

"What if she knows our dirty little secrets?" Jimmy asked nervously.

"Don't be scared," Galen jibed. "Being a stooge isn't a secret. You jump when Lilith says jump."

Jimmy turned red. "Take that back."

"Why? You carry out her dirty work. I know that for a fact. Try thinking for yourself." Galen enjoyed watching Jimmy squirm. They were both as timid as mice when it came down to it, but at least Galen was top mouse.

Meg ignored them. "I imagine the presence knows us at both our best and our worst. That's what God sees. So if she belongs with God, we can expect no less."

This was the first open declaration about God that anyone had made except for Galen's sarcastic outbursts.

After an uneasy silence, Jimmy said, "I believe in God. Is that a crime here?"

"Stop it," Lilith said sharply. "We need to stick to business."

Galen shot Jimmy a look that said, "I told you so." Jimmy's face began to color again.

Before the spark was fanned into a flame, Mare raised her hand. "I have an idea, and I think it will work."

She had been so quiet that stepping forward came as a surprise. The stares she received made her uncomfortable, but she pressed on. "I propose that each of us touch the object, being open to whatever happens. Let it communicate that way."

She gave Frank a meaningful look. They both knew that something was bound to happen.

"Good suggestion," he said. "Let's find out exactly what the presence wants to tell us."

"I want to go first," Jimmy said eagerly. He had lost confidence during the week. He wanted the room to be filled with a golden glow again. The light made him feel that he belonged in its shimmering aura. There was another thing too. What if a disciple of Jesus really lived in the shrine? It wasn't impossible. He heard stories in the neighborhood, where a ghoul, a *demonio necrofago,* crept into someone's body at night while they slept. When Jimmy was a child, the windows in his bedroom had always been shut after sunset, no matter how sweltering it became in August.

"The first to go will be Galen," Meg announced, to Jimmy's disappointment.

"I'm not touching that thing," Galen protested.

"Then don't," Jimmy said, seeing a chance for himself.

Mare took a deep breath. "I haven't told anyone, but I've touched it before, and I had an experience, so maybe I should go first."

Meg shook her head. "It has to be Galen."

Everyone looked puzzled, but Galen felt her words pierce his heart.

Behind his polished Trotsky glasses, his eyes were exhausted, and if you looked deeper, he felt defeated. No matter how hard he tried, he couldn't push the memory of Iris away. He was tormented by images of her body buried in the ground and the grisly process of decay. A doctor had prescribed sleeping pills and an antidepressant, which sent Galen into a chemical haze. Worse, the pills made the images in his dreams more intense and harder to bear.

After the funeral her father had sent a long note to Galen, basically a kiss-off, declaring that the marriage to his daughter had been a sham. Galen skimmed over the caustic accusations. As immature as he was emotionally, he recognized that Iris's father was using blame to disguise his utter helplessness after she died. But a phrase, one of the few that didn't take aim at Galen, read, "She was a saint, but none of us recognized it."

Tears welled up in his eyes. Galen didn't believe in saints, and he loathed sentimentality. He had shut himself off from feeling anything—this had been his habit long before Iris got sick. He had turned to science to keep from sinking into the swamp of emotions. No one ever told him that tears are a release, after which something better comes. To him, tears were a crack in the dam, and unless you patched the crack, you would be washed away in the flood.

So the group didn't know the courage it took for him to suddenly say, "All right, I'll go first. Just don't blame me when nothing happens."

Jimmy shook his head. "Have some faith, bro."

Lilith said, "If God is God, a little skepticism won't stop him. Have at it, Mr. Blake."

If using his last name was meant as a little jab, Galen ignored it. The golden chapel was within his reach, and he pulled it closer until it sat squarely before him.

"See? I touched it. Nothing happened."

"Great, pass it on," Frank said. Mare wasn't the only one who had experienced the shrine's powers.

"Wait," said Mare, putting her hand on Frank's arm to quiet him. "I know you'll probably hate this word, Galen. But there has to be a communion between you and her."

"What garbage!" he snorted. "Either it works or it doesn't." He was already regretting being put on the spot, and by his own doing. It had been foolish and stupid to volunteer.

"He's losing his nerve," Frank taunted. "Predictable."

Jimmy's fear of confrontation came up. "Nobody should do what they don't want to. Can't he just come along for the ride?"

Frank shrugged. "Sure, let him be ballast in the boat. He's not good for much else."

By now Frank was annoying people as much as Galen. But no one disagreed with Jimmy's point. It wasn't compulsory for any of them to participate.

Galen felt his heart thumping, and it began to grow sore again. Against his will, he gave in. With a cryptic smile he closed his eyes and folded his hands around the shrine. Somewhere in the back of his mind, he framed a wisp of hope that Iris might speak to him. He didn't believe in communion, but who knows? Maybe this could turn into some kind of séance.

Behind his closed eyelids, he became aware of a faint light. At first he didn't notice it, because there is always a residual glow in the eyes—no one is literally in the dark. The glow began to swirl and grow brighter. Within seconds a woman's face was starting to form. Galen's heart skipped a beat; his stomach was in knots.

But as the image became clear, he saw it wasn't Iris. The woman had dark hair and eyes. Galen could hear her speak to him, even though her lips didn't move. *You have been suffering so much. There is no need to. Find a way out. I will show you.*

By rights his heart should have sunk when it wasn't Iris. But the woman, who looked no older than a girl, sounded so sympathetic that Galen was drawn to her. She had such a radiant smile. He wanted to speak to her, but he didn't know how.

What should I do? he thought.

A moment passed in silence that seemed like an eternity. He was afraid to open his eyes, certain that she would disappear.

Kill God.

Galen was too dumbfounded to respond. Had he heard wrong, or was this some weird, spiteful mockery? Without changing her smile, the woman communicated again.

Kill God.

A single word sprang to Galen's mind. *Why?*

It can end your suffering.

With a start his eyes opened on their own, and he squinted at the light as if he'd been asleep for an hour. People were staring at him with expectant looks on their faces.

"Did you see her?" asked Mare, who had an intuition that this would happen when anyone touched the golden shrine.

Galen nodded, still speechless. The woman in his vision hadn't faded away gradually like Marley's ghost or the Cheshire Cat. She was there one minute and gone the next.

Lilith looked askance. "Something's wrong. He could be in shock."

"I'm perfectly all right," Galen tried to say. But nothing came out, and the room started to swim. A veil lowered over his eyes. The next moment, he was lying on the floor, and Jimmy was holding a cup of water to his lips.

"You fainted, man. Good thing there's carpet." Then, with a conspiratorial smile, "This is the second time. Maybe you should stay away from me."

Apparently Galen had slipped slowly off his chair and wound up on the floor. "I'm all right," he mumbled. When he glanced to his left, Mare was there kneeling beside him.

She asked again, with quiet urgency, "You saw her, didn't you?"

Galen waved away the question. "Let me up." He accepted the water and gulped it down before getting to his feet, still unsteady.

"You were brave," said Jimmy, patting him on the shoulder. "So tell us."

Galen waited until they had all taken their seats again. "I got a message. But you're not going to like it."

"Just spit it out," Frank said impatiently. He wasn't entirely buying the little scene Galen had just put on.

"I saw a face. It was a young woman, and she said, 'Kill God.'"

Instantly Frank exploded. "I knew it! This guy's nothing but trouble." He jumped to his feet, pointing his finger at Galen. "Tell them about the crazy stunt you pulled. You got arrested, right? It's time we heard all about it."

"Kill God," Galen repeated, in a firm, steady voice.

A wave of confusion ran through the group. Lilith told everyone to keep calm, but no one could hear her above the building chaos. Frank weighed the idea of punching out the obnoxious little twerp. Mare was downcast, which stirred Jimmy's heart. For a fleeting moment he thought he should be with her, not Frank.

Galen looked on, at first with a dazed expression, as if he didn't really know what he had just said. In fact, two impulses were fighting inside him. One was awe that he had encountered the presence in the shrine, actually seen her and talked with her. The other was triumph—he was back in control of the group, just like at the first meeting. The mixture was intoxicating.

A voice inside him exulted. *You're not weak. You're powerful. Go for it.*

So he did. "I can only tell you what she said to me. You're all believers, at least you pretend to be. Now we have something to believe in together. Let's kill God. I'm ready."

"You should be ashamed of yourself," Lilith scolded.

Galen saw fear and revulsion in the eyes of the others. He felt the rush that comes when you've been deprived of attention all your life. Even bad attention is better than no attention at all. *More!* the voice inside told him. His other feeling, the one of awe before a looming mystery, couldn't compete. Galen was about to open his mouth, ready to crow louder. Yet a flicker of the woman's image returned, and he stopped himself.

In the general outrage, it took a while for anyone to notice that Meg had kept silent. She didn't even look distressed.

"Kill God. Yes, maybe that's a good idea," she murmured.

Frank exploded anew. "What? This guy went on a rampage to manipulate us. He's got an agenda. If you don't believe me, I can give you proof. Another reporter wrote the whole story up. There was a crazy plot, but it fizzled, and Galen weaseled out. Go on, tell them."

Galen fixed him with a cold stare and said nothing. So Frank told the story himself, of the botched act of art terrorism, as he dubbed it. He was so worked up that the incident spilled out in a garbled fashion, but they were all transfixed.

"Now you have it," Frank said. "Vote him out, and be done

with it." He didn't dare look over at Mare. Even this worked up, he knew her eyes would make him feel ashamed of himself.

The first to reply was Lilith. "Those who hate God are sometimes the greatest seekers."

"What? Not this character," Frank exclaimed.

How would you know? thought Galen, without speaking up for himself.

Then Frank felt Mare's hand touching his, and he deflated, slumping back down into his chair.

They waited for Meg to speak. She and Lilith were the only ones who seemed to know the territory. Quietly she said, "If we are a mystery school, we'll be guided in ways we don't understand."

"But isn't God the mystery?" Mare asked. "That's what we're here for."

Meg shook her head. "I never said that. We're here for the truth, and we have to have the courage to go where the trail leads us. If the message is 'Kill God,' I can't change it. I'm sorry."

This was no way to calm the group. Lilith stared at her in amazement.

"There is no reason for me to disbelieve Galen," Meg continued in a steady voice. "We all saw how shaken he was. Unless he's the greatest actor in the world, he wasn't following an agenda."

"His hate isn't acting," Frank protested.

"I don't see hate," Meg said. "I see someone who has suffered a great deal. If he did something extreme and reckless, it was only an expression of pain."

Galen felt exposed, his momentary power grab fading. If he agreed with Meg, the truth would be out. Then what? He'd return to his mouse hole. He wasn't going there without a struggle.

"Nobody at this table has a license to shrink me," he snarled. "You think I'm the only one in the whole world who hates God? Wake up." Now he felt some juice returning. "Why are you people so afraid of two little words? 'Kill God.' If God can't protect himself from someone like me, he must be pretty pathetic."

"No argument with that," Frank muttered to himself.

Meg didn't budge. "The message wasn't for the whole world. It was for you personally, Galen. If I were you, I'd take it seriously."

He couldn't wriggle out. She was a better player at this game than he was. Galen realized this with a sinking feeling; his sense of defeat began to creep back in. He tried a new ploy.

"It's a trick or some kind of code. No one can kill God. He's already dead," he said.

"What if he's not dead enough?" asked Meg.

Galen looked confused.

"There was something you hated enough to get arrested over. You must have thought God was alive then," she pointed out.

He shifted uncomfortably. "I wasn't myself. I did something stupid."

Meg remained dogged. "You can't escape the fact that you hated God, so there had to be something or someone to hate. Maybe that's who you need to kill."

"All right," Galen sighed. "I hated the God that kids are brainwashed into loving and worshipping. That God is a fraud, a cheat. He doesn't exist." Galen felt himself getting emotional. "That's the real truth, more than saying God is dead. He's a figment of our imagination."

"Which you set out to destroy, so that people wouldn't be fooled anymore," Meg prompted.

"Someone had to stand up. My only mistake was thinking I could lead the charge. I'm too insignificant. I'm a nobody."

Running himself down like this came easily to Galen, once he decided to be perfectly candid.

"Then I'd say the presence you met knows you quite well," said Meg. "She's telling you to finish what you set out to do."

Galen turned his head away, and while his stubborn silence lasted, Meg addressed the others. "Why not destroy a God you hate? No one here is naive. Horrible things happen every day, unspeakable things, while God stands by and does nothing."

No one disagreed with her. Their faces looked anxious and guilty.

"Don't be afraid to attack such a God," Meg assured them. "It's time to kill him if that's what it takes to get at the truth."

Galen wanted to sulk, but something new hit him. "Is that why you left the convent?" he asked. "You saw through the hoax?"

Meg's reply was cryptic. "I left for the opposite reason, but this isn't about me." She looked around the table. "When the disciple gives any of you a message, you become the mind and heart of everyone in the group. We look to you to uncover the next piece of the puzzle."

Her little speech caused a shift. Galen was no longer the fly in the ointment. Hostile as he was, at that moment he was holding the flashlight whose beam could melt the darkness. This wasn't the same as respecting him, but it wasn't outright disgust anymore.

He felt the change and said quietly, "I'll try." He paused. "This is the damnedest thing, isn't it? A wimp leads the pack. I promise to let you down."

For the first time he got smiles from the others, even a tight, begrudging one from Frank.

Meg was pleased. "'Kill God' means eliminating everything false about God, all the images and myths and childish beliefs we never bother to really think about. Get rid of that God; wipe him out."

She turned to Galen. "That's why you went on your rampage. So keep going."

Suddenly Galen's anxiety returned. He was being led into the unknown. His old wounds would be reopened. At that very moment he could feel them starting to seep, their black poison oozing out.

Meg saw the pain in his face. "Be brave," she whispered. "Can you destroy forever the God who hurt you?"

The room grew deathly quiet, waiting.

"I don't know," Galen mumbled, all but inaudibly. He wanted to clutch at his heart and close up his wounds again.

"You can. It's only an image," she urged.

But he knew otherwise. An image can't be the source of so much pain. An image can't turn someone's life into a desert devoid of love.

He managed a choked laugh to keep himself from crying. "This is harder than I thought."

"I know. It wouldn't be a mystery school otherwise," said Meg. "It would be kindergarten."

You have to see what I lost, Galen thought. He willed Meg to see Iris in all her beauty. Without hating God, he'd be left with no ties to her, no way to keep her with him, even in a shriveled, pathetic way.

Now it wasn't possible to hold back his tears.

"You fear your own emptiness," said Meg gently. "Everyone does." She gave the group a meaningful look. "Why else would they cling to images so desperately? They don't want to tumble into the void. Who will catch them—God? But no one else can. That's the mystery."

Everyone in the group held their breath. They had been fixated on watching Galen unravel before their eyes, but this was a total surprise. Meg's gaze went from one to another.

"When you destroy everything that is false, whatever remains must be true." She waited to let her words sink in. "Do you all understand?"

There were a few nervous smiles, but no one replied.

"To meet God as a reality, you have to reach the zero point, where there is faith in nothing. It's frightening, but totally necessary. At the zero point every false idea about God has been abandoned. You cry with all your heart, 'Show yourself as you really are. I'm finished with fakes. Either show yourself, or I am lost.'

"When you can say that, God hears you. He knows your search for the truth is serious. If God is truth, he has no choice but to reveal himself to you. That's what Galen has guided us to today."

Galen felt a wave of emotion on hearing this. It was as if a tangled web had been transformed into a luminous path. Iris's love was part of the path, and so was his despair after she was taken from him. Every blow had brought him closer to the zero point. Galen had never had much faith in anything, but even the shreds had been stripped bare.

I'm clean, he thought.

"Scraped to the bone," said Lilith, picking up what he was going through.

Galen didn't spare a thought for how she was able to tune into his mind. He was too grateful to be emptied of the poison that had been eating him alive.

CHAPTER 15

A week passed, and the next meeting was ready to start. Galen came in late. He looked more rumpled than usual, as if he'd slept in his clothes. Frank didn't wait for him to find a seat.

"You got pretty bashed in last time," he said. "Rough week?"

"Sort of," Galen replied guardedly.

There was silent tension in the room. *Why is it focused on me?* he wondered. For the first time, everyone sat together. To Galen it looked like a jury watching him, the reluctant witness giving suspicious testimony. Meg sat back impartially, her hands folded in her lap. Only Mare seemed to look at him with sympathetic eyes, so he sat next to her, in case he needed an ally.

"What's going on?" Galen asked. "I haven't done anything to you people."

"True, but something was done through you," Meg said. She swept her hand over the group. "What you experienced when you touched the shrine spread to everyone."

"Like a virus," Frank added. "And you're the carrier."

This was totally unfair, but Galen felt a grim kind of satisfaction.

"What are you smiling at?" asked Frank sharply.

"Nothing."

Lilith spoke up. "We can't start until somebody explains things."

When no one else volunteered Mare said, "I can only speak for myself. Right after the last meeting, I was on edge. It felt like I was in danger. When I got home, I kept checking to make sure my door was locked. The slightest sound made me jump, and then—" She was on the brink of revealing something, but couldn't.

Jimmy looked the most agitated. "All week I wasn't myself. I felt, like, empty. When I passed myself in the mirror, it was like looking at a zombie. I can't believe you did this to us, man."

Galen was taken aback. He had experienced the same emptiness, but he thought he was alone.

"You don't have a clue what this is about, do you?" asked Frank with disgust. "He's not going to cop to anything."

Meg turned to Frank, and for such a gentle person, her tone was severe. "And what are you ready to cop to?"

Frank sat back in his chair. "I didn't mean—" he stammered.

Frank was getting close to something important—Meg's antennae were always out. Nothing slipped by her. He looked at Mare for support, but she felt helpless about her own situation.

Every night when she went to bed, Mare couldn't close her eyes without feeling that she was suspended over a bottomless pit. Below her she saw only blackness. By Wednesday, she was so anxious and bleary-eyed that she called Frank. He came over. He sat up in bed holding her until she fell into a fitful sleep. He waited to kiss her cheek until she nodded off. It was the tenderest moment between them so far, but what if coming back this evening only made things worse for her?

After an uncomfortable moment Meg said, "Frank is as afraid to show weakness as Galen. But it's not about who's weak or strong. All of you have had a terrible week. It's to be expected. Remember, when a door is opened, we all walk through it."

"Including you?" asked Mare.

It was the first personal question anyone had put to Meg. She took no offense. "I didn't suffer with the rest of you, no," she admitted. "That's not my role."

"You seem to know everything. So why didn't you protect us?" Jimmy asked.

Lilith replied before Meg could. "Don't be childish. She's not your mommy." Jimmy's face colored red, something that happened too easily.

"It's all right," said Meg. "Galen didn't like his experience; none of you did. But you had to experience the zero point. There was no other way."

"You said that reaching the zero point was positive," Mare reminded her.

"And it will be, I promise. At some level we all want to be protected. We crave love. We cling to life as something precious. The zero point strips those things away. The loss is just the same as losing God."

Meg's presence was reassuring, but at the same time she kept aloof. No one had seen her outside the meetings. She stayed apart from Lilith, despite their old friendship. Even Mare hadn't heard from her, and when Mare left messages on her phone, they weren't returned. On Thursday her mother phoned.

"I heard from my dead sister at last," she began. "Your Aunt Meg ran away because she'd had enough of the convent, plain and simple. She waited long enough, I'll say that."

Mare was cautious. "Did she tell you anything else? Will we see her?"

"No, she's rid of us. There's some trip she has to take right away. She might call when she comes back. Don't hold your breath." Mare's mother sounded irritated rather than distressed.

So Meg's intuition had been correct. The family wasn't greeting her return as good news, and when she excused herself from visiting them, they didn't insist. They were more comfortable with an empty place at the table.

The mood in the room was darker than it had ever been. "I don't think we're going to make it," Jimmy mumbled.

"The zero point is very bleak," Meg said. "But it's not the end. It's a prelude."

"To what?"

"To being filled with grace."

Jimmy's eyes widened, but Frank was still disgruntled. "What about me? I don't care about God. Why do I deserve to go through hell?"

"I think that's the point I'm making," Meg said. "The disciple pulled the rug out from everyone. Fair is fair."

He let it rest there. Mare wasn't the only one who didn't want to reveal what had happened to them. On Monday Frank was sent on assignment to interview homeless single mothers. Beneath an overpass on the edge of town, he found an encampment. The women looked shattered; their kids were gaunt and forlorn.

The photographer who came along was upset. "I gotta shoot all of this," he said. "Some of these kids need a doctor really bad. That little guy over there, his teeth are falling out. Nobody cares."

"Yeah, it's a crime," Frank muttered. He stood back, not taking the tape recorder out of his pocket.

"So where should we start?" the photographer asked.

"Anywhere. It doesn't matter," Frank replied. He felt strangely detached. The roar of overhead traffic on the interstate jangled his nerves. He wanted to get out of there.

The photographer was furiously snapping candid shots. When Frank didn't move, he said, "Something up with you, man?"

"No, I'm fine." Rousing himself, Frank approached one of the gaunt-eyed mothers, who was huddled inside a filthy blanket with a two-year-old wrapped in her arms. She glared at him suspiciously—visitors to the camp meant that social services would be following close behind, or the police.

"Why are you hassling us?" she demanded.

"I'm not hassling anybody. I'm just a reporter." She told him to buzz off. Frank shrugged and moved on to the next one.

The photographer kept shooting, but he was growing annoyed. "You have to get them to open up."

"I know my job; you just do yours," Frank snapped. He continued to go through the motions a while longer; they got back in the car and left when a cold drizzle started to come down.

The city editor frowned when he read Frank's copy, which was about as emotional as the transcript of a water-board meeting. "Bighearted, that's you," he said. Frank was sent back twice until his story began to show some empathy. He didn't dare reveal how little he actually cared or how frightened this made him feel.

Frank didn't tell his story to anyone, but Meg seemed to see through him.

"Let me tell you what you've all been feeling," she said. "In the absence of God, there's a hole inside you."

Frank felt himself shrinking inside. So that was what it meant when he looked on those homeless mothers without a shred of pity. The memory sent a chill through him.

Galen objected. "There's another explanation. Feeling empty exposes how alone we are. God has nothing to do with it."

To everyone's surprise, Lilith was almost as doubtful. "I want to believe you, Meg. You say fair is fair. A pretty cruel fairness, if you ask me."

Unlike the others, Lilith wasn't referring to a rough week. No one could have guessed what she'd gone through before they met her. She'd kept faith for almost thirty years. Not a word escaped her lips about the strange dream of the Black Death or the golden light that appeared in her bedroom. Lilith had kept up a good front—marriage, kids, career, all of it—while inside she was secretly in turmoil. This turmoil never completely left her, even during her happiest moments. Her heart always felt like a cave with a cold wind blowing through it, terrifying.

She was comforted by the fact that her husband didn't have a clue about what she was going through. He worked in the insurance business. He carried a card with a slogan he'd made up: "Insure and be sure." Lilith thought this was feeble, but didn't criticize, just as he never criticized her for being too strict with their two daughters.

One Sunday in front of the television he put the golf tournament he was watching on pause. The girls were off to college now. No one was at home except Lilith.

"I wonder who you are," he said. His tone wasn't accusatory, but bemused. "I don't know you."

She was flabbergasted. "I haven't changed, Herb."

"All right." He clicked the golf back on. "But if you ever want to tell me, I'm here."

Lilith felt unmasked and nearly trembled. She grabbed the remote from his hand and turned the TV off. "What are you saying? Do you want a divorce? Are you going to sleep in the spare bedroom from now on?"

Her husband looked bewildered. "Of course not. I love you."

They kept sleeping in the same bed, but Lilith doubled her armor plating. She wasn't about to lose everything. Her life was going to look ordinary if it killed her. Letting Herb in on her secret was unthinkable, like asking him to fly with her to Neptune.

But hiding out wasn't working well enough. She began a lonely search for the truth. Her only clue was the golden object that had appeared in her bedroom so many years earlier. She started to haunt the university library, poring over books about the plague years. Nothing similar to her dream of the six bodies radiating out in a circle was ever recorded.

What next? The golden object was in the shape of a church. Lilith knew what a reliquary was, so she researched pilgrims in the Middle Ages. She discovered hundreds of accounts, then thousands, and tens of thousands, most of them written in foreign languages. That route proved impossible, like everything else she had tried. Lilith remembered the exact moment when she gave up her search.

She was sitting at a long oak table in the library reading room. Before her tottered a tower of volumes devoted to Paris in the eleventh century. They smelled of dust and wilted scholars who never got married.

I'm lost, Lilith thought.

Then from over her shoulder a creaky voice said, "I didn't know I had competition."

She turned around to find an old man with a white goatee, a polka-dot bow tie, and suspenders.

"I study the period too, you see," he explained. "But I'm not selfish. If you need more books on mystery schools, I'll return mine forthwith. I keep them too long anyway."

"Mystery schools?" Lilith said, baffled.

He pointed to the leather-bound volume at the top of the pile. "I peeked at the title. *Mystery Schools, the Ecclesia, and the Role of Magic.* I hope you don't mind."

Lilith's puzzled expression made him hesitate. "You don't think his thesis is sound? I quite agree. Magic indeed."

With a squinty smile the stranger began to walk away, humming to himself. Lilith wanted to run after him. She had never heard of mystery schools, but the words gave off an electric charge. She'd stumbled on some kind of clue, she was sure of it. She started to bolt from her chair, but immediately something stopped her. Scholars like him would be no help to her. She wouldn't even get over the first hurdle, making them believe in her dream, so strange and so long ago. Yet she wasn't discouraged. Pure instinct would lead her to the next clue. Being the only road left, it was the one she had to follow.

The remaining clues didn't come quickly. They arrived at long intervals usually by happenstance, like a falling autumn leaf landing in your hair or the shadow of a raven crossing your path. Each clue made her excited; each long lapse until the next clue was given drove her mad with frustration. But Lilith was dogged, and when the haul was finally gathered in her net—a flotsam of overheard remarks, chance encounters, and arcane discoveries—she finally understood. It could only be the thirteenth disciple who was leading her on. No biblical historian believed in such a personage. The two Aramaic sources hidden in the depths of the Vatican library had been completely discredited. Yet Lilith believed, and when she found Meg, she felt vindicated—no, triumphant. Everything was real, if you only knew where to look.

So why would the disciple now throw her into desolation all over again? The others might have a hole inside, but not her. It was unfair, cosmically unfair.

Yet only one thing mattered now. If the group fell apart, things would only get worse. "I apologize for my moment of weakness. The zero point is where we have to start," Lilith affirmed.

Galen spoke wearily. "We've chewed this thing to death." He pointed at the shrine in the middle of the table. "I went first. Who's next? We need a volunteer."

When no one made a move, Meg threw up her hands. "The disciple made you feel uncomfortable for a week, and now you're ready to run away?" No one looked happy.

"So what do you want us to do?" asked Mare.

Meg's answer was unexpected. "We're going to start acting like a real mystery school. Touch the shrine."

"All of us?" Mare asked.

"Yes. Follow my lead." Meg lightly touched the roof of the golden chapel with her fingertips. "She's been awaiting us for centuries. We have to show her she didn't make a mistake." One by one they followed Meg's example, even Galen. The shrine started to glow again.

It wasn't dead; the presence inside had been listening. The glow pulsated faintly, sending out waves of peace. For all their hands to fit on the shrine, their fingers had to intertwine.

"Our Kumbaya moment. I knew it was coming," Galen joked. But his words were lost as the walls of the room melted away. A breeze ruffled their hair.

"I know where we are!" Mare exclaimed. This seemed improbable, because it was a moonless night. She didn't need moonlight to recognize the man standing in the narrow cobbled alley. He was always there. She said Jesus's name, but as before no sound came out. Mare pointed, and the others looked in his direction, silent presences to an unfolding scene. For Mare it was different this time—she was living the scene with him, from inside his mind.

It was cold for spring, even sheltered by the walls of Jerusalem. Jesus's hands were trembling. He could barely see them in the dark, but he felt their fear. Sunrise would be his death sentence, and even his body knew it. What his hands dreaded were the nails. He could do nothing about that. Maybe he should spend the last few hours before dawn asking his hands for forgiveness, then his heart, his eyes.

Instead, he kept walking through the city's labyrinth of hidden streets and alleys, which wove through Jerusalem like arteries and veins. He asked for peace. He prayed, "Our Father, who art in heaven," but the fear wouldn't leave his body.

Just hours before, his hands and heart obeyed his will. It was possible to remain calm at the Passover *seder* with his disciples. Jesus recited the ritual text but added, "When you eat this bread, you partake of my body. When you drink this wine, you partake of my blood."

The words had just come to him, as if out of God's mouth. The disciples looked bewildered. Every part of the *seder* existed to remind them that they were Jews. The meal brought Moses and Abraham into the room. It made the exodus from Egypt a living memory, even though their ancestors fled from captivity centuries ago. At Passover, with Roman soldiers, clubs in hand, patrolling Jerusalem, the Jews were reminded again that they had no power in their own land except the power of memory. It was the one thing the hated occupiers couldn't seize and control.

How could Jesus say, "This meal is about me"? It was beyond outrageous. If there had been a Pharisee in the room, he would have run back and told the temple priests that they had a danger-ous zealot in their midst.

The disciples were following a miracle rabbi, and such men were inspired by God. (The Pharisee would have condemned them simply for thinking such a thing.) Jesus's words always meant more than they seemed. He was constantly pushing the disciples to grasp his meaning. They rarely succeeded, but at least they could argue about it. To be Jewish is to argue endlessly, and so the room grew full of questions and doubts. This time Jesus didn't give them any answers. He sat silently watching. The flick-ering candles made his shadow quiver on the wall. And then he jumped to his feet.

"There's a spy in this room. He knows who he is, but I won't remain in his presence."

"Master, stay and point him out," Peter cried, his voice rising above the din of the confusion.

"Why, so you can attack him?"

"Shouldn't we?" asked Judas in the calmest of voices. "We'd be carrying out the will of God."

Jesus looked away. "I'm going."

The disciples sprang to their feet, blocking the door so he couldn't leave.

"Please, master, think of us. Stay and teach us," Judas pleaded. "This is a holy night."

When a man contemplating suicide has made up his mind, he goes calmly about the small tasks that attend death. He buys a coil of rope and borrows a stool of the right height. He bars the door with a heavy table and sits down to carefully tie the noose. A kind of fatal courage descends on him. It's the same with traitors. The closer they approach their sin, the more brazen they become.

"Let me leave this place," Jesus insisted.

The disciples moved aside except for Iscariot. He put his face close to the master's so that the others couldn't see him smiling. "You are the son of God. You can't be afraid of one of us."

Without reply Jesus quitted the place. He descended the narrow stairs that led from the cramped upper room to the street and was gone. In his mind he now saw every moment of what lay ahead. The Father had granted him that. Judas would flee the room on a feeble pretext. The disciples would wait in bewilderment until the master returned, and after midnight Jesus would ask them to pray in the garden.

Aimlessly his footsteps had taken him to an alley walled in by tall houses, leaving only a sliver of night sky overhead. The closeness pressed in on him, and he stopped wandering. "Thy will be done" gave him no strength. He rebelled against his sacrifice. *Father, I implore you. If you love me, listen to me now.*

The moment the words escaped him, Jesus's face grew hot despite the chill of the night. He was begging. It was the one thing he had taught his disciples never to do. A Jew never begs from a loving God. The Father knows everything his children need and gives it out of his loving grace.

But Jesus's mind was panicking. *Save me, save me!*

The plea was too late. From the far end of the alley, which was hidden by a winding curve, he spied a glimmer of light approaching. Judas's betrayal must have happened earlier than Jesus saw, and the rough hands of soldiers would be dragging him away. The miracle rabbi faced his worst fear. It was not the dying, but dying in doubt.

The light came closer, rounding the curve. Strangely, there was no sound of tramping boots. And the light didn't flicker like torches.

"Oh," a woman's voice said. The light stopped moving closer.

"Don't be afraid. I won't hurt you," Jesus said. His heart was racing, the way it always did when a mystery sought him out. He hadn't run into a prostitute, who would have boldly approached a man walking alone at night. There was a hesitation; then the woman moved toward him, and in the light he saw that she was just a girl.

"Let me pass. I'm needed," she said. The girl groped her way, as if there were no light. Jesus was transfixed with amazement. "My father was injured when a brick wall fell," she said. "They couldn't move him for hours. I ran to get medicine for his wounds."

She told all this with a slight nervousness in her voice. Otherwise, she seemed unafraid. "I wish I had a torch to see you by. I carried one, but it went out."

She doesn't know, Jesus thought.

There was light everywhere, and it emanated from her. This was what amazed him.

"You are blessed," he said.

"Thank you, *rebbe*." No one had ever blessed her outside of the temple, which meant this stranger must be a priest.

Jesus hesitated. He knew this light. It was the Shekinah of the scriptures, the light of the soul. For it to shine radiantly from the girl meant something. He waited for God to tell him what to do.

And then he did.

"May I speak with you?" Jesus asked.

"I would, but the medicine—" she replied doubtfully, holding up the packet of herbs that were nestled in the sleeve of her gown.

"Your father is healed."

"What?" The girl felt the chill air creep down the alley, making her shiver.

"Your father doesn't need you, but God does." Jesus didn't wait for her to object. The urgency of the hour was upon him. "I have a teaching for you. Pay attention. The Jews prove that they are God's children by two means. What are they?"

The girl wasn't poor. Her family had hired religious tutors for her brothers, and she was allowed to listen in from the other side of a curtain.

"The word and the temple," she replied. "The word binds God to us. Making sacrifice in the temple binds us to him."

Jesus shook his head. "Is that enough? Words are not eternal, and the temple may fall into ruins."

"Pardon me, *rebbe,* but the word *is* eternal."

Jesus smiled to himself. The Father had led him to the right person. He said, "Yes, the word is eternal, but it can be forgotten among men. I tell you a mystery. There is one thing beyond the word—the light. Death cannot touch it. I am the light. Be sure of it. This truth will lead you to heaven."

The girl was baffled, and she still couldn't see the face of the stranger. He turned to walk away, and at that she felt a sharp pang in her heart. She cried out, but he kept walking. She ran to catch up, but a second pain shot through her chest, and she stumbled.

Overhead a window opened, and someone leaned out, waving an oil lamp.

"Who's down there?" he cried, irritated and sleepy.

By then the stranger had reached the end of the alley and disappeared into the night.

The scene was cut off like a broken movie reel, and their hands sprang away from the shrine. Eyes opened. The group gazed at the golden glow, still faintly pulsating.

"Don't speak," Meg warned. "The thirteenth disciple was a young girl, an innocent. She was entrusted with a mystery. Now the same mystery has been passed on to us."

After a moment the golden glow faded. It took away the disciple's presence. Everyone had felt it.

Galen got in the first word. "We've been asses, all of us."

"Definitely," Jimmy seconded.

Meg smiled. "You couldn't help yourselves." She didn't say how close they'd come to failing. Now the fear in their hearts was losing its grip.

"We have one last thing to discuss," Meg said. "We stepped through time tonight. What was the lesson waiting for us?"

Their answers overlapped.

"Jesus is real."

"We're not crazy."

"The light."

The last was from Lilith, and Meg agreed. "Our only salvation is the light. This coming week, I want you to go into the light on your own." There was a murmur of assent. They could feel the protection that encircled them like enfolding arms.

Mare had a question. "How will we know what to do?"

"It can't be planned in advance," Meg replied. "Give in to the light. That's my best advice."

"I don't mean to be a buzzkill," said Frank, "but giving in led to a pretty horrible week last time."

"Then give in more," said Meg. "The disciple knew absolutely nothing. She was sent into the light blindly, if I can put it that way."

Just like me, Lilith thought to herself. What she had considered a curse was a blessing in disguise.

They dispersed in a mood very different from the way the meeting had begun. Meg stayed behind to lock up. Trusting in the thirteenth disciple meant that the group trusted her. She knew that, and it made her keep some secrets to herself.

"Everything looks good so far," she said to the empty room. Her charges had passed through an invisible veil.

Who really knew what a mystery school should be? Monks in hooded robes kneeling before the cross. Heavy incense in the air. The shields of Crusaders and their dulled swords lining the walls. There was something to be said for stage props.

A mystery school couldn't be ordinary people in an ugly basement meeting room, with greenish skin from the cheap fluorescent lighting.

But this time it was.

CHAPTER *16*

The next week passed neither slowly nor swiftly for Meg. She was barely aware of time anymore. She had grown so used to silence that time was no longer useful. It had withered away like the convent garden in winter, leaving bare sticks where sweet fruit once hung. When she came back into the world, time wasn't waiting on the doorstep to greet her.

She was due at the next meeting of the mystery school, but Meg lingered in the huge sitting room of Father Aloysius's house, a cool, gloomy place he rarely entered when he was alive. The good priest preferred a modest rectory. Carved lions' heads silently growled at her from the corners of heavy Victorian furniture. Some of the gilt-framed pictures on the wall were still draped with cloth, but even years of neglect hadn't been able to dim the trappings of family wealth.

Father Aloysius never mentioned that he was leaving Meg the house, a mansion, really. Toward the end, knowing he had little time left, he defied his doctors by visiting the nuns one last time to bless them. The sisters were shocked by his appearance, how gaunt he looked.

"Now we have to discuss the disciple," he said when he and Meg finally found time alone. Their weekly meetings were held in the ramshackle toolsheds and boarded-up cottages scattered around the grounds of the convent. On this final visit, they sat side by side in a garden shed on a rickety potting bench, the last relic of the Italian gardeners the estate once employed. Their breath fogged in the cold air. None of the outbuildings had heat, and the cracked windows were never repaired.

"When I'm gone, the disciple will have no one to talk to but you," Father Aloysius said.

Meg looked doubtful. "But I don't really know who she is. Have you actually seen her?"

"Oh, yes. But you already know the most important thing. She's the keeper of the invisible gospel." The old priest gave Meg a sharp look. "This would be a bad moment to lose faith."

"I don't want to," Meg mumbled.

He sighed. "You think you haven't done anything these past ten years? You have. You've allowed the presence of God to come to you. Now his presence is with you. It's in you every moment."

Father Aloysius took a drag on his cigarette. He'd never kicked the habit, but he had lived long enough to see e-cigarettes come along. "An electronic nicotine delivery system. What a thing," he mused with a touch of regret.

Meg felt a wave of emotion. "What will I do without you?" she cried.

"You'll leave this place. That's the first thing. You must continue the disciple's mission, and you can't do it sealed away behind these walls."

Sitting there in the frigid drafty shed with her hands tucked into her sleeves for warmth, Meg watched as Father Aloysius opened a worn leather valise he'd brought with him. From inside he lifted a wrapped object. He unwrapped it carefully to reveal the golden shrine, which she'd never seen before.

"We live in a terrible time for miracles," he said. "They're endangered, like the bird of paradise. When you get back to your cell, commune with this precious object."

As much as she trusted him, Meg was struck with fear. Being a bad Catholic had never gone this far.

Father Aloysius put his hand, which was sinewy and strong despite his sickness, over hers. "I'm not asking you to practice black magic, my girl."

"I'm not sure I'm ready for white magic," Meg said with a nervous laugh. "This could all be a mistake."

"If God makes mistakes, then there is no God."

Meg shook her head. "That's not good enough, Father."

"It has to be, for now."

The old priest's chest was suddenly wracked with an alarming cough, and before her eyes he turned weak and exhausted. He draped one arm over Meg's shoulders, and she helped him out of the shed. The walk back to his car was painfully slow.

"It doesn't really matter who spies on us now, does it?" he said with a grim smile. "We're both about to disappear."

At the parking lot, he rested for a moment before getting behind the wheel of the battered black town car.

"I don't think about death," he mused. "I wait in quietness. What will come will come."

There was nothing more to say. It would have been a blessing if Meg had witnessed what came next. As he drove down the winding road that led away from the convent, Father Aloysius remembered when he was ten years old, dangling his feet in the cool blue water of the town swimming pool. His best friend, Ray Kelly, pointed to the high diving board silhouetted against the sky.

"Double dare you to jump off it," he said. Neither of them had ever worked up the courage to climb that high. But Aloysius, who got his peculiar first name because a strong-minded devout grandmother had insisted on it, couldn't refuse a dare. He climbed the ladder, and heads turned as a skinny little boy tiptoed gingerly to the edge of the board. No matter how light his step, the board jiggled under his feet. Peering down, he saw the water, which looked miles away. His fear told him not to jump, but what could he do? His reputation depended on not climbing back down the ladder.

Now he stood at the edge of another leap, having tiptoed toward it for seventy-eight years.

I have no choice, he thought. *It would ruin my reputation if I backed down now.*

Meg waited until dinnertime to retrieve the old valise that contained the miniature golden church. She excused herself from the table, saying she had indigestion, and then hurried through the dark to the rickety garden shed. The valise was hidden under a tarp behind a rusty old mowing machine.

She got back to her cell undetected and shoved the valise under her cot. If she didn't attend evening prayers a medical sister would check up on her.

Returning to the group, Meg mumbled that she felt much better, thank you. All through prayers the only thing she could think of was Father Aloysius's mysterious instruction: "Commune with this precious object." What did that even mean?

The sisters went directly to bed after the last prayer. There was no socializing, because the next round of praying began very early in the morning. Meg sat on the edge of her cot, allowing for a safety margin. It was very unlikely that another sister would tap on her door, but Meg waited until the corridor was completely silent and empty.

Dragging the valise out from under the cot, she was struck by its heaviness. She had been too anxious carrying it in the dark to really notice its weight, but when she opened it and lifted the object, still wrapped in a torn piece of white sheet, it almost slipped from her grasp.

For a split second she panicked at the thought of the clattering sound the object would make if it hit the stone floor. She caught it just in time, sat down quickly, and placed it in her lap. She forced herself to breathe while waiting for her heart to stop racing. Too nervous to turn on her reading lamp so late at night, Meg stared at the object in near darkness. *It must be quite valuable,* she thought, *but if that's the only reason for its existence, Father Aloysius wouldn't have cloaked it in secrecy.*

This thought brought his face to mind, and Meg felt a wave of sorrow. She would never see him again. There was great pain around that. She hadn't wanted to face it all day. A final ending brought fear and grief, even though her old friend was still alive. If she weren't a cloistered nun, she could even telephone him to hear his voice again.

It would have been easy to give in to self-pity sitting there in the dark. Meg resisted, focusing her attention on the miniature church.

What do I do with you now? she thought.

It was a rhetorical question, directed at no one, but Meg had the sense that someone heard it. Not that this was possible rationally, only that her doubt receded a little. She felt understood, much the way Father Aloysius, among all the people in her life, made her feel. But it proved unsafe to bring his face to mind a second time. She found herself crying, and she pulled the golden church close to her and embraced it, using it to hold on to the old priest.

Suddenly she saw a hill in her mind's eye, with three crosses outlined against a stormy sky. To witness three bodies hanging from crosses would be unbearable. She had been there before, and her heart pounded. *Please, not again. I can't.*

Voices buzzed around her, and the image went in and out like a weak television signal. Meg had a faint hope that she could escape, until all at once her cramped cell disappeared, and she was there. She had returned to the Crucifixion, but she didn't see the bodies, only the young girl running away from them.

The scene jumped ahead. Now the girl was in the city. There were no crowds in the narrow streets she ran through. Passover took the Jews to temple; few went to gawk at the spectacle on Golgotha, the "Place of Skulls."

The girl ran blindly, hardly able to see the way through her tears. Meg hovered near her, so close that the disciple's racing heartbeat felt like her own. The girl fled until she was exhausted; she collapsed in the shade of a twisted olive tree just beyond the city walls. For a while nothing happened. Her ragged breath began to subside. Her fear subsided with it, and she was able to think. Her thoughts came through clearly to Meg.

He was a stranger. Now he's dead. I don't have to do anything.

The girl became aware of a shadow passing over her. She looked up, embarrassed to be caught when her emotions had run away with her.

It was him.

She was so startled that childish words sprang from her lips. "Aren't you supposed to be dead?"

Jesus smiled. "That depends on how you look at it."

The figure Meg saw was short and dark, with a general look she thought of as Mediterranean, not even Jewish. The girl had only seen the stranger at night. His voice was gentle, the same as when he found her in the alley. But he looked shockingly ordinary. To Meg, Jesus could be the Iranian who owns the neighborhood dry cleaner's.

The girl was bewildered. There was no possible way he could have escaped.

"I saw what they did to you," she said.

"To men's eyes, I'm still there," Jesus said. "It will not be finished for a while."

He sat down beside her in the shade of the olive tree, which made dappled shadows on his face.

"The one who speaks to you, who appears to you now, he is the only one you must pay attention to. The men who think they can crucify the light are mistaken."

The girl looked stricken. This man could be a magus who had worked a spell on her. Or demons might have entered her body. Or she had lost her mind. None of these explanations fought for her attention, however. Taking a deep breath, she accepted what she saw.

The stranger sensed her acceptance. "You have heard it said, many are called, but few are chosen. You have been chosen, and through you others will be too."

The girl wanted to protest, but Jesus got up and began to walk away in the direction of the Place of Skulls, which couldn't be seen over the city walls and houses in between.

The night before the girl had run after him. This time, though, she sat still, nearly collapsed on the ground. Meg wanted to reach out and hold her in her arms. She knew how insignificant the disciple felt at that moment. Meg was haunted by the same feeling herself.

Suddenly the disciple's head exploded with doubts. "Tell me what to do!" she cried out in a panic.

Jesus was already too far away to hear. But her mind answered for him: *You will be guided, as he was guided.*

In an instant, the flashback vanished. Meg was sitting on her cot back in her cell enveloped in darkness. She became aware of the heavy little church in her lap, her hands wrapped tightly around it. In a moment she regained her wits and even managed a faint smile. She had managed to commune with it after all. The metallic surface of the object felt warm. She knew what her duty was now, and although it was impossible, the object began to glow faintly, as if it too understood.

CHAPTER *17*

The meeting room in the hospital basement was stuffy at the best of times. Waiting an hour for Meg to appear made it seem stifling.

Frank looked at his watch for the fifth time. "She's not coming, so what do we do?"

It wasn't the simplest question. When they arrived the door was locked. Lilith had an extra key. They got inside, and the golden shrine had been placed where it always sat, in the middle of the table. They were baffled.

Now Galen leaned forward and laid his hand on the chapel's smooth roof.

"What are you doing?" Frank asked. His tone wasn't hostile. Last week's session had melted away any rivalry. The mood was more suspenseful than anything else.

"I want to see if something happens when she's not here," Galen replied. "Maybe the mojo comes from Meg."

"And?"

Galen shrugged. "Nothing."

"I think she's deliberately leaving us on our own," Lilith remarked. "We should start without her."

The group wasn't enthusiastic about her suggestion.

Frank jumped to his feet. "We were instructed to go into the light this week. Did anyone succeed?"

Silence.

"Me neither. Meeting adjourned."

"Wait," Jimmy protested. "We should talk about it some more. This week was a lot better for me. I didn't see a zombie in the mirror."

He got a few weak smiles. No one else spoke up. Mare said what they were all starting to think. "What if she's gone, and she's not coming back?"

"Don't get carried away," Lilith said tartly. "Jimmy's made a start. Who else wants to share their experience?" Silence. She shook her head. "This is quite peculiar," she muttered.

"What about you?" Jimmy asked.

"I'm afraid not."

In fact, Lilith had been dead serious all week in her search for the light. She was more ambitious than anyone else in the group, or just more driven perhaps. The disciple must have planned some extraordinary experiences for her. An illumination? A great epiphany? What would it be?

Lilith mulled this over in the big house where she and Herb lived. He had never questioned her again about things he couldn't understand. Their two grown girls had left home for other cities, to attend graduate school or follow a job opening. They were Herb's daughters, really. They had the same literal mind, which made them feel safe. *Too safe,* Lilith thought. She had been tempted many times to reveal herself to them, especially when they faced a crisis.

When Tracy, the older girl, was in high school, she was seeing a boy who suddenly began to lose weight and feel tired. She got irritated when he canceled two dates in a row. He was never home when she phoned. When they finally connected, the first thing he said was "I have bone cancer."

The news devastated her. Lilith stood in the hallway outside Tracy's bedroom, hearing her cry on the other side of the door. Any mother would have gone in to comfort her, but Lilith was conflicted. She didn't feel anything for the sick boy, who was probably doomed. Malignancies progress with vicious swiftness in someone that young. Lilith turned away from the door and went downstairs.

She sat at the kitchen table, still feeling nothing. These were the years when looking into her heart made her afraid. She had a sudden impulse. She should ask why she didn't feel what normal people felt. She silently put the question out to the void.

A voice in her head replied, *Because you know. Because you can see. I will show you.*

Lilith's heart beat faster. *Show me now. I'm ready.*

But no more came. She was bitterly disappointed. Why was every experience a tease? She got up from the table and went up to her daughter's room.

"Tracy, honey, are you okay? May I come in?"

The door opened, and Lilith went over and sat on the bed hugging the girl and comforting her. It went well, because Lilith had learned long ago that other people can't read who we really are. That night, after making sure Tracy had fallen asleep, Lilith had a dream, the kind she thought of as a "special" dream. She saw the boy, Greg, lying in a hospital bed with tubes sticking out of his body. He was asleep, his face pale and worn. Lilith saw him from a bird's-eye view, as if hovering in the air over his bed.

"I'm here to take you home," she whispered.

He stirred in his sleep and moaned softly without waking up. Then a wisp of light emerged from the top of his head. Lilith felt like his mother, tenderly coaxing him not to be afraid. The wisp of light became a silvery thread, and as it emerged, it grew longer, extending up to the ceiling. The boy in the bed stopped moaning or moving. And there the dream ended.

Tracy came home early from school the next day, her face streaked with tears. Greg had died suddenly in the hospital that night. His heart had stopped. The doctors were mystified, but they were spared from telling him that his cancer had spread so far that it was untreatable.

For days Lilith went around feeling good and bad. Good because she had gone on an errand of mercy. Bad because it was just a dream. The experience refused to go away, urging her on. But it took a long time before she screwed up the courage to visit the hospice unit at the hospital, where she proved to herself that she could actually witness someone's spirit leave the body.

So it was true that she hadn't seen the light that week, but the whole truth was that she had seen it many times before.

Another half hour passed in the meeting room. It was hard for the group to accept defeat.

"It's not our fault," said Frank. "Meg didn't tell us enough."

He glanced over his shoulder in case she had come through the door. "As long as Meg's not here, I have a question for everyone. How into Jesus are we supposed to be? The scene we saw last week, it's not in the Bible as far as I know. Do any of you have a clue where this is coming from?"

"I told you, it could be her mojo," said Galen. He had backslid over the week. "Maybe she's a hypnotist. Don't look at me that way. It's a better explanation than believing we met Jesus."

Lilith shot him a sour look. "Bravo. Our archskeptic wants to burn a witch at the stake."

"I didn't say that," Galen shot back. "Don't put words in my mouth."

Frank shook his head. "The bottom line is none of us saw the light."

"Then you looked in the wrong place."

Heads turned. Meg was standing in the doorway listening. "I'm pleased at your honesty, but you gave up too soon."

She walked in and took her place at the head of the table. "I suspected you wouldn't succeed. For some reason that must be what the disciple intended."

"To keep us in the dark?" asked Mare.

"She wanted you to search as hard as you could in all the ordinary places," Meg replied, "until you realized how elusive the light really is. It's nowhere and everywhere. It shines as brightly in a coal mine as in a cathedral."

Their bafflement made her smile. She had a touch of the theatrical about her. "If I'd followed you around this week, how much looking would I have seen? Frank was at work, and so was Jimmy. Mare and Galen mostly watched TV and worried about not having a job. You four barely made an effort." Turning to Lilith, she said, "But that's not so with you, is it?"

"I told them before you came in, I didn't see anything either," said Lilith reluctantly.

"But you didn't tell the whole truth. I'm sure of it." Meg had a touch of the interrogator in her too.

"I didn't go to the store for lightbulbs, if that's what you mean." Lilith's instincts told her to guard her secret. That's how she had survived. But Meg was waiting to hear something from her.

"There was never a special place to go. The light is the same as the presence. If you feel the presence, you are in the light," Lilith said.

"Indeed." Meg nodded approvingly.

"But that's no help," said Mare. "There was no presence outside this room."

"That's the mystery, when something is everywhere and nowhere," Meg replied.

"More riddles," Galen grumbled.

She ignored him. "Imagine, all of you, that you are a fish. You're not satisfied being an ordinary tuna or halibut. You want to be spiritual. One day you swim to the mouth of a deep cave where a wise teacher is supposed to dwell. You don't swim inside, in case this is just a trick and there's a shark waiting to devour you. 'Tell me how to find God,' you plead. And from deep inside the cave, a low voice says, *Get wet.*

" 'What is this?' you think. You ask again. 'I desperately want to see God. Tell me the real answer.' But the same reply rumbles from the cave: *Get wet.* You swim away discouraged and disappointed. You find other teachers who tell you all kinds of things to do. But in the end you never get wet, and God remains a mystery."

Meg looked around the table. "Who sees what this parable means?"

Jimmy spoke up. "The fish is already wet, only he doesn't know it, because all his life the water was too close."

"Right."

While Jimmy enjoyed the pleasure of getting the answer, Lilith argued back. "Now that we know we're in the light, how do we actually see it?"

"With these."

Meg held up a drugstore shopping bag. Inside were half a dozen pairs of plastic sunglasses. "One each. They're all the same."

Frank picked out a pair with neon-green frames. "I wore el cheapos like these to the beach when I was eight."

"Not exactly like these," said Meg. "Don't analyze. Just wear them tomorrow. Agreed?" She didn't wait for answer. The meeting came to an abrupt end as she got up and departed without a backward glance.

As he walked Mare back to her car in the parking lot, Frank twirled the plastic sunglasses in the air, like a kid with a whirligig. Something about the evening had put him in a manic mood.

"Get your God glasses here," he shouted, imitating a carnival barker. "Don't wait for the last trumpet, folks. It's a downer."

Mare didn't do anything to stop him, but she didn't laugh either. After the night when he held her until she fell asleep, they should have grown closer. Frank wondered why they didn't. Maybe the mystery school was too much to handle on its own.

His manic spell vanished as quickly as it had appeared. "Are we actually supposed to wear these stupid things?" It was a moonless night, too dark to try them on.

"Why not?" said Mare. "The worst that can happen is nothing."

"I dunno. Maybe the worst is that we get sucked in too deep," Frank said. "You really don't mind going along, no matter what?" Now he was restless and uneasy. Every meeting left him feeling that way.

They found Mare's car. Frank searched for an excuse to keep her from driving away. "We should talk more, about everything. Us and what's happening."

Mare didn't go there. "What's really bothering you?"

"You're kidding. All of us should be bothered. I mean, jumping down the rabbit hole is nothing compared to this."

"Galen's scared too. I could see that tonight," Mare said.

"I'm not scared," Frank bristled. "Maybe, just maybe, he had a point about your aunt's mojo. Our minds are being bent, and someone's doing it."

To his surprise, Mare said, "Let's go to my place. You can stay the night and pick up your car in the morning."

Frank nodded and got in on the passenger side. Ordinarily he would have been thrilled at the invitation. He was drawn to Mare, just as he had been in college. Everything physical about her was perfect in his eyes, and whenever he made her smile, he felt as though he'd scored a small victory. But she sparked his insecurity. Mare was deeper than he was, and Frank didn't think she ever let down her guard, not completely. She spent the meetings looking on, saying little. The weirdness they were going through might not be good for her.

They were way past the stage where he would swoop in with a charm offensive. In a serious tone he said, "I meant it about getting in too deep. I'm concerned about your welfare." As soon as the words came out, he regretted it. "I sound like your father. Sorry."

But she didn't mind. "I don't worry about getting in too deep. I worry that I'm another Aunt Meg."

He was too surprised to react right away. Despite the winter cold, the roads were clear. Frank wasn't holding tight to the door handle, fighting the urge to grab the wheel the way he had the first time Mare drove to her apartment.

She didn't need a response from him. "My aunt gave her life away. I don't know what happened in the convent, but I know she's a total outsider. I can see it in me too."

"So we're not eloping?"

Mare laughed. "Don't be freaked out, but I plan on sleeping with you tonight."

Frank's heart skipped a beat, but his mind didn't go, *Score!* He even held back. "I get the feeling I'm your lab rat. To make sure you're still normal, not like Meg."

"Maybe." Mare said this in a neutral tone, keeping her eyes on the road. The pavement looked clear, but black ice is nearly invisible.

When they got to her place, events unfolded in a pattern familiar to Frank. He enjoyed undressing a woman and admiring her body, confident that she admired his too. Mare turned off the overhead bulb; she lit a candle so the room wouldn't be dark.

They silently agreed that sex was going to be a reprieve. Thinking about the mystery school was forbidden; thinking at all was forbidden. Frank loved the caressing part of being in bed, and this wasn't his first time or his fiftieth—he could stand apart a little, watching how a woman behaved in bed. He was considerate about giving Mare pleasure. He stayed in her as long as she wanted; he was proud that he had enough control to extend their lovemaking without rushing or stealing his own pleasure first.

What he didn't expect was that she would draw him in so deeply or how she did it. She was a quiet lover. When she made soft sounds, they weren't needy or selfish. She wasn't a little girl or a pliant body submitting to his will. He couldn't figure out what she was. The flesh took over after a certain point, and he surrendered to skin hunger, letting himself be carried away by its sensations. At the moment of climax he was alone, not united with her or anyone or anything. It wasn't the moment to question where this feeling came from.

After the physical rapture passed, always too quickly, they kissed and held each other. Each wanted to postpone the return of ordinary existence—when someone's arm has started to fall asleep from the head resting on it, and sweat feels a little clammy, and the bathroom calls. Frank was a realist, and lovemaking was just an interlude, a kind of midnight vacation. *Would this time be more?* He fell asleep thinking about it.

He woke up alone in bed. Mare was taking a shower, and the broken blinds let in bright sunlight. He had slept a long time. Sitting up, he was surprised to see the neon-green sunglasses lying on her pillow. Curious, Frank held them up. *More mojo or something truly unknown?* He didn't know which was better or worse.

At that moment Mare emerged naked from the bathroom, looking beautiful and ridiculous, because she was wearing a pair of the plastic sunglasses. "Don't laugh at me," she said. "Just put them on."

Frank obeyed. At first the greenish-black lenses blocked out everything. He would rather have gazed at her.

"Do you see?" Mare whispered.

"See what?"

And then he did. The air was filled with glittering gold sparks. At first they were like a shimmering mist. In a few seconds, this changed. Everything in the room started to glow, exactly like the glowing chapel.

"Awesome," Frank murmured.

"Wait. Don't talk," she urged.

Nothing changed. Frank wondered if he had to focus harder. Maybe he didn't know what to do. As soon as these doubts entered his mind, the glow faded, turning back into the misty shower of gold.

"I think we have to relax completely. That's the secret," said Mare, sensing what was happening.

"It's not that easy to relax with a gorgeous naked woman in the room."

"Then look away."

He did, reluctantly. Now he was facing the door, and it started to glow. The effect was warm and embracing, just as it was with the chapel. Then the door was gone, and the next instant the walls. Frank gasped. He was staring at the outside world, and everything gave off a lustrous golden light—the bare trees, the dirty snow, the chain-link fence. He turned his head, and in all directions it was as if the real world had melted away, leaving only the vaguest outlines around things.

Neither of them moved. They were transfixed by the beauty. And there was another thing. The light wasn't shining from things.

Everything was the light, and nothing but.

CHAPTER *18*

Jimmy woke up the next morning at his usual hour, just before dawn. The sun was peeking over the horizon when he stepped off the bus at the hospital. There was no time to test what the plastic sunglasses would do, so he had stuffed them in his jacket, along with the candy he passed out to sick kids when the staff wasn't looking.

After ten years at the same job, his routine proceeded automatically. As Jimmy emptied wastebaskets and tidied up rooms, he felt what the patients were feeling. Helplessness and fear were epidemic in the hospital. Patients rarely saw their doctors, and when they did, usually for a few anxious minutes, they were like guilty defendants waiting to be sentenced. They strained to read the doctor's face as he glanced at their chart; they waited for the next word out of his mouth, which could send them home with a smile or plunge them into a dark abyss.

Jimmy felt their distress, and he wanted to do something—but what? He had gravitated toward the children's floor, and over the years he'd become a fixture there. This morning he walked into the largest ward, where excited cries of "Señor Lucky!" greeted him. Quickly he was surrounded by six- and seven-year-olds. One little hand reached into his pocket for candy and came up with the sunglasses instead. They had bright pink rims with sparkles, and suddenly three kids wanted to put them on at once.

Startled, Jimmy grabbed them from the little girl who had found them.

"No, *querida,* these are just for me."

She started to cry. The noise level in the room rose rapidly, and Jimmy knew a nurse would be running in very soon. Mumbling "Sorry, sorry," he got out of there. He scurried down the corridor, avoiding eye contact with anyone he passed.

He was panting, his heart racing, when he made it into the safety of the men's room. Jimmy didn't know why he was so agitated. He'd reacted as if the sunglasses were cursed. But they couldn't be, not when it was Meg who handed them out. He stared at them with uncertainty for a moment before putting them on.

There was no instant effect, and then the outer door to the washroom creaked open. A doctor entered; he didn't acknowledge Jimmy standing at the sinks. Nervously Jimmy left, obeying his usual instinct to remain invisible.

In his distraction, he didn't remember that he was wearing the sunglasses. Diego, another young orderly, was loitering beside a gurney in the hallway. He smirked and gave Jimmy a thumbs-up. "*La vida loca,* eh man?"

Jimmy reached up, but before he could take off the glasses, a rush of golden light filled the air. He froze in place. The process wasn't gradual, the way it had been for Frank. One minute the hospital corridor was there, the next it vanished, replaced by a shimmering glow. The walls melted away. People were illuminated from the inside, yet only for an instant before they vanished too.

Disoriented, Jimmy staggered forward a few steps.

"Hey, watch it."

Jimmy felt his shoulder graze somebody, but he couldn't see who.

"Sorry," he mumbled, or thought he did. The glowing light absorbed him completely. Sounds were blurred and far away. He barely sensed it when a hand clapped him on the back.

"Orderly, stop daydreaming. I just said I need you."

I can't help it, Jimmy thought. *I'm floating away.* He had the uncanny feeling that his feet were lifting off the ground, and every fiber in his being wanted to break free, rising up and up, wherever the light wanted to carry him, like a feather in the wind.

From a distance he heard fuzzy words, more impatient this time. "You coming or not? This kid is seizing."

An alarm went off inside, and Jimmy tore away the sunglasses. The world took a second to return. One of the residents was rushing past him into a private room. On the floor lay a small boy writhing in convulsions. The doctor knelt beside him, clasping his writhing limbs. The boy was only nine or ten, but it was almost impossible to hold him still.

Looking over his shoulder at Jimmy, the doctor issued a torrent of instructions. "I need a nurse, stat. Tell her to prep an IV. We'll inject Dilantin and phenobarb. I'll also need a tongue depressor, and bring restraints in case we have to tie him to the bed."

Seeing no response from Jimmy, the doctor snapped, "You got all that?"

Jimmy wanted to rush off to do what he was told, but the afterglow of the light filled him; he wondered if he was still floating.

"Damn it," the doctor shouted. "Go!"

Suddenly Jimmy's body was galvanized. He hurried to the nurses' station, and within minutes the boy received an injection. The worst of the seizure passed, and he didn't have to be restrained in bed. In the immediate aftermath, the resident, who was younger than Jimmy, gave him a hard look.

"I know you have a good reputation. You don't need to explain anything, but the next time you don't jump when I say jump, I'm ordering random drug testing. You get my drift?"

Jimmy nodded, putting on his most contrite face. But inside he didn't feel humiliated or guilty. In the middle of the crisis, a brave thought had come to him. *I can heal this boy. Once everybody leaves, that will be the right time.* As if struck by lightning, he instantly knew that he, Jimmy, the lowly orderly, was a great healer, the answer to every sick child's prayers.

It was all he could do not to shout his thanks to God. There was too much activity around the epileptic boy's bed, so Jimmy left. There were many other sick children in the wards. His epiphany told him he could cure them all.

They're getting into trouble. I'm sure of it, Meg thought to herself anxiously. Before she handed out the cheapo sunglasses, she knew that seeing the light with your own eyes was a glorious experience. But that didn't save it from being perilous too. One way or another, each person in the group was stumbling.

"Keep them safe," she murmured.

Even after all this time, she still wasn't quite sure who she was talking to. It could be the disciple or the light or just herself. She lay in bed staring at the ornate ceiling overhead, which was painted like an azure sky with cherubs peeking out from billows of rosy clouds. The bed alone was larger than her cell at the convent.

A beam of morning light found a gap in the heavy velvet draperies. Meg got out of bed and pulled them aside. She was looking directly into the sun, and for a second its dazzle filled the world. But this was only a hint at the golden light that really did fill the world, no, the cosmos.

Meg hadn't told the group what to expect. How could she put it into words? Only Father Aloysius had come close.

"The light is alive. It's intelligent beyond anything our minds can understand. It knows us better than we know ourselves," he told her. "So going into the light can be very simple or very complicated. It's simple if you surrender. It's complicated if you resist."

They were meeting behind the estate's old dairy barn. Meg couldn't recollect what year this was, but summer had arrived, and she smelled new-mown grass in the air.

"I used to hate the idea of surrendering," she admitted.

"Resisting is much easier," he replied. "But you already know that."

"I suppose." Meg was reluctant to talk about her inner struggles.

"You're very special in many ways," Father Aloysius remarked, "but not in this. Everyone who glimpses the light is thrown into confusion. I certainly was."

"You, Father?"

He laughed. "I was the worst, quite giddy and beside myself. I fancied I was in love with every girl on the street. I came close to proposing marriage to the housemaid. She was from Brazil, and I planned to surprise her with two plane tickets to Rio." He smiled at the memory. "Did I mention that I was eleven?"

He was in an expansive mood. In the warm summer breeze the priest's white hair was like a dandelion puff against the sun. (This became Meg's favorite image of him after he died, the one she recalled whenever she wanted to remember him.)

"You see, the light doesn't care if you are young or old," he said. "It will undo you whenever it wants. The light exposes everything you've hidden from the world."

"Then what?" Meg asked with feeling. "You're left to crash on your own?" She still had days when she was lost, twisting in the wind. One part of her hated God for leaving her that way.

Father Aloysius sensed what she felt. "Be calm, child. I came to you, didn't I? Someone always comes. The light never works for anything but the good. It has no other purpose."

Meg wasn't sure she believed him, but she didn't argue. It was better to be grateful that he had come at all.

Now the tables were turned. The mystery school would be twisting in the wind unless she came for them. Meg dressed quickly. Ten minutes later she was in a taxi heading for the hospital, where Jimmy would already be hard at work. An impulse told her that he was the one who needed rescuing first.

By now, she was used to surrendering. She surrendered to her visions and to the golden chapel. Nothing mystical felt outlandish anymore. (Most people would be bored if the mystical weren't outlandish.) She didn't second-guess the disciple when she guided Meg to the drugstore for those sunglasses. Meg was told that their magic was temporary. After a day, they would go back to being cheap plastic sunglasses. Then the group would be in free fall.

The taxi left her at the front entrance of the hospital. Inside there was a bustle of people. The line in front of the reception desk was three deep. She passed through the lobby unnoticed and headed for a bank of elevators.

Meg didn't know which floor Jimmy worked on, but she remembered that he stopped every morning in the children's ward to cheer the kids up. He pretended to be Señor Lucky, the pony that the hospital owned so that children could ride on its back. She decided to try there first.

When the elevator doors opened, Meg stepped into a corridor painted in bright primary colors, with rainbows and baby animals at play. A dozen doors stood on either side, but she didn't have to peek into them. At the far end of the corridor was a chair with Jimmy sitting in it. He was slumped, hanging his head.

Meg knew that his stillness was deceptive. She rushed down the hallway, and as she got closer, she saw that Jimmy was clutching the plastic sunglasses in his hands.

"Jimmy, what's happening?"

He didn't look up, for the simple reason that he didn't see her. He had gone into a tailspin, sunk deep into himself, and it was entirely his fault. After his epiphany, he had returned to the big

room where Señor Lucky should have handed out candy instead
of running away. The atmosphere was calmer now, but the kids
didn't rush to his side. They were a bit wary of him.

Jimmy smiled magnanimously, spreading his arms out the way
Jesus did in the illustrated Bible stories his grandmother bought
for him when he was little. "Suffer the little children to come
unto me." That's all it would take. One touch, and they would be
healed, one by one.

"Come on," he urged. But they were too nervous.

Too impatient to wait, he went to the bed of a girl with leu-
kemia. She had a shaved head because of her treatments and slept
most of the day, her body wasted and weak. She would be the
first. Jimmy placed his palm across her forehead. He sent waves
of love into her. Whether it was this or feeling his touch, the girl
woke up. She looked at him, and Jimmy held his breath.

"How do you feel, baby?" he whispered.

"I hurt."

"You don't feel better now?" Jimmy asked.

She shook her head. "I hurt everywhere. Why are you bothering me?" She wasn't angry with him, just sleepy and cross. Turning her head away, the girl fell back to sleep, but not before Jimmy
saw the expression in her eyes, which was vacant and lost.

Oh, my God. Jimmy felt himself crash to earth. He had made
a terrible mistake. He tried to bolt from the room, but his knees
buckled, and he barely made it into the corridor. If a chair hadn't
been sitting there, he would have collapsed. He felt nauseous; far
worse, he was sick at heart. What had come over him? A pang
of fear struck his chest. What if someone had walked in on him?

As he slumped there, a woman started speaking to him. As if
swimming toward the surface from a great depth, Jimmy managed to look up. He recognized Meg.

She bent down and softly said in his ear, "You're not Jesus
Christ. Sorry to disappoint you."

He was relieved and bewildered at the same time. "Then who am I?"

"You're one of us. And a very beautiful soul."

Jimmy managed a grateful smile. Then a fresh spasm of nausea came over him, filling his mouth with its bitterness, and he started to cry.

Meg called an emergency meeting that evening, and one way or another every member was rounded up. She was guided to rescue them, as she had been with Jimmy, but she needed help.

Lilith was likely to be the one who hadn't run amok. Meg called her at home. It took three tries before she answered.

"How are you feeling?" Meg asked. She assumed that Lilith had tried on the sunglasses.

"What?"

"Are you feeling anything unusual?"

"I feel very well," replied Lilith. "Very well indeed." She sounded like herself but mildly confused. "Listen carefully," Meg said in an urgent voice.

"All right."

"You're not God. You're not a saint or an angel or waiting for the rapture. I know you're trying to decide which one applies. None of the above. You are still Lilith. Do you understand?"

Silence at the other end. Then in a quavering voice, sounding more vulnerable than Meg had ever heard her, Lilith said, "If I'm not God, wouldn't God tell me?"

"No, he's busy. I'm telling you instead. You got a blast of reality, that's all. It's wonderful, but you need to come to your senses. We've got to find the others, and quickly."

Luckily, Lilith came down to earth after three cups of black coffee; her years of experience had kept her from becoming delusional.

Mare was fairly stable also. They found her at the bus stop near her house. As the buses rolled up, she stood at the door, her hand raised in benediction. "Bless you," she said to the passengers getting on and off. "Be at peace."

A few people smiled at her. The rest were used to crazies in the city; this one seemed harmless. Only one man was irritated enough to say, "Get yourself some help, lady."

Mare was surprised to see Meg and Lilith at the curb. "Were you sent here too?" she asked. "Everyone is a child of God. I see it. Why don't they?"

"They've got other things on their mind," said Lilith. "We need to get you home."

"Why? I've found my calling."

"Maybe so," Meg said. "But now is not the time."

"What does that mean?" Lilith asked, looking puzzled. She'd caught the look that passed between them.

"Never mind. Let's get her away from here."

Mare had rushed out into the cold wearing only a light jacket and now she was trembling. Like Jimmy she had the plastic sunglasses clutched tightly in her hand. Meg immediately grasped what they were doing to her niece. The look that passed between them had history.

It went back to the legendary Thanksgiving Massacre, as the Donovan family took to calling it. A distant cousin was being ordained, and Mare's family filled two cars, driving a hundred miles to attend what Mare's grandfather Tom referred to as a going-away party.

"He'll miss the best part of life, I'm telling you," he said.

Mare, who was six, wondered what he meant. Her grandmother told Tom to shush.

Tom, who was "black Irish," loved the I.R.A. cause and resented priests. At the party he made a nuisance of himself. He knew better than to make cutting remarks about the church, so, instead, he made mischief by goading the soon-to-be priest into drinking too much.

"Another nip can't hurt you, or you're not a Donovan," he said. The young man, barely out of his teens, did what he was told. Finally someone intervened and told Father Ronnie, as they had already started calling him, to get some fresh air. He walked out alone, tripped over a tree root in the back yard, and hit his head. The result wasn't terrible, a gash on the forehead and a mild concussion. But the gash bled profusely, the parents exchanged hot words with Tom, and that side of the Donovan family was never welcome in the house again.

The disturbing part wasn't the fight, because Tom never liked his snooty, devout cousins to begin with. The disturbing part occurred on the way home when Mare, sitting in the backseat, started to scream, "Stop the car, stop the car!"

Her outburst was completely out of character. Her mother looked around from the front seat. "What's gotten into you?"

Mare began to cry, and no one could calm her down. "Please, please," she whined.

"Do you have to go?" her father said, looking at her in the rear-view mirror.

"No."

"Then what is it?"

Mare remembered that she was going to blurt out, "We're all going to die." A brutal image had flashed through her mind, showing a railroad crossing and a car twisted into a hideous wreckage. At that moment she heard the bells signaling an approaching train, and the flashing red lights for the gate were only a hundred yards away. She was too frightened to speak, squeezing her eyes shut in terror.

"Look out!" her mother warned.

There was a loud horn blast from the locomotive barreling toward the crossing, instantly followed by a sickening crash.

"Look away!" Tom ordered as he slammed on the brakes and leaped out of the car. Ahead of them a driver had tried to beat the crossing gate, but he had misjudged by a matter of seconds. It was enough. In the horror and confusion at the scene, no one found time to question Mare about why she had cried out. She felt incredibly guilty, as if she could have saved the people who died. The newspaper said the driver had been drinking heavily at a holiday party.

In the aftermath, her mother remembered how Marc made such a fuss, but Thanksgiving was the next day, and there was the main event to discuss, the big row over the soon-to-be priest. Mare never came up.

Aunt Meg poked at her turkey in silence and then took her niece into the back yard while the table was being cleared. "You notice things, don't you? Things other people don't."

Mare was alarmed. "I try not to."

"Why? It's not a bad thing. Did your mother tell you it was?"

Mare bit her lip. "All right, go back inside," her aunt said. "Brush the snow off your shoes first."

At the age of six, it didn't occur to Mare to wonder about Aunt Meg's motivation. All she got into her head from that traumatic Thanksgiving was a recurring nightmare. The sound of crunching metal woke her up shaking.

The plastic sunglasses reawakened this bad memory, which thankfully fled as soon as Mare started blessing the bus passengers.

Now she heard Meg say, "Come with us. We don't want a blessing overload, do we? It might blow the circuits."

Mare looked confused, but she allowed herself to be led away docilely. When Meg and Lilith got her back home and into bed, she fell asleep instantly.

"On to the next one," said Meg with a touch of grimness.

They found Frank sitting in his car in the newspaper parking lot. He was blasting heavy-metal rock at a deafening volume and didn't hear them approach. Lilith rapped on the driver's-side window. Frank lowered it.

"Why are you here?" he asked. He looked badly shaken.

"To see how you're holding together," Meg replied.

He grimaced. "The glue's not dry yet."

"What happened?"

Frank had made a fool of himself. At Mare's apartment the effect of the sunglasses had been overwhelming, but somewhere in the back of his mind he remembered that he had to go to work. He took off the glasses and stumbled to the bathroom. A cold shower helped. He dressed to leave, but Mare paid no attention, perched on the edge of the mustard yellow sofa with a giant grin on her face.

"I'm going now," he said. "Don't keep those things on too long."

"Uh huh."

The streets were clear, but Frank's driving was shaky, and he stopped by his young reporter buddy Malcolm's place. Malcolm was surprised to see him.

"I need you to drive," said Frank, hoping he sounded normal. Perhaps not. Malcolm gave him a puzzled look and took the wheel.

"You've got that political thing in an hour," he said. "Maybe I'll come with."

"Sure, fine," Frank mumbled. He had no idea what the political thing was. He kept staring out the window at the passing scene. Instead of a grimy city, his eyes drank in a whoosh of colors that was almost musical.

"Heavy night?" Malcolm asked. "You look wasted."

The concern in his voice made Frank try to focus. He shut his eyes and concentrated. Things came into view.

"The political thing is a press conference?" he said doubtfully.

"Yeah. Boy, I'm glad you asked me to drive."

At a hotel downtown, a right-wing candidate running for Congress had scheduled a pointless press conference. He was behind in the polls and wanted to agitate about abortion and gay marriage. The only media who showed up were Frank, Malcolm, and a college-aged girl from the local-access TV station.

The candidate looked miffed. He was a local fundamentalist minister who was bewildered that his old hot-button issues had turned cold. He took out his sheet of talking points, but before he could speak Frank raised his hand.

"Questions can come later," the candidate's PR assistant said.

Frank stood up anyway. "I just wanted to tell Reverend Prescott something. You're beautiful, man."

The candidate, an imposing figure in his late sixties with snowy hair, scowled. "What did you say?"

Frank felt himself slightly tottering. "I said you're beautiful. Actually, you're totally full of it. You've become a laughingstock. But God doesn't care. He loves you."

Frank started to sit down, but had a second thought. "I love you too."

Malcolm looked around nervously; the local-access girl giggled.

With a sense of dreamy detachment Frank watched the candidate's face turn purplish red. The PR assistant, who knew all the local reporters, grabbed the microphone and shouted into it.

"Get the hell out of here, Frank. I'm calling your boss. I hope your little stunt is worth losing your job over."

"No worries. God loves you too. Creep."

No one heard Frank add this parting remark, because Malcolm was dragging him out of the room. Nothing was said in the car on the way back to the paper. But when he got out, Malcolm was visibly angry.

"Sorry, man," Frank mumbled.

"If you want to commit public suicide, it's okay by me," Malcolm said. "But leave me out of it. I don't want to get hit by the shrapnel."

Frank watched him stalk off, then he turned the music on in his car full blast to clear his head. Time passed; he didn't know how long. The next thing he was aware of was Lilith rapping on the window.

"Can you turn that down?" she said.

"He's still in shock," Meg guessed. They gave Frank a few minutes. He clicked off the music and stepped out of the car.

"Jesus, what a mess," he moaned. "I'm ruined."

He didn't want to talk about his grim mood. The two women decided to wait in the parking lot while he went inside to learn his fate. Frank was back in two minutes.

"I can't believe it. My editor was ready to kick my ass down the street, but he got a call from the owner of the paper. Turns out he hates this wack-job preacher. I might get a raise." Frank shook his head. "There is a God."

Lilith shrugged. "Give the boy a gold star."

Which left only Galen. They swung by his house, but his car was gone, and no one answered the door.

"The painting he tried to deface," said Lilith. "Maybe he's gone back to kneel in front of it."

"No, that's not like him," Meg replied. "Everyone reacts according to their nature. That's how it works."

Guessing where he might be was impossible, but on the first try Galen answered his cell. He sounded calm. Too calm.

"I haven't tried the sunglasses on yet," he said. "I'm still supposed to, right?"

Meg hesitated. She had no right to reverse the disciple's instructions. "Let me come to you first. Where are you?"

"I'm walking into the planetarium."

"Why?"

"I used to like it as a kid. Seemed like a safe place to trip."

Meg said, "Wait there. Don't do anything."

She rushed Lilith back into the car. "I have a bad feeling about this," she said.

When they got to the planetarium, the ticket seller told them the next showing was delayed. In the distance Meg saw two uniformed guards entering the auditorium.

"I'm going in there," she whispered to Lilith. "Create a distraction."

Lilith's idea of a distraction was to empty her purse on the floor and then beg the ticket seller to help her find a diamond ring that had fallen out. It was feeble, but good enough for Meg to scurry past the gate. She hurried into the empty auditorium, which was dimly lit. The domed ceiling was devoid of stars. She heard a commotion in the middle of the room and, once her eyes adjusted, Meg spied the two guards. They were prying Galen off some kind of machine. She ran up and saw that he had wrapped himself around the star projector. He was wearing the sunglasses.

"Let there be light," Galen was mumbling. "And there was light."

The burly guards were having a surprisingly hard time pulling him loose. One said, "C'mon, mister, you don't want to be doing this."

When they pulled harder, Galen began to squeal and held on tight. Meg intervened. "I'm his sister. Let me try. He's frightened."

The guards didn't give her permission, but she shoved past them anyway, which got her close enough to snatch the glasses off Galen's head.

"I took him out on a day pass. He's under care," she explained.

The guards looked suspicious. At least Galen had let go of the projector. He slid to the ground, softly murmuring "Wow" over and over.

"Your brother needs better doctors," one guard said. He was older and seemed to be in charge.

"Oh, I agree," said Meg. "I appreciate your understanding. And, of course, if we're allowed to leave, there will be a generous contribution to the planetarium."

"Whatever," the younger guard grumbled. "I'm going to lunch."

Between them, Meg and Lilith dragged Galen away. He pawed at Meg's purse, where she had stowed his sunglasses.

"Mine," he babbled. "Mine, mine, mine."

But they managed to keep him from getting at them.

"All gone," he moaned softly. His head lolled to one side, and he fell asleep.

CHAPTER *19*

When the emergency meeting convened that evening, the group looked like five cats scooped out of the river and wrung out. But there were no visible signs of derangement. Meg took a careful look around.

"Everyone is all right?"

"We're safely back in our cages," Lilith said drily. "I'm using a metaphor."

"Maybe," Frank grunted. He was still badly shaken, and he suspected the others were too. But no one wanted to exchange notes, not until things settled down.

Meg picked up Lilith's drift. "It's not a physical cage you're trapped in. The bars are mental. They block out the light. Deep down that's how you want it to be, because living normally means everything if you plan to survive. The disciple has shown you a way out, an escape route."

"So we can enjoy living abnormal lives?" Frank asked. He pulled his plastic sunglasses out. "Help like this I don't need, thank you very much."

Despite his protest, Meg sensed that none of them regretted a moment of their time outside the cage.

She said, "I had a great teacher, and one day he gave me a piece of advice. 'Don't judge anyone for who they appear to be. Get a sense of their soul. One kind of soul is masked from view, and it gives off no light. Another kind of soul sometimes peeks out from behind the mask, giving off a flickering light. The rarest kind of soul hides from nothing; it's out in full view. That's you.'"

"Beautiful," Mare murmured.

"You think so? I didn't. I felt exposed and guilty," Meg said.

"Guilty for what?"

"For being a fraud. If you don't have a clue who you really are, your whole life's a fraud, isn't it?" She gave each person around the table an astute glance. "Now you don't have an excuse anymore."

They grew quiet, and then Lilith stood up. "I want to apologize. I've been seeing the rest of you as ordinary people. The sight was extremely disappointing, let me assure you."

"Thank you, Missus God," Galen muttered under his breath.

"I'm not deaf," said Lilith. "You've all done such a good job hiding your light that you fooled me. No longer, and so I apologize."

She said none of this with a smile. If anything she looked angry as she sat back down. *All those wasted years,* the voice in her head began to say, but she turned her attention away, refusing to listen.

Jimmy held up his sunglasses. "These things freaked me out. I'm with Frank. Just take them back."

"No need," said Meg. "They were just an invitation. God's not going to push himself on you."

"Is it really so bad being a fraud?" asked Jimmy, which got a nervous laugh. "Seriously, I don't know how to change."

"I'd be worried if you didn't want to keep fooling people," Meg replied. "It's taken years to get your act down pat. But the disciple thinks you're ready, all of you."

"I'll bite," Galen said. He hadn't tossed in a complaint, because he didn't really have one. The light had treated him more carefully than the rest.

Meg felt a silent agreement all around. If they had hesitated, she was prepared to make the same promise Father Aloysius once made to her: "One taste of the light isn't the same as living there. When you live there, you won't need hope or faith. You'll know everything."

Back then, her anxiety wasn't assuaged. "I don't want to know everything."

"Yes, you do. You just don't realize it yet," he told her.

The golden shrine was sitting in its customary place in the center of the table. Meg placed her hands on it. The others followed her lead without being told. The room began to fade away. The shift into another reality happened smoothly this time, although they had no idea what would greet them on the other side.

This is what they saw. The thirteenth disciple was traveling on a road in the desert, empty in both directions. An old servant was leading the sleepy donkey she rode on, its clip-clop sending up puffs of dust. Spring had come into full bloom around Jerusalem. For a magical three weeks, splashes of yellow and purple brought joy to the landscape. But here the only vegetation was drab, low scrub.

"The place must be near," she said anxiously.

The servant shrugged his shoulders. "Who can say?"

This stretch of the road to Tyre was usually filled with traders and their caravans. Trade attracted bandits. But there were no hills or cliff faces for them to hide in for the next few miles, and Jerusalem could still be seen in the distance, a hazy blue mirage.

The servant eyed the sun's position in the sky. "If we don't see a house soon, we'll have to turn back." He didn't want to suffer the consequences if his mistress got waylaid.

Where could a house hide in such flat, unsheltered land? The answer came around the next bend—a deep ravine intersected the road like a slash in the skin.

"There," she said, pointing to a trail that led into the ravine.

The servant looked perplexed. "There's nothing down there but snakes and devils."

"In a few minutes there will be snakes, devils, and us."

Grunting, the servant goaded the donkey with a switch. The trail wound its way around rocky outcroppings. Once they reached the dry floor of the ravine, which had been cut by centuries of flash floods, the bed veered away from the road.

Ten minutes later they came upon their first human being, a man sitting on a sandstone boulder whittling on a stick. The servant wondered if the point of this activity was to show that the man had a knife.

When they were in close range, the man spoke cryptically. "I had a feeling."

The thirteenth disciple didn't hesitate. "Me too."

The man got to his feet, revealing how tall he was. His robe, tied with a sash at the waist, was good-quality hemp, but not the fine-spun linen the girl wore. He had a neatly trimmed beard and eyes that studied her with sharp clarity.

"Do we need to speak alone?" he asked, eyeing the servant, who didn't exactly seem pleased with their encounter.

"I'm staying," the servant insisted.

"It's all right," she said. The girl knew that age had made him somewhat deaf. Her father's granaries and fields were too busy at planting time to spare any of the young men. He wouldn't have sent anyone if he'd known she was going to hunt for one of Jesus's disciples. The miracle rabbi had caused trouble among the Jews, which tightened the Roman grip. Killing him only made the occupiers search harder for more of his kind.

She dismounted and approached the man. "What shall I call you?"

"Simeon. Or if you are more Roman than Jew, Simeonus."

"Simeon, then. Do you have a hiding place nearby?"

"Yes. Bandits dug out some caves. With everything stirred up, rebels use them now. You're safer here." Simeon gestured toward the boulder he'd been sitting on, the only thing that could pass for a seat. The girl perched herself on it while he sat cross-legged in the dust.

"I've seen everything," she began. "Just as I saw how to find you today."

She was sparing his feelings. In a vision she had seen Simeon run away when the Roman soldiers seized Jesus. He hid in a hole in the poorest slums of the city, weeping uncontrollably. But that's what attracted the girl to him. She had wept uncontrollably too.

"What do you want from me?" he asked.

"I wish I didn't want anything. My family should be offering you a hiding place, someone as holy as you."

He shook his head. "You think I'm holy? I betrayed the one I promised never to betray. Now I have no way to go in the world. I used to fish in Galilee, but that's too far behind me."

"So you live as God pleases," she said.

Simeon sat back. "I live as my master taught, because I know he forgives me."

He spoke with total sincerity, and this encouraged the thirteenth disciple. The donkey wandered toward a tuft of grass lodged in a crevice, and the old servant sat in the shade with his straw hat pulled down over his eyes.

"I spoke with Jesus," the thirteenth disciple said. She took a deep breath. "He was on the cross when he came to me."

She expected Simeon to jump to his feet, in either anger or amazement. But he remained calm. "What did he tell you?"

"He told me he was the light of the world. Do you know what he meant?"

"He meant what he said."

Simeon spread his arms out. "All this, and everything we can see, is light. When the spirit completely fills us, we are the light. Jesus taught this."

"So you could become the same as God?"

He was alarmed. "Those words are blasphemous."

"Your whole life is blasphemous. I don't care. Let me follow you."

Simeon shook his head. "Someday I'll return to Jerusalem, God willing. I don't want your father stoning me for ruining his daughter."

"How can you ruin me?" She asked the question without flinching, staring directly into his eyes.

"By taking away your faith. With faith, you can still be a Jew."

"No, I'm like you. Neither of us can go back to how we were."

Simeon frowned. He'd never heard a woman speak like this. She could have explained to him about listening behind a curtain while the rabbis taught her brothers. She could have pointed to her heart, which many days was like a burning ball of fire. But there was no time.

He said, "It's rare to see a woman on the cross, but not impossible. You must go. I have nothing more to tell you."

The sun had already sunk below the lip of the ravine. She stood up, brushing the pale desert dust from her shift and sandals. "I know what I've seen. Whether I'm cursed or blessed, I'm one of you."

"Then I pity you." Simeon's eyes grew moist. "Jesus may never return to us. Don't put yourself in danger. Just go."

He saw how crestfallen she looked, and his voice softened. "If you're one of us, the Lord will guide you. Even in the shadow of the death."

She paused. "I know why you're sick at heart. It's not because you betrayed your master. It's because he left you behind. You blame him. You think it's unfair."

How did you know? he thought. To be so blessed when the master was alive and then abandoned like a stray spark blown from a bonfire into the night. How could she know?

When he didn't reply, her tone turned grim. "As long as you wallow in grief, you have no master, and no hope."

Her words would come back to haunt him in all the tomorrows leading to his death. Simeon waited while she woke up her drowsy old servant. He accompanied them to the trailhead and watched the donkey climb to the road. The little party had to make it back to Jerusalem before the night and its lurking dangers swallowed them up.

With one impulse, they all took their hands off the golden shrine. As often as the disciple had taken them back in time, it was still hard to believe. Lilith looked at the others. Did they realize that the hunted fugitive in the ravine was Simon Peter? Or that he would only meet his master by being crucified in Rome? All the disciples died violent deaths. If the girl shared their life, she must have shared their doom. Lilith decided not to mention any of this. She steered the group in a different direction.

"You said that going back there would help us make a choice," she reminded Meg. "What is it?"

"Living as God pleases," Meg replied, quoting the disciple. "Without doubt or fear."

Her words were meant to inspire them, but that wasn't the outcome. Jimmy looked anxious. "It sounds too hard," he said. "Look at them squatting in a ditch. They were miserable."

"And hunted down," Galen added. There was a general murmur of agreement. "The disciples were promised heaven, and then overnight they're criminals on the run."

Lilith was irritated. "For pity's sake, why can't you see past that?"

"Maybe I do," Galen shot back. "I'm sorry horrible things happened. But history is a nightmare we spend our whole lives trying to forget."

This was perhaps the deepest thought any of them had expressed, certainly the gloomiest. Jimmy felt sorry for Galen. But his gloominess wasn't the only way.

"If everything's so horrible, maybe it doesn't have to be," Jimmy said. "I'm an optimist."

"For how long? Eternal optimism is insanity if nothing ever changes," Galen declared.

When Jimmy didn't respond, Meg said, "You're looking at the world from darkness. But the light never abandoned us—we abandoned it. Is that what you want?"

She wasn't throwing a challenge in their faces, but one was implied.

Frank put into words what they were all thinking. "Okay, so I look into the light and say, 'Come and get me.' Is it going to make me crazy again?"

"I'm not a fortune-teller," Meg replied. "In this new life, every day is an unknown. The alternative is totally predictable. You stay behind bars."

They could tell she meant business, but they couldn't see where she was taking them. Meg didn't know either. Ever since Father Aloysius died, she had abided alone in a deserted kingdom. She was the queen of her own solitude. Now the kingdom was beginning to be populated. Five shipwrecked travelers had washed ashore by the light of the moon. They had no idea if they belonged in this strange land. It was time they found out.

Meg looked around the table, sizing up each castaway. "When you see me, do you see somebody who's like you?" She didn't wait for a reply. "I'm no different from you, I promise. Except in one thing. When the disciple says, 'Live as God pleases,' I get it."

She reached into her handbag and took out a small change purse. "Enough talk. There are five pennies inside this purse, one for each of you." She spilled the coins out; they clinked as they landed on the table. "Take one, and regard it as precious. If you lose it, that means you want to go back to your old life."

In silence the pennies were passed around. Galen eyed his, then he flipped it in the air. "Heads. Now what?"

"It's not a game," Meg warned. "The disciple gave plastic sunglasses a secret power. She's done the same here."

Frank shook his head. "This whole thing about walking away. It sounds like a threat."

"It's not," Meg insisted. "The instructions are simple. Carry your penny around for a week, and when you return, you'll be changed."

Galen was annoyed. "Every time you explain things, nothing gets explained."

If he expected more clues, Meg didn't offer any. "You're on your own," she said. "Just don't lose your penny, no matter what. If you do, don't bother to come back."

The group dispersed, going their separate ways in the fading twilight, more bewildered and fretful than ever.

CHAPTER *20*

That night Galen slept fitfully and woke up tangled in the sheets. He had twisted them tighter trying to burrow into the bed, like an animal digging its way out of danger. The meetings did that to him, and he hated it. But there was nowhere else to turn. His days were empty without the mystery school.

Standing in the bathroom, he looked at himself in the mirror, saddened by the puffy roundness of his face, his absent hairline, and his bloodshot eyes. *Why was nothing working?*

Nobody owes you anything, he reminded himself. *Get a grip.*

Back in the bedroom he pulled on the pants and shirt he'd flung over a chair. A bright spot glinted out of the corner of his eye. He leaned over and picked up the penny, which had fallen out of his khakis.

Really? he thought. It wasn't clear what another dose of magic would do. He'd already floated through the universe. He was tempted to throw it away the minute he got to the hospital parking lot. Galen had a deep suspicion of magic. It was primitive and mindless. As a child, he recalled random visits from a whiskery, smelly uncle, the last of the farming stock his mother came from. When Galen was ten, Uncle Rodney pulled him aside and produced a dollar bill from his wallet.

"I got somethin' real important to show you," he said. His tone was conspiratorial. He pushed the boy's hand away when Galen reached for the money. "This isn't for you, no sir."

Uncle Rodney gave the bill a snap. "This is the first dollar I ever made. It's sacred to me. If I ever lose it, Lord knows what will happen."

"You'd have one less dollar," said Galen.

"No! Much worse. I'd probably go bust."

"Why?"

His uncle frowned. "What do you mean why? Don't you believe in luck?" His breath smelled of chewing tobacco and bad teeth.

Galen turned and fled, much to his uncle's disgust. The only luck was bad luck—the boy knew that very well. Fortune was a secret enemy, and no matter how often you begged her to be kind, her treachery could never be appeased.

This recollection distracted him from throwing the penny away. He thoughtlessly pocketed it along with the rest of his loose change, which he'd neatly laid out in rows on the dresser. The winter sun was bright and high in the sky. Time to go out.

Because he was sulky and absent-minded, he didn't notice that he was headed in the wrong direction, away from the bus stop. Galen hung his head, mechanically counting his steps, when a stranger bumped into him. The next second, he felt something wet and hot. The man had spilled coffee down Galen's front.

"Watch it!" Galen snapped. He looked up, and it was no stranger. It was Malcolm, the kid reporter, who had rushed out of a Starbucks without looking where he was going.

"Jeez, are you okay, man?"

"I don't know." The coffee wasn't boiling hot, but it was Galen's habit to make someone else squirm for a change when he had the chance.

Malcolm looked genuinely apologetic. "Listen, I have a little time. Can I get you something to eat? How have you been?"

What is this? Galen thought. The last person who had said a kind word to him was Iris. The memory brought a stab of pain. His natural instinct was to brush the kid off and scurry down the street.

Before he could do this, Malcolm said, "You've been keeping out of trouble, I hope."

Malcolm's cell phone rang. He held up his hand, saying, "Just a second," and answered it.

Galen's hand wandered into his pocket, touching the change he was carrying. At that moment an unusual thought came into his head.

This kid pities you. Is he wrong?

Galen didn't know how to react. Malcolm's call was brief, and when he said good-bye, his face had fallen.

"I guess I have more time on my hands than I thought," he muttered. "They cancelled my assignment."

Galen's hand lingered in his pocket. In the back of his mind he knew he was touching the magic penny.

Without a second thought he said, "You're going to be fired tomorrow."

"What?" The kid backed away a step.

"Tomorrow morning the city editor is going to let you go. That's why he took your story away."

"Jesus." Malcolm looked badly shaken. He had a sinking feeling that he was hearing the truth. "What am I going to do?"

The words came out involuntarily. The last person on earth he wanted to share his trouble with was the nut job from the museum fiasco.

"I know you think I'm a loser," said Galen, "but I can help. Come back here after they fire you." He saw the doubt written on

Malcolm's face. "Sometimes weird people like me actually know something. You and me, we're a lot alike," he added.

"Wow, it's that bad?" Malcolm mourned. Galen was older than his father. He resembled a dumpling in wrinkled khakis. He probably had nothing to do but wander around all day pestering people. How could they be alike?

But by then Malcolm was starting to feel panicky. He turned away mumbling, "I have to make some calls" as he punched numbers into his cell phone. He wandered down the sidewalk without saying good-bye.

The voice in Galen's head said, *He'll be back.*

Which wasn't good news. Galen was almost as shaken as the kid. Some impulse he couldn't control had taken over. Why else had he said those things? He wasn't the kind to meddle in other people's affairs, ever.

Retracing his steps, Galen scurried home to clean the coffee stains off his jacket and scarf. This took only a few minutes, and afterward he didn't feel like mingling with the crowd at the mall anymore. *Who does that anyway, besides losers?*

The next morning he went back to the corner where the Starbucks stood. It took half an hour to talk himself into going; this time the only coin he put in his pocket was the penny. The day was gray and windy. There were gusts of sleet, and Galen almost turned back. A lifetime of missed opportunities told him not to.

Amazingly, Malcolm was there, sitting on the steps of the coffee shop. He looked miserable. "All right, I got sacked. So tell me the wisdom of the weird."

He followed Galen inside. As they stood in line, neither spoke. Galen felt cold with panic. Why had he lured this kid into meeting him?

The voice in his head returned. *Don't worry. It will be like talking to your double.*

Galen laughed, and Malcolm whipped around. "Something funny?" He looked irritated and as nervous as Galen.

"Potentially," Galen replied. "We'll have to wait and see."

After they took a table, Malcolm didn't make eye contact. He gulped his coffee until Galen said, "Slow down. No one's keeping you here."

"I've been thrashing this out in my mind," Malcolm said. "You took a lucky guess yesterday, didn't you?"

It would have been easy to say yes, and that would have been the end of it. But Galen remembered Meg's image of living behind bars. For the first time in his life, he asked for guidance.

Malcolm mistook his silence. "I thought so," he said, pushing his coffee away and starting to get up. "It was nice knowing you."

"If you stay, you'll get your job back."

"Bull."

"What have you got to lose?"

"I dunno, my self-respect?" Malcolm hesitated, perplexed, but he sat back down again. "What's the plan?"

Galen clasped his hands together under the table to keep them from trembling. "Go back to the paper. But you have to take me with you."

"Now?"

"Yes." Galen managed what he hoped was a confident smile. "I'll know what to do when we get there."

"Because you've run your life so spectacularly that way, right? Jesus!"

Malcolm didn't mute his insolence. He felt entitled to it, being young and employed. Except that the second part wasn't true anymore. The gap between them was closing. Wearily he got up and let Galen follow him out of the coffee shop, not looking over his shoulder.

They drove in silence through the cold, gray day. In the newspaper parking lot, Galen expected the kid to get cold feet, but he marched the two of them upstairs to the newsroom. The city editor's desk had several reporters gathered around it, drinking coffee and shooting the breeze. No one looked Malcolm's way.

Coming to his senses, he shook his head. "This is ridiculous. Why did I listen to you?"

Without replying, Galen walked up to the desk. "I'm Malcolm's father. He's sick of being on obits, but he didn't want to tell you."

The city editor was Galen's age, but robust-looking, as red-faced as an Irish boxer. Behind him on a coatrack hung a trench coat and a fedora. He thought of himself as an old-school newspaperman.

"He should have had the guts to come to me himself," he said.

"He was afraid he'd get fired," Galen said.

"Fired?" The editor pointed to the circle of men around his desk. "These hacks would go first."

He grinned wickedly at the reporter lounging on the corner of the desk. "Isn't that right, Nicky?" The man stood up, faking a smile. No one looked very happy.

By this time Malcolm had walked up. He couldn't believe what Galen was trying to pull off.

"This isn't my fault," he said apologetically.

His editor looked annoyed. "You call in sick yesterday, and now I don't see any copy coming across my terminal." He tapped the computer screen in front of him. "Your old man's got a point. Forget obits. Someone else can pick up the slack. I want the story on police corruption you promised me."

He seemed oblivious of the fact that he'd fired Malcolm earlier that morning. The reporters around the desk had all witnessed the scene, had watched Malcolm clear out his desk. Without comment they drifted back to their cubicles.

To keep the kid from opening his mouth, Galen dragged him away. It wasn't easy.

"He doesn't remember a thing," Malcolm whispered. He sounded very agitated.

"Do you want him to remember?" Galen hissed.

"I want an explanation."

Galen searched his mind for one. "He can't remember because it never happened."

"You're crazy."

"I must be." Galen had no idea why such a bizarre explanation had come out of him. "Keep moving, and close your mouth. You'll catch flies."

Malcolm could have said, "It's winter, there are no flies." But he was dazed. Galen dragged him through the nearest door, which opened onto a stairwell. They both felt weak and sank down on the steps.

"This goes a lot farther than weird. Really. I guess I should be thanking you," Malcolm managed to say.

Galen shook his head. "I didn't do anything. I was just there."

"So you're not, like, a shaman or whatever?" Malcolm took a hard look at Galen and laughed. "Of course you're not." He got to his feet. "I meant that in the best possible way."

Galen shrugged. "I doubt it."

Malcolm opened the door to the newsroom, anxious to get back to work before his job vaporized again. He bit his lip, trying to think of something else to say. Nothing came, so he smiled weakly and left, letting the stairwell door bang shut behind him.

Galen took the magic penny out of his pocket and held it up to the light. It looked completely innocent, and the voice in his head said, *Sometimes being here is all it takes.*

CHAPTER 21

The morning after the meeting Frank woke up in his bed and looked over at Mare, who was still asleep. They spent two or three nights a week together now, alternating between his place and hers. Each made room for the other's toothbrush and emptied half a drawer. It wasn't the first time for either of them. Frank got up and started a pot of coffee in the small galley kitchen. A bouquet of last week's flowers, daisy mums he'd bought half price at the supermarket, needed throwing out. The penny lay on the kitchen counter where he'd left it, looking harmless. But the sight of it bothered him.

"You're tricky, aren't you? You've given me a way to bail out. What if I take it? You don't control me."

Who was he speaking to—the disciple, God, Meg? He didn't have a good reason to drop out of the mystery school. Seeing is believing, and Frank had seen things he couldn't wrap his mind around. So he didn't try. That was the long and the short of it. He drifted with the group, waiting for a flash from God. For all he knew, the line was dead.

Mare came in, yawning and drowsy. She noticed Frank staring at the penny.

"A penny for your thoughts," she said. Her temp agency hadn't left a message on her cell, so she had the day off. She could curl up in bed again after Frank went to work.

"I don't know where we go from here," he mumbled. The coffeemaker beeped, and he poured two cups without looking into Mare's eyes. If he dropped out, he was sure that Mare would stop seeing him.

She didn't answer immediately, making a small business of dosing her coffee with milk and sugar.

"No one's putting pressure on you," she said, sounding as reasonable as she could.

He took her hand. "It's not just us. It's everything. We're on a roller coaster with a brick windshield. We can't see an inch ahead."

"Maybe we're not meant to," she said.

"So you aren't the least little bit worried?"

Mare picked up the penny. "Don't make any decisions until you've given it a chance. Meg promised it wouldn't make us crazy."

She put the coin in his hand and closed his fingers around it. Perhaps she also kissed him on the cheek, but Frank didn't notice. As soon as the penny touched his hand, disturbing images filled his mind, moving as fast as a movie spooling on a berserk projector. The coffee cup almost slipped from his hand. The images were gone in two seconds; he felt dizzy. He snatched his hand away and dropped the penny back on the counter.

"You're right. Listen, I'm late. Let me jump in the shower." He got the words out with difficulty.

For some reason Mare, who noticed everything, didn't question his behavior. She had already moved away and was sitting at the little breakfast table that caught the best morning sun. Her fingers absently picked through the droopy bouquet, looking for any flowers that might be worth saving.

Frank made his getaway and popped into the shower, running the water as cold as he could stand it. The flickering images didn't return. The stinging cold of the water made him shiver. By the time he got out, his body was numb enough to dull his brain. He no longer saw the mangled children's bodies, the blood on the road, the police cars. The wail of ambulance sirens was now so faint that he could barely hear it.

The drive to the paper usually took ten minutes, only there was roadwork, and traffic was diverted to the bypass. As soon as he pulled onto it, Frank became anxious, and by the time he'd merged into the center lane, his hands were shaking on the wheel. He reached into his jacket pocket where he stashed a cigarette for emergencies. He pulled out the penny instead. He hadn't put it there. His intention was to pretend that he'd forgotten it rushing off to work. This had to be Mare.

Before he could think, a low-sounding horn blasted in his ear. Frank had drifted half out of his lane, and he quickly swerved back as a tractor trailer bombed past on the left. In front of him was a gray minivan. Two little girls in the back turned around and waved. Frank started to sweat. He saw that the driver was a woman, perhaps a soccer mom taking her kids to school. Frank leaned on his horn.

"Pull over!" he shouted, waving his arm toward the shoulder of the road to show the driver what he wanted. The woman sped up, ignoring him. Frank gunned ahead, moving closer. The kids were still looking at him, no longer smiling.

"Pull over!"

This time the woman listened. When she stopped on the shoulder, Frank pulled in behind her. He didn't get out. There was no way to tell if the two girls were the mangled bodies he'd seen. The woman emerged from the minivan, looking perplexed. She walked to the back of her vehicle, checking the tires and the tail lights. Her face wore an exasperated look. She shot

Frank a rude gesture with her middle finger, got back in, and sped away.

God help you, Frank thought. After a few minutes he had settled down, but he felt nauseous. He was late to work, but he didn't get back on the road. In thirty seconds, he thought, the stream of traffic would suddenly slow. In a minute and a half the first patrol car would fly past, moving cars out of the way with its sirens. The ambulance would be close behind.

Actually, it was forty seconds before traffic slowed, but everything else unfolded just as he saw it. Frank's nausea grew worse. He could have gotten out and talked to her, given the woman his bizarre explanation and not worried that she would call him a lunatic.

If he stayed there on the shoulder, a cop would check what was going on. Reluctantly Frank pulled back on the highway. Traffic was moving again, slowly. After a mile he saw the flashing blue and red lights of the patrol cars. An officer was waving everyone into one lane. The tractor trailer had jackknifed, blocking the rest of the road. Frank wanted to close his eyes, but he kept looking, and as the single file of cars crawled past the accident site like a makeshift funeral cortege, he saw two crumpled sedans. A bewildered man stood beside a stretcher that was being hoisted into the back of an ambulance.

But that was it. No blood on the pavement, no mangled children. The gray minivan was nowhere in sight.

The security guard stationed beside the reception desk always nodded when Frank came in. This time he said, "You okay, buddy?"

"I'm great, I think," Frank muttered.

The guard, a retired policeman with a gray buzz cut, laughed. "You're the one who'd know," he said, rather puzzled.

Frank didn't stop to chat. Feeling dizzy, he got to his desk in the newsroom and sank into the chair. *What the hell?* His confused thoughts whirled around, trying to make sense of what had happened. It was like being at the Laundromat watching clothes tumble in a dryer. Only in this case he was tumbling with them. The only thought he could seize onto said, *I told you so.* Frank knew exactly what this meant. The moment he agreed to join the mystery school, something bizarre would drag him under, a freak occurrence that would ruin his chance for a normal life.

He felt afraid, more afraid than he had a right to be. Wasn't he some kind of hero? He'd saved two little girls from a horrible death. Frank wanted to feel good about that, but his fear wouldn't let him. He took the penny out of his pocket and stared at it. Maybe if he threw it away immediately, he'd be safe.

At that moment the buzz of voices in the newsroom, which was always there like background static, dropped out. Very clearly Frank heard two reporters talking from twenty feet away.

"Anything on the police scanner?"

"Not really. A truck jackknifed on the bypass."

"Anybody killed?"

"Nah. There's no story."

"Too bad. Better luck next time."

The two reporters went back to work, and the buzz of voices in the newsroom rose again. Frank was disgusted. "Too bad." "Better luck next time." It could have been him talking. He regarded the penny again, this time with uncertainty. The two reporters were wrong. There was a story, but Frank couldn't tell it.

From behind him a voice spoke. "Why tell a story when you can live it?"

He knew it was Lilith before he turned around. No one else did that annoying mind-reading trick.

"Don't throw the penny away. You're just getting the hang of it," she said.

Frank had no reply. He was too fixated on how Lilith looked. In place of the gray tweed suit he'd always seen her in, she was decked out in bright pink, with a wide-brimmed yellow hat and a feathery thing he thought was called a boa.

Lilith laughed and did a twirl. "Who doesn't like the circus?" she said.

Frank could see out of the corner of his eye that people were staring. A few at the far corner of the newsroom stood on their chairs for a better look.

"We weren't supposed to go crazy," he reminded her in an undertone. "You're not yourself."

"Thank God." Lilith laughed again, a bright sound that was as strange coming from her as the outlandish outfit. She raised her voice so that everyone could hear. "Come with me, darling. When the going gets tough, the tough go to lunch. My treat."

He followed helplessly as she swanned her way past the cubicles. At least they'd be out of sight in a minute. He had to hope that his editor was on the phone in his office and wasn't viewing the spectacle.

At the reception desk, the girl on duty said, "How did you get in?"

Lilith didn't stop, trailing an answer behind her. "Magic, my child. Magic."

Frank seriously considered phoning for medical help, but as soon as they were outside, Lilith dropped the act. "The things I do for you," she muttered in her normal starchy tone.

"For me?" Frank was astonished.

"You were wavering. I didn't want to lose you."

She seemed amused by his doubts, which annoyed him. "I can make up my own mind. I'm a big boy."

"Lucky for you. Rusty never got to be a big boy, did he?"

This enigmatic question had an astounding effect on Frank. His face turned white, and a tremor shook his body.

"You couldn't know about that," he said in a strangulated voice.

"But I do."

He leaned against the wall next to the exit, trying to catch his breath. A flood of half-buried images filled his mind. It was the summer he turned fourteen, and his father took Frank and his younger brother, Rusty, fishing. He roused them early in the morning, saying the bass wouldn't wait, and a few minutes later the brothers were in the backseat of the family Jeep, still trying to wake up. Rusty, who was ten, whined about it. He leaned against Frank, trying to use his shoulder as a pillow, but Frank pushed him away roughly.

The lake was as smooth as glass when they got into the canoe, and Frank was proud at how well he could balance standing up to push them away from the shore. His ankle socks had gotten wet running through the dewy grass—why did he remember that? The morning chill quickly turned into midday heat. Frank enjoyed fishing with his dad, and Rusty had fallen asleep at the other end of the canoe.

Neither of them, Frank or his father, paid attention when a shadow passed over the sun. The fish were biting too good. But then the shadow didn't pass, and looking up, they saw thunderheads approaching.

"Start paddling," his father said. They were pretty far out from shore; the dock was at least five minutes away. The storm didn't care. It was upon them in no time, bringing a sharp wind that roughed the surface of the lake. Frank saw his father's jaw set; they started paddling harder. The first clap of thunder woke Rusty up, and Frank knew that his younger brother had an undue fear of lightning.

"Fraidy cat," he teased.

Is that what caused Rusty to jump to his feet? It was such a strange, impulsive thing to do. He lost his balance as a wave rocked the boat. Frank saw the little boy's mouth form a silent "Oh!" before Rusty went over the side. His father, sitting up front, hadn't seen it.

"Dad!" Frank's shout pierced the wind, which had started to howl.

When he turned his head and grasped the situation, his father dropped his paddle and jumped into the water, where Rusty was flailing, his wide, frightened eyes showing white. If only Frank hadn't felt the same surge of adrenaline as his dad, but he did, and they dove into the water at the same instant. His father reached Rusty first, holding his head above the waves.

"Just breathe. It's going to be okay," he said. The little boy clung to him, gasping and spitting out water.

Frank didn't see fate closing in. The whole thing was disguised by tiny coincidences. Here, there were three. The canoe was empty, making it hard to climb back in. The mountain-fed lake was frigid in early June. His father had gained twenty pounds over the winter and was out of shape. Very innocent coincidences, really, but the result was inexorable. Their first attempt to climb into the canoe tipped it over. There was no bucket to bail it out with—everything inside the boat sank out of sight the minute it capsized—and when they righted it, the canoe rode too low because of the water it had taken on.

The rest happened in slow motion as Frank experienced it. Rusty started crying, whining about how cold he was. His father, who wasn't a good swimmer to begin with, used all his strength to hold his boy and the side of the canoe at the same time, but the cold water made his hands go numb. He lost his grip with the next big gust of wind. Rusty's panicked eyes landed on Frank, who was clinging to the other side of the boat. They didn't accuse him or say good-bye. It was just the gaze of a scared child, who then slipped away, leaving one last sight of his hair waving like seaweed in the current before disappearing.

Frank was the strongest swimmer in the family, and he dove repeatedly to find his brother, over and over until he was so exhausted there was a chance he might drown too. By then the sun had come out again, and the surface of the lake calmed down, as if nothing catastrophic had occurred.

"Come back," said Lilith sharply.

The sound of her voice pulled Frank up from the depths of memory. "Why is this happening?" he asked. He wore a pained expression, which Lilith ignored.

"If you're going to walk away, you need to see what your choice is really about," she said.

"It's about leaving the rest of you high and dry," Frank snapped. What right did Lilith have to stir up his worst memory? "Be honest. That's why you came here."

She shook her head, pressing on. "Do you really think you survived that day? You lost everything. Can you even remember when you had faith or hope?"

"I don't need faith," said Frank, trying to sound defiant.

"All right," said Lilith. "But you need something besides guilt. It's led you in the wrong direction. You've become a bystander to your own life."

"That's not true." Her words felt cruel, as if she were prying open an oyster while it squirmed inside its shell.

"You learned how to wear a mask. What other choice did a kid your age have? But masks have a funny way of fooling the people who wear them, don't they?"

Frank wanted desperately to run away, but he felt weak and shaky. "Don't," he pleaded. Deep down, he was shocked that he could fall apart so completely.

"I know you feel blindsided," said Lilith, watching him closely. "We're on a fast track to the truth, the whole group. Did you really think you'd get left out?"

Frank heaved a sigh. His mind started to clear; he didn't feel as if the ground was wobbling under him. It would be solid in a minute, safe to stand on again. "I want to be left alone. Why can't you see that?" he said.

"Because it's not what God has in mind," Lilith replied.

Frank turned his head away. Lilith knew he didn't read the Bible, so he wouldn't know a phrase she had grown up with: "For He is like a refiner's fire." The divine flame had a long reach, and now it had touched another stranded soul.

CHAPTER *22*

Much had already happened that day before Lilith went to the newspaper to find Frank. She came down to breakfast in the morning wearing her outlandish pink and yellow outfit. She had dug it out of a box in the attic where the girls' old Halloween costumes were stored.

Herb looked up from the *Wall Street Journal* and faintly raised an eyebrow. "That's nice," he said. He was a cautious soul.

Lilith stroked the moth-eaten feather boa draped around her neck. "I needed a change."

No more was said, which was for the best.

Lilith had gone to bed anticipating that something wondrous would happen. Instead, she woke up feeling grumpy. There was no magic in the air. She waited, staring at the ceiling. Nothing. Getting dressed, she did feel something unusual, but it was trivial. She felt dissatisfied with the clothes in her closet. Going up to the attic was almost an afterthought. What could she possibly find there? Yet she was guided to poke through the old Halloween trunk, and as soon as she saw the boa, pink dress, and yellow hat, she had to try them on, even though this impulse was completely perplexing.

As she looked in the mirror, she thought, *I'm a cross between a drag queen and the Easter parade.* The fact that she didn't immediately take off the absurd costume must have been the penny's fault. With the same feeling of being guided, she got in the car after breakfast and started driving. It surprised her when she arrived at the hospital parking lot. She almost didn't get out. A voice inside warned her that she was about to make a fool of herself.

"Enough of that," she muttered. "Get on with it."

She walked briskly to the ER entrance and went inside. The waiting room was jammed already, and it wasn't even ten. Everyone was sunk in their own problems, so the only ones staring at her outfit were kids who had been dragged along by a sick parent. One little girl who was four or five pointed at Lilith and began to laugh loudly, a piercing bratty laugh that embarrassed her mother.

"Don't point," she scolded. The mother turned to the woman next to her, who was idly thumbing through a magazine. "Looks like somebody's off their meds." The two women followed Lilith with their eyes as she found an empty seat in the corner.

Lilith ignored their stares. Her attention was caught by the grayness that enveloped the room. The smell of sickness was mixed with apprehension. Everyone was braced for bad news, and not a small number would be getting it when their name was called. Lilith sat down, finding it hard to meet anyone's eyes. She resisted the urge to consult the magic penny for clues; it was safely nestled in her purse, wrapped in a handkerchief.

Then the waiting room became dead quiet. No one talked or moved. Before Lilith could register how strange this was, time stopped. The woman who had been reading a magazine was frozen with a page half-turned. The bratty little girl was posed bending over to grab her doll, which had fallen on the floor. The charge nurse at the front desk who was lifting the phone receiver to her ear never got it there.

Lilith was so startled that she leaped to her feet, which proved two things at once. She could move, and when she did, the freeze-frame stayed the same. She eyed everyone in the room, as if suspecting that somebody might be faking. But they remained eerily still. Lilith wasn't easily shaken, much less frightened. The scene fascinated her. She walked over to the bratty little girl, picked up her doll, and placed it beside her on the next chair. The child didn't stir. Lilith touched her hair, which was short and blonde. The hair moved like silk stands at Lilith's touch.

She took her hand away quickly. It felt wrong to disturb anyone. At that moment she heard footsteps approaching down a hall. Someone else was able to move, and Lilith suspected it could only be one person. A set of swinging doors swept open, and she was right.

"Did you do this?" Jimmy said. He was dressed for work in blue scrubs tied at the waist.

"It just happened," Lilith replied.

Jimmy nodded. Joining her in the middle of the room, he held up his penny with a puzzled smile. "What now?"

Lilith thought for a moment. "Let's see what the rest of the world is doing."

They went to the nearest window, which looked out over the parking lot. No one was visible. In the far distance cars were moving on the four-lane road that fed into the hospital.

"So it's just us. What if someone comes?" Jimmy said.

"They won't. Not for a while." Lilith looked around the room again. "We're in this alone, however long it lasts."

"Okay." This didn't seem like a satisfactory reaction, so Jimmy added, "There must be something we need to see. What are we missing here?"

"Missing?" All Lilith saw was a tightly packed room of department-store mannequins.

"Like that," said Jimmy. He walked closer to the little group with the bratty girl, her mother, and the woman flipping through a magazine.

"See? They're not all the same. Look closely."

It took Lilith a second, but she saw. The girl was brighter than the two women, like a photograph printed two shades lighter. The effect wasn't noticeable unless you looked for it. But once you did, you could see that the two women were slightly gray and dull.

"That's odd," Lilith murmured. She had witnessed a light when the spirit left the body. So had Jimmy, but not this.

Jimmy gazed around the room. "They're all so gray, except for the kids." He was right. The children in the waiting room weren't grayed out like the adults. They shone from within. Suddenly the freeze-frame didn't feel creepy anymore. These were souls on display, and the reason for stopping time was that it made it easier to notice, the way a sleeping person looks peaceful when the cares of the day are lifted.

Jimmy moved closer to the mother and held his hands above her head.

"What are you doing?" Lilith asked.

"I don't know. I just feel this urge."

He didn't touch the woman, but instead swept his hands in one motion down her body, beginning at her head and ending at her toes.

"There," he said. "Better."

Wisps of gray like tangled threads were now gathered around her feet, and the woman looked a fraction brighter. Jimmy kicked away the gray threads, which dissolved into dust. Then he did the same sweep for the woman holding the magazine, and it had the same effect. Grayness gathered at her feet, and her frozen image became visibly brighter.

Lilith hadn't moved.

"Go ahead," he said. "You try."

She leaned in close to the mother, examining her neck, where a dark irregular mole was visible. "That's why they came to the ER," Lilith murmured. "Cancer?"

Jimmy nodded. "Poor woman."

Lilith bit her lip, feeling a moment of indecision. Then with a fingertip she rubbed the dark mole. When she took her finger away, it was gone, like a blot erased from a sheet of paper.

"Wow," Jimmy exclaimed softly.

Lilith spotted an old man across the room, bent over in his seat leaning on a walking cane. She went over and saw that his knuckles were lumpy and red.

"Arthritis," she said. She started to smooth out his fingers, as if reshaping modeling clay. Jimmy watched until every inflamed bump was gone.

"That's incredible," he said.

Lilith stood back and examined her handiwork. "Indeed."

Jimmy did a silent head count. "There must be sixty people here. Are we supposed to do them all?"

Lilith might have said yes, but she didn't get a chance. Without warning the freeze-frame ended. The waiting room became animated. The old man leaning on his cane looked up at Lilith with surprise.

"Is it my turn yet?" he asked, mistaking her for a nurse.

"You've had your turn," Lilith replied, walking away quickly. The old man paid no attention. With a bemused look on his face, he was rubbing his fingers. They were smooth, just as she'd left them.

Jimmy followed Lilith to the exit. They faced each other in the bright winter morning.

"Why didn't we finish?" he asked.

She shook her head. "I'm not sure. Maybe it was just a demonstration."

"Of what?"

She held up her hand. "Don't talk. Let it sink in."

They sat down on the bench used by people waiting for a taxi. Jimmy's thin cotton scrubs gave no protection from the cold, but he wasn't shivering. A car pulled up to the entrance, and an old woman was helped out of the front seat into a wheelchair. She wore a woolen cap pulled down over her ears; her eyes were rimed with red.

This was something Jimmy saw every day, but now it looked unreal.

Lilith read his thoughts. "We were sent into the miracle zone," she said, "just for a moment."

"To see if we want to stay?"

"Something like that."

Lilith got to her feet. "I have to go. Frank is wavering. He can't stand this much truth. I'm going to try something drastic."

Jimmy nodded. "Is that why you're dressed like cotton candy with a banana on top?"

Lilith smiled. "Maybe I wanted them to see me coming."

"Or God did," said Jimmy. But Lilith was already hurrying across the parking lot to her car. Suddenly he realized how cold it was outside. The electric doors to the ER whooshed open, and he went inside, rushing to get back to work. Everything had returned to normal. People sat around waiting, staring at their watches or going up to hassle the nurse at the reception desk. There were no signs that the miracle zone had ever existed, except for the gray tinge that lingered on everyone he passed.

CHAPTER *23*

After the door closed behind Frank, Mare went back to bed, but she couldn't fall asleep again. She was too uneasy. The rising sun cast a shadow of windowpanes across the coverlet. Frank's apartment had the creaking floors and peeling paint of a veteran in the rental market, but Mare loved the elaborate plaster work on the ceiling. If you had the imagination, you could pretend you were in a Paris hotel.

She stared at it now, pondering. The magic penny would change Frank's life. Mare foresaw this, which was why she had slipped it into his pocket unawares. It would reveal things that would shake him to the core. She knew this too, because knowing came easily to Mare, all her life. As a girl she had laughed out loud one evening when a movie title came on television: *I Know What You Did Last Summer.*

I Know What You Did Next Summer, she thought. *That's a much better title.*

She opened the drawer of the bedside table, where she'd placed her penny. She couldn't help averting her eyes. She was afraid of its magic, because it spelled the end of her secret. Mare had skillfully kept her secret hidden even as so many others were coming to light. She'd only slipped up once, when she was at the bus stop, seeing the light in every passenger who got on the bus. "I've found my calling," she said before Meg shushed her.

The time for secrets was over, but what about Frank? That was more complicated. It had been easy to keep things from the two or three serious boyfriends who came into her life and left again. Like them, Frank had felt like an intruder at first, but Mare had grown to love him. He was confused and hurt whenever she kept her distance.

"We spend the night, and then you don't call for days," he complained. "Why?"

Because I have to, she thought.

If she married him, her gift would become a threat, and not just to Frank. She had no control over her far-seeing. What if she saw that he would cheat on her? It would make for strange vows at the altar: "I do thee wed, for better or for worse, in sickness and in health, until you step out with Debbie from the gym."

Mare pushed the thought out of her mind. She took the magic penny from the drawer and folded her palm over it. She might as well face whatever it wanted to show or say. There was a message, but it wasn't magical: *Throw me away.* With a sigh of relief she got out of bed and tossed the coin into the wastebasket. It was like a last-minute reprieve.

But almost immediately a voice in her head said, *This is your test.* What did that mean? Mare anxiously waited for more, but nothing came. She suddenly knew that she had to act. Her test would mean something crucial for the whole group.

Quickly throwing on some clothes, she walked outside into the bright, brisk winter morning. She paused, peering up and down the street. Where was she supposed to go? It was entirely her choice, but the test consisted of making the right choice. She closed her eyes. Nothing appeared. She couldn't wander at random.

How do you find the route to an unknown destination?

Mare waited for an answer. Nothing.

All right, a clue, then?

Again nothing, no puff of wind, no glint of sunlight off a car windshield, no chance remark from a passing stranger. These were signs she had followed all her life. The world spoke to her, and it was time for Mare to realize that it didn't speak to everyone. To a normal person, looking for signs was like believing in omens—not something you did if you wanted to appear sane.

She would have to create her own clues. Mare looked inward, this time expecting nothing. And a faint image came through. She saw a gleaming silver thread lying across her palm. She took a step to the right, and the gleam grew dull. She took a step to the left, and it became brighter. So left it was. She'd stop at every corner to check which way to go next. It was a start.

When she was four, riding in the front seat of the car, her mother came to a lurching stop when another driver cut her off. Instinctively she reached out with her right arm to hold Mare back in her seat, forgetting that she was wearing a seatbelt. A few days later, when the car came to another sudden stop, Mare reached over from the passenger side to hold her mother back.

"What are you doing, honey?" her mother asked.

"Keeping Mommy safe."

Her mother laughed, but was strangely touched. Protecting Mommy became a little game between them. Her mother didn't notice that Mare was reaching out before the brakes were hit. She anticipated what was about to happen. The only one who saw this was Aunt Meg when her car wouldn't start one morning and she needed a ride to work, but she said nothing.

Lost in memory, Mare was forgetting to consult the silver thread. She looked down at her palm, and the thread had turned a dull gray. She had to retrace her steps a couple of blocks until it began to brighten again. It pointed down a broad thoroughfare leading to one of the swanky parts of town. Feeling tense, she quickened her pace. But for some reason memory wouldn't release her. It kept pulling her back to the past.

At some point when she was a child, Mare's gift started to betray her. She couldn't remember what finally caused her to bury it. Maybe she said something wildly inappropriate, like telling one of her mother's friends that she would never have children. Stuck in her recollection, though, were sharp looks directed her way. She felt different, but not special, the girl who burst out laughing before a joke reached the punch line.

She was secretly relieved when she grew up to be pretty. It was the best of disguises. She could go on a date with the high-school quarterback and cheer for him even when she knew the game would be lost. Behind a shy façade, Mare learned about human nature in all its unpredictability, which for her was entirely predictable.

She heard the word "psychic" for the first time in a psychology class in college, where the professor said the paranormal didn't exist. It was a fiction to mask neurosis. "Given the choice between feeling magical and feeling crazy," he said, "most people choose magical." By that time Mare had let her gift wither, so she didn't care if it was unreal. The important thing was that it was gone—until the day she went to the convent in search of her dead aunt.

Mare returned to her test. An hour dragged by as she followed the silver thread. Mare didn't know this part of town very well; most of its houses were built by old money. Where the money stuck around, the three-story brownstones were expensively kept up. Where the money flew away, old people lingered in tattered gentility and stashed bottles of gin. Deep into this mossy territory, which felt vaguely like a damp forest, Mare felt something new. The silver thread burned, and its glow turned almost incandescent.

It wanted her to stop. She looked around, but nothing unusual stood out. The neighborhood was empty, quietly moldering. Then a teenage boy in a hoodie and cargo shorts pedaled up the street on a bicycle with a bag of groceries in the front basket. He stopped at the corner opposite Mare, not glancing her way, and rang the bell beside a wrought-iron gate with brick pillars as big as phone booths. After a few seconds someone buzzed the gate, and the delivery boy pushed it open.

Go. Now!

The voice in her head was urgent. Mare took off. Five seconds, and she'd be too late. She caught the gate just as it was about to click shut. The delivery boy turned around, startled.

"Those are for me," Mare said, reaching to take the brown paper bag from him. Stalks of celery and a baguette of French bread stuck out the top.

"You live here?" The delivery boy sounded more confused than suspicious.

"Yes. I didn't want to search for my keys. It's okay."

He wouldn't let go of the groceries. "I always give them to her, the older lady."

"My aunt," said Mare, hurriedly reaching in her purse. She needed to get rid of him before Meg answered the door.

"Here." She produced a twenty-dollar bill from her wallet. The delivery boy gave her the grocery bag just as Mare saw, over his shoulder, the heavy oak front door begin to open.

"Neatly executed," said Meg. She stood in the doorway dressed in a suit, as if she were going to her job at the bank. She didn't look the least bit surprised to see Mare. "This was the only time today I would have answered the doorbell." She gave a thin smile. "A person has to eat."

She turned back into the dimly lit house, leaving Mare to shut the door behind her and follow. The drawing room was immense and forlorn, the furniture shrouded in dusty sheets. The dining room table was uncovered, set for one. A massive silver candelabra sat in the middle. Mare gawked.

"You get used to it," said Meg.

The kitchen was laid out with a scullery, a butler's pantry, and zinc sinks big enough to bathe a sheepdog in. Meg put the groceries down on a massive butcher-block table. "Do you want lunch? You've been walking for hours."

Mare shook her head. "I'm too nervous."

"Don't I know it? When I was new at the convent, meals were the worst. A sister would say, 'Pass the ketchup,' and I'd hear, 'We all know you're a fraud.' I was lucky to keep anything down."

She caught the look on Mare's face. "Don't feel sorry for me. I was a kind of spiritual con artist, pretending to be a good Catholic."

"Did you ever fit in?"

"No. A nun may be many things. Disobedient isn't one of them. I did all the right things. My disobedience was of the heart."

Meg started unpacking the groceries, speaking as casually as if the whole situation wasn't extraordinary. "I really didn't know what to expect, but I had to be there, you see."

Mare fell into the rhythm of putting vegetables in the refrigerator and canned goods in the pantry. It seemed pointless to ask how her aunt acquired the huge mansion. "Why did you have to be there?"

Meg looked bemused. "For the longest time I had no idea. But now I see. It all led to this moment. You understand? No, how could you?"

Suddenly Mare felt a wave of resentment. "We're family. Why have you been hiding from us? My mother is worried sick. I can't tell her you're not dead without producing you."

"She's not all that worried. She just doesn't like surprises."

Meg took a seat at the butcher-block table and waited for Mare to sit down. "I kept myself hidden, so that you could pass this test. If you already knew where I lived, there would be no test." She paused. "Are you sure you won't eat something? Here." Meg pushed a bowl of apples across the table.

"In a minute," Mare replied. She wasn't satisfied with the

answers she was hearing. "You don't have a right to do all these things to us—not just me, the whole group. We're like rats in a maze." She caught herself. "That didn't come out right. I don't want you to feel guilty."

Meg gave a curt laugh. "Guilty? That's all I could feel when this began. I saw ordinary people thrown on a magical mystery tour, with no idea where they were going. It was outrageous."

"Maybe it was a power trip for you."

For the first time since Meg had reappeared, she was offended. "Watch yourself," she said sharply. "And eat. You're tired and cranky."

Reluctantly Mare picked out an apple and bit into it, while Meg went into the pantry and returned with a bag of potato chips. She watched her niece pick at them without enthusiasm. At the far end of the table was a lead-crystal vase with white roses picked from the garden. Meg gave them a sidelong glance. She waited to see if Mare would follow the glance. She did.

The roses had begun to glow, just as the golden shrine did. A soft radiance surrounded them. Mare stared, her mouth forming a silent "Oh."

"You can do that?"

"Who else? I'm not who you think I am."

The glow subsided, and the roses went back to normal. Mare sat back, stunned. A surreal image came to her. She saw Aunt Meg radiating the same white light, then vanishing into nothingness.

"All along, I thought—"

"That a magical talisman had dropped out of the sky? I've told you before, all of you, the shrine is just a distraction."

"But you didn't tell us it was a distraction from you."

Meg laughed. "The shrine isn't really old, probably Victorian. Someone I dearly loved, an old priest, bought it at an antique store and had it plated gold. He probably ruined its value."

While revealing this, Meg closely watched Mare's expression.

"You feel cheated, don't you? You wanted miracles, and now you think I'm some sort of illusionist."

"I don't know what I think."

"If it's any help, I'll tell you what an old priest told me. 'Either nothing is a miracle or everything is.' You understand?"

Mare shook her head.

Meg reached down the table and plucked a white rose from the vase. "This flower is made of light. If it weren't, I couldn't make it glow. A miracle exposes the light inside all things."

She didn't wait for Mare to reply. "I'm not telling you something you don't already know. You're a seer. Pushing it out of sight like dust under the carpet doesn't change the fact."

Mare felt a tremor of fear run through her. "I don't want to be a seer."

"Really, after all this? Frankly, I'm disappointed."

Meg stood up, tossing the rose on the table. "At the next meeting, tell the others it's over."

"You don't mean that!" Mare exclaimed.

Meg's face looked stern. "What do you care? The magical mystery tour stops here. All passengers off the bus, please."

Mare was bewildered. "Why?"

"Because there's somewhere I have to be."

Her aunt was about to pull a third vanishing act? Mare was about to get angry when Meg seemed to relent. "I'll let you come with me. When you get back, you can decide about the group."

Abruptly she left the kitchen, and when she returned, Meg had a sheaf of papers in her hand. "Sign these first. I'm giving you the house and the money that comes with it." Meg held out a pen. "Where I'm going, I won't need them."

Mare felt a fresh wave of anxiety. "You're making me dizzy." She wanted to get up from the table, but her knees felt watery. "Let me come back tomorrow. Once I think this over—"

Meg didn't let her finish. "There's no need. You passed the test.

If you could follow the invisible trail that led to here, you're the rightful owner."

She pointed to the first places where Mare needed to sign. Feeling helpless, Mare picked up the pen and scrawled her signature.

When the signing was done, Meg looked satisfied. "Now, then, shall we go?" She reached across the table and took Mare's hands in hers. "You know how by now."

Mare didn't hesitate. If everything was about Meg, she had to be trusted.

"One thing will be different," said Meg as their hands locked in a firm clasp. "This time we can talk to each other."

The kitchen vanished and was replaced by a long-ago scene. They were on a bustling street in Jerusalem, and Meg had been right. Mare could see her standing there. But the passing crowd took no notice of either of them. They were invisible, as before.

"Notice something?" asked Meg. "Look in their eyes."

Mare looked first at a fruit vendor ten feet away and his customer, hurriedly putting figs into a sack. She looked at a mother dragging her two small children into a side street, then at a bearded rabbi with a silver chain around his neck.

"They're all afraid," she said.

"All but one."

Meg led the way, weaving in and out of the crowd. She walked briskly; it was all Mare could do to keep up.

"Why are they all so scared?"

"It's like dogs getting frightened just before an earthquake. They can feel destruction coming."

At the end of the street, where it opened on a small plaza with a stone well in the center, there were no women drawing water. Instead, a squad of Roman soldiers guarded the well, scowling at anyone who came near.

Meg nodded toward them without stopping. "There have been rumors about the Jews poisoning the city's water supply."

Now Mare was beginning to see images in her mind's eye. A Roman soldier committing a sacrilege on the grounds of the temple. Jews running riot, the city boiling over. A veil of blood covered these images.

"Are we here to stop it?" she asked.

"No, Jerusalem will fall."

Meg stopped before an imposing two-story house on the corner, surrounded by a stone wall with well-tended olive trees beyond it. "I'm almost afraid to go in," she murmured.

"Why? Who lives there?"

"Who do you think?"

The iron gate in front of the house was slightly ajar, which made no sense amid the restless fear in the streets. Meg slipped through it and waited for Mare before locking the gate behind them. The courtyard contained a lush garden with a fountain and flowers planted in neat square beds. *A paradise garden,* Mare thought, dredging up the name from some distant memory.

Meg didn't give the garden a glance, but hurried to the front door. It too was slightly ajar. She and Mare entered and were met by a rush of cool perfumed air. A smaller inner courtyard faced them, bathed in sunlight, enclosed by a gallery of fretted marble.

"So beautiful," Mare whispered.

"It's her home." Meg pointed to an alcove nearby where the disciple sat, contemplating. The girl they knew was almost unrecognizable. She looked older now, middle-aged; but it was her, and the way she raised her head made Mare believe she knew they were there.

If we talk to her, she'll be able to hear us, Mare thought. Immediately a warning voice in her head said, *Don't.*

Meg barely glanced at the disciple before turning away. She retreated to a dark corner at the far end of the gallery. After a moment the disciple sighed deeply, stood up, and left, her purple silk skirts rustling as she walked.

Once it was safe to talk, Mare said, "You were right. She doesn't look afraid."

"She can see ahead, past the danger."

"So she'll save herself in time?"

Meg shrugged. "She's not worried about herself. She's past all that."

"I want to talk to her." Impulsively, Mare started to follow the disciple's footsteps into the depth of the house. Meg held her back.

"You've been talking to her the whole time," she said.

"What?"

Meg held her hand up, asking for silence. Her voice was already far away, and as dim as the shadows were in the cool, sheltered gallery. Mare saw doubt in her face. Her aunt had come to a cross-roads, and she couldn't decide which way to go.

The silence didn't last long. "We part here," Meg said decisively. "You can embrace me. I believe that's customary."

The strangeness of these words made Mare go cold. "You're leaving me?"

"I'm staying here. It's not the same thing."

The blood drained from Mare's body. "You can't!" she exclaimed. Weak as she felt, her voice was loud, ringing down the marble halls of the gallery.

"That's right, shout some more," Meg murmured. "Shout all you want."

Mare might have, but she froze, hearing the approach of running feet. From around the corner came the disciple. Someone was following her—a servant?—but she waved him away. Now she could definitely see them, and the sight made her pause.

"It is done," said Meg.

The disciple nodded and began to approach.

"You see," Meg said, "I sent myself on a mission." She waited for the disciple to come nearer. "It took ten years in the convent to realize that. You couldn't expect me to believe it, not for a long time."

"Please," Mare pleaded, "just tell me what this is all about." She was suddenly overcome by a sense of loss.

Meg pointed to the disciple. "I am her. Now do you understand?"

Then she stepped forward, quickly covering the short distance between her and the disciple, who stood motionless, expectant. Just before there would have been a collision, Meg's body was transformed. It turned into pure light, like a movie image being replaced by the light of the projector. This took barely a second, and then there was only the disciple. She trembled slightly, making no sound.

"You," Mare whispered.

The disciple hadn't acknowledged that she was there, and even now she did no more than raise her hand. A farewell? A blessing? Mare couldn't tell, her sight blurred with tears. Suddenly there were voices approaching. They sounded alarmed. The disciple spoke sharply in Hebrew (Mare supposed) and strode toward them. She disappeared into a clutch of servants coming from deep inside the house.

Now Mare's tears flowed freely. Meg had been like a visitation, poised between two lifetimes. There was no way to explain how such a thing can occur. A breeze blew across Mare's cheek from the inner courtyard. She blinked to clear her eyes. A neat rectangle of white roses stood close by, and they began to glow.

Before Mare could blink again, she was back in the kitchen at the butcher-block table. She looked down. A half-eaten apple was starting to turn brown beside a withered white rose. Time had passed, but how much? Hours? Days? She couldn't tell. She could only tell that she'd come back a different person. Her secret gift, all the hiding, her dead aunt who wasn't dead but a conveyor of wonders—none of it mattered anymore. Something did, though, the one truth Mare could live by without fear or doubt.

Either nothing is a miracle or everything is.

CHAPTER 24

When Frank arrived for the next meeting, the door was ajar. Inside he found the room dark and empty. Before he could turn on the lights, a voice said, "Please don't."

"Mare?"

The sound of her voice rattled him. "Where have you been?"

She wasn't at his apartment when Frank came home. That was two days ago. She didn't answer her cell phone or return any of his messages. He was getting more and more worried. "You didn't want to talk to me?"

"I needed to be by myself."

"I thought everything was good with us."

"It's more than us."

This cryptic exchange told him nothing. "Listen, talking in the dark is creeping me out. I'm turning the lights on."

Frank flicked the wall switch, and the buzzing fluorescent fixtures came on, casting a greenish pallor everywhere. He saw Mare seated at the head of the table where Meg always sat. The golden shrine was in front of her.

"Did Meg tell you to bring it?" he asked.

"In a way. She's not coming back."

Mare didn't wait to see if this news upset him. She already knew it wouldn't. "You're not coming back either, are you? None of you are. You just want out."

Frank was bewildered. "How did you find out? Have the rest of them been talking to you?" A note of suspicion crept into his voice. "I don't like this, not one bit."

Mare spoke insistently. "Does it matter? In an hour there won't be a mystery school."

"Jesus." This wasn't remotely what Frank expected.

"It won't be long now," Mare said. "Try and calm down."

She was asking the impossible. After his experience with the magic penny, bringing back the boating accident that had ruined Frank's life, his mind was reeling. He couldn't come to terms with anything, not his work or Mare or the past. Every night when he tried to sleep, he kept seeing Rusty's pale, frightened face sinking out of sight. Frank felt stranded, and the woman he needed to be there wasn't. His dark mood attracted comment in the newsroom, but it didn't improve. Everyone gave him a wide berth, even Malcolm.

The only solution, he finally decided, was to walk away from the mystery school. It led into too many weird and painful places. Maybe he still had a chance for a normal life.

"You couldn't at least answer my messages?" Frank asked.

Mare held up her hand to keep him from asking more questions. "Everything will be settled once the others are here."

Her calm tone was eerie. *You're not yourself,* he thought, staring at the woman who had been sharing his bed three nights ago. Just thinking about her, he felt the warmth of her skin.

"Why are you acting this way? You're treating me like a stranger."

"I care about you, but this isn't the time."

Mare looked deep into Frank's eyes, trying to communicate that he had nothing to be afraid of. It didn't work. He threw himself into a chair and pounded the table with his fist.

"You're leaving me. I knew it!" His hurt flared into anger. "And don't sell me some crap that it's more than us." He was already exhausted, and this outburst spent his last ounce of energy. Heaving a ragged sigh, he lowered his head in sorrow.

Maybe none of them will understand, Mare thought. *Even after all that's happened.*

She remembered that she had almost given up too. She didn't want to be a seer. Meg had replied, "Frankly, I'm disappointed," but Mare wasn't going to show that Frank had disappointed her. An invisible force had taken over, immense, powerful, beyond emotion. *The way being alone at sea must feel,* Mare thought, *when the wind has died and the moonless sky falls away to infinity.* Pure wonder pulled her away.

"You two don't look like happy campers."

Sunk in their own thoughts, they hadn't noticed Galen appear in the doorway. He was smirking, but he didn't follow up his remark with a jibe at Frank.

Not that it mattered. Frank was beyond caring. In a dull voice he said, "Take a seat, little guy. Mare's cooked us the last supper."

Warily Galen walked around the table and sat down away from Frank. "I don't get the joke."

"It's not a joke," Mare said. "This is our last meeting. Aren't you here to say you've had enough?"

Galen didn't ask how she knew. "I haven't made up my mind yet."

She smiled. "You have, but you wanted to shock the group. They won't be."

Now they heard footsteps in the corridor, and after a moment Lilith and Jimmy appeared. If they were about to say something, the tension in the room stopped them. The two newcomers exchanged glances and sat down at Mare's end of the table.

"You've all had a magical week," Mare said. "So have I. I went where I never imagined I could go. Coming back has been a hard adjustment. I don't know how to live in the normal world again."

Was she talking about the journeys they took with the golden shrine? Why her alone? The very fact that Mare had usurped Meg's place was baffling.

"I need details," Lilith said. "Did all this happen because of the magic penny?"

Before Mare could answer, Galen interrupted. "Wait, I was gypped." He reached into his pocket and produced his penny. "Mine only worked once."

"Stop," Lilith said irritably. "Your situation isn't on the table right now."

Frank spoke up. "I'm with Galen. Mine lost its juice too." Not that he sounded sorry.

"Stop!" Lilith repeated, louder this time.

"It's okay," Mare said. "The penny was only meant to work once."

"How do you know?" asked Jimmy. He was upset and voiced the question bothering all of them. "Where's Meg, anyway?"

"Mare's not saying," Frank grumbled. "She's the new quarter-back, and that's it."

No one was ready to believe this.

"You really should tell us what's happened," Lilith said, trying to sound reasonable. She took Jimmy's hand to reassure him, but she was hiding her own insecurity. It felt like the whole situation could unravel.

Mare surveyed their anxious faces. Reaching down, she found the canvas bag resting at her feet. She took out a hammer and rose to her feet. There was barely time for anyone to guess what she was about to do. With a swift, decisive motion she raised her arm and brought the hammer down hard. It struck the golden shrine in the center of the roof, midway between the four spires. With an agonized noise, halfway between a metallic screech and a groan, the roof imploded, and the walls of the miniature church crumpled.

"Oh, my God," Lilith whispered, horrified. The others were too stunned to speak. The shrine was their only link to another reality.

"All of you wanted out," Mare declared. "Now you're free."

"What are you talking about?" Jimmy exclaimed. None of them realized that they had all come to the same decision. Strong magic had touched them, and the aftershock was too much to bear.

"It was our choice," Lilith protested. "Who gave you the right to smash the shrine?" They waited for what Mare would say next.

"I found Meg in her hiding place," she began. "She has a big house on the other side of town. We talked, and then she took me on a journey, back to the disciple." She paused with a doubtful expression.

"And then what?" Galen snapped impatiently.

"I left her there."

It was an answer that told them something and nothing at the same time. Before the room could fill with questions, Mare continued. "Is it possible for someone to vanish into the past? That's what I'm telling you. Meg isn't dead; she didn't run away."

Frank interrupted before she could explain further. "It's all pointless. Meg started something, and now she's not here to see it through. That's what you're telling us." He got up with an exaggerated shrug of indifference. "Anyone who wants to join me in a beer, I'm buying."

"Wait, there's another way," said Mare. "It doesn't have to end like this."

"Meaning what?" Frank demanded, on the verge of turning belligerent. He made no move to sit back down again.

"Meg didn't bring the mystery school down," she said. "Smashing the shrine didn't either."

Jimmy looked forlorn. "It was us. We did it."

"No, it also wasn't you," Mare replied.

Everyone was quiet, waiting tensely. Instead of more explanation, Mare said, "It's time for one last journey. You don't have to go. You can walk out the door this minute, but if you do, the mystery school is over for you."

Jimmy pointed to the crumpled shrine. "How can we go anywhere? You let the disciple out."

"I don't think it's like Aladdin's lamp," Frank said drily.

"Maybe it is. You don't know," replied Jimmy defiantly.

"We can take this journey by ourselves, without the shrine," said Mare. "Trust me."

The group was confused. How could they trust someone who had barely participated in the past, who seemed to go along meekly with whatever Meg said? Mare hadn't explained her sudden change. They felt as if they barely knew her.

There might have been an argument, but Lilith, who sat closest to Mare at the end of the table, took her hand. "I'm willing." She gestured for the others. "One last time? It's only fitting."

They all knew what she meant. Traveling back to the time of the disciple was the one thing that bound them together. After a moment a circle was formed, with everyone holding hands. In the middle stood the golden shrine, smashed like a toy in the hands of a spoiled child throwing a tantrum. It gave off no radiance, but as Mare had promised, there was no need.

First they heard the screeching cry of seagulls, followed instantly by the glare of sunlight over the water. They were standing on the crest of a hill, with the ocean half a mile down below. Was it the coast of an island or the mainland? It was impossible to tell. The hill was crossed by a narrow footpath. A pair of gulls sat on tilted posts that were once part of a fence. They didn't fly away when the group appeared or even stare at them inquisitively.

"We're invisible," said Galen.

This they were used to, but the absence of human life was puzzling. It took a moment before there was any indication of people coming up the path, and then it wasn't foot travelers, but a litter being carried by two panting servants. At first a speck, the conveyance grew larger as it approached. The servants dripped with sweat; the headbands they wore couldn't keep it from streaming down their faces as they pushed their way up the hill.

The litter was brightly painted, and the wood finely carved with deer and foxes and other animals. Whoever rode inside was hidden from view by drawn curtains. A woman's voice spoke in Hebrew, sounding urgent.

"She's telling them to hurry. There's little time," said Mare.

"How do you know what she said?" asked Frank.

"I just do." Mare couldn't explain why she could suddenly understand a foreign tongue, but there was no time for discussion. "We have to follow them."

Once the litter crested the hill, the bearers carried their mistress faster. The group trailed behind under the bright hot sun. Even without a burden they began to sweat and pant.

The members of the mystery school followed for more than half an hour without saying a word. Around a bend blocked by a thick grove of trees, they suddenly spied their destination, a huddled collection of docks used by local fisherman.

The woman in the litter parted a curtain and peered out. She was gray-haired and aristocratic looking, although much of her face was wrapped in a white linen shawl pulled around her head. The shawl was covered in a thin layer of dust, implying that they had been traveling since morning. She barked an order, and the message was clear to everyone. "Faster!"

The bearers nodded, but were too exhausted to pick up the pace. One man was much older than the other. Perhaps they were father and son. Galen sank to the ground in the shade of the trees. Frank looked at him over his shoulder. "Don't quit on us," he said. Back in the meeting room he was ready to walk out, but now he was caught up in the adventure.

"Forgive me for not being young. My mistake," said Galen. He waved at the parting litter. "Let them go. They're dog-tired. We can catch up."

Frank might have tried to jerk Galen to his feet, but Mare said, "It's all right. We're all tired. Let's take a minute."

They gathered together, some sitting on the ground, others leaning against tree trunks. It was a relief to be out of the sun.

"As long as we're invisible," Jimmy said, "I wish we'd brought some invisible water."

"I know," said Mare, but her mind was on something else. "You saw who the old woman was, didn't you?"

"The disciple," said Lilith. Not that this was a surprise. "What has she been doing all these years?"

Lilith had studied about the early Christians, and she knew that women at first could preach in the churches alongside the men. Did the disciple do that? Or had she fled Jerusalem on an endless journey to escape the persecution that doomed the other disciples to violent deaths?

"Think about it," said Jimmy. "If we're here, somebody had to start the mystery school. It must have been her."

Mare nodded. Jimmy's reasoning was logical, but he'd missed something. She said, "There's a crisis. She's racing to find someone before he sails. Everything's at stake, for her and for us."

The group exchanged glances. Apparently this was another thing Mare just knew. To keep from being cross-examined, she got to her feet and started quickly down the path. Everyone followed. Galen, who could have used another ten minutes in the shade, brought up the rear. The walking was downhill, but they were drenched in sweat by the time they caught up with the litter, which was now less than a hundred yards from the water.

The two bearers showed signs of buckling, with the younger one muttering encouragement to the older. The disciple suddenly rapped on the roof of her compartment and jumped out almost before the bearers came to a stop. She ran the rest of the way to the water, kicking up dust with her slim lambskin sandals.

"Jonas, Jonas!" she called.

"Her son," Mare explained, running after her.

At the docks several fishing boats were moored, but only the largest, whose square-rigged sail was being raised by two sun-baked fishermen, was getting ready to depart. At first no one else was visible, and then from around the edge of the rising sailcloth a head appeared. The man was middle-aged, and as he stepped forward he frowned.

"He wanted to get away without facing her," said Mare.

The disciple stopped, her way blocked by the large scattered rocks on the shore. Mother and son faced each other silently for a moment before he barked an order to the fishermen, who stopped hauling up the sail. Looking angry, Jonas leaped from the prow of the boat into the water, not bothering with the rickety dock. He waded knee-deep until he reached the sand, then made his way to the disciple. Once he was close, she began to speak, not raising her voice but sounding very intense. There was an offshore breeze that carried her words out to sea; only some of it could be heard from where the group stood.

"She's begging him not to leave," said Mare.

"That's pretty obvious," Frank snapped. "What's the point? It's not like we can stop him."

Mare ignored this. "I need to get closer. You don't have to come if you don't want to."

With some reluctance they straggled behind her.

It was slow going to get nearer. The shore rocks were packed close together, inviting a twisted ankle if your foot slipped the wrong way. But they could see that the conversation was becoming heated. The disciple's son grew red in the face.

From inside his tunic, which was cinched at the waist, he pulled out a rolled parchment. One could see that he wasn't young, his hair already thinning, crow's feet around his eyes wrinkling as he squinted in the bright sunlight. He unrolled the scroll and started reading aloud. From the way he barely glanced at the writing, he must have had it memorized.

Mare wasn't close enough to catch what he was saying. The wind swallowed his words. But a voice in her head began to recite with him. Unbelievably, she knew the text from childhood.

> And behold a pale horse, and he that sat upon him, his
> name was Death, and hell followed him. And power
> was given to him over the four parts of the earth.

The thirteenth disciple looked distressed and tried to grab the scroll from his hands. Her son snatched it back, turned, and marched into the sea. It was shallow along the beach. He waded through the water until he reached the boat. The two fishermen leaned over the bow and pulled him up. The disciple's face filled with tears. She didn't wait for the sail to be raised, but picked her way back to her litter. The two bearers had come to her side by now and helped her over the rocks. They stumbled several times before reaching open ground.

Mare stood and watched them for a moment.

As vigorous as she had looked before, the disciple suddenly seemed very frail. She paused, as if sensing a presence. Her gaze met Mare's. Did she recognize her? It was impossible to tell, for a second later the old woman looked away.

Meg's not there, Mare thought. She felt a pang in her heart. At least it was good to know; Mare no longer had a reason to look back.

The two bearers exchanged worried glances as the disciple collapsed into the cushioned seat inside the litter. She was panting and had no strength to pull the curtains. They did it for her, then took their places front and back between the poles. The litter was lifted, and the bearers retraced their steps up the winding dusty path.

Mare regarded the fishing boat, which was now rigged and ready. One fisherman minded the rope line that tied the boat to the dock, the other sat at the tiller. The disciple's son, still scowling, said nothing. He held on to the mast as some strong swells moved in, rocking the craft. For a moment he seemed hesitant, but his resolve quickly returned. He nodded, the mooring was loosed, and the fisherman on the dock pushed the nose of the boat away before jumping in.

This was all Mare needed to see. "The disciple will never convince him," she told the others. "He thinks God has a message for him. There's a new cause, and he can't wait to join it." Her instinct made her certain of this, even if she couldn't explain why.

Now that the excitement was over, Galen's doubt wasn't going to be squelched. He swept his arm over the landscape. "We don't belong here. None of this fits anything."

"Would it fit if this was the island of Patmos?" asked Mare quietly.

A flicker of recognition lit in Lilith's face. "It's where St. John wrote the book of Revelation."

"So what?" asked Frank. "That's just a legend. There probably wasn't a St. John. The church needed a scare tactic to keep the sheep in line."

Mare pointed at the departing boat, which had caught the wind and was moving quickly with bellied sail. "He's sure the final days are near. It makes him feel incredibly strong. He's going to be one of the saved, and it infuriates him that his mother doesn't believe him."

At that moment they heard the unmistakable buzz of fluorescent lights, and instantly they were back in the meeting room, sitting in a circle with joined hands. It took a moment to get their bearings. Galen wore the same dissatisfied look that he wore by the sea.

"Her son may be an idiot and a fanatic," he declared. "But his side won."

Frank chimed in. "Absolutely. The crazies came up with a bizarre myth about the end of the world. He raced off to hear the last trumpet, and his kind are still packed and ready for doomsday. Armageddon has them pumped."

This was a harsh indictment, but no one contradicted it. After a moment, Jimmy weakly muttered, "I still believe."

"It's over," Galen shot back. "The disciple failed. Her own son wouldn't follow her. We were there, we saw it."

"We did see it," Mare acknowledged. "Now you have a send-off, which is what you wanted, isn't it?"

Her tone was cutting, something no one had ever heard from her. They stared as she stood up in front of the smashed shrine. "Fairy tales don't always have happy endings. So leave. If anybody wants to stay behind, I know the real ending."

"We're not stupid," Galen grumbled. "You're baiting the hook." There was general dissatisfaction, but none of them moved toward the door.

Mare waited to see that everyone really intended to stay. "The disciple didn't fail that day. What did we really see, one woman against the force of history? The odds against one woman would be impossible."

Lilith was the first to catch on. "So she had to find another way. She had to go around history if she wanted to beat the odds."

With a beatific smile, Mare spread out her arms. "She found a way. It's us."

They'd never heard her be sarcastic; it was much weirder to see her being grandiose.

"Careful," Lilith murmured.

But Mare had kept her secret too long; she was bursting to tell them everything. "It took forever, but I pieced it all together. Don't you see? Every piece of the puzzle fits."

Galen slouched back in his chair, arms folded across his chest. "I must be stupid, because I don't see anything."

"It's quite astounding," Mare said. "God was sending revelations, but the disciples became confused. They were constantly fighting over what the messages meant. But the thirteenth disciple caught on. Everything was about the light. When a vision of Armageddon appeared, it came from fear. The light never promotes fear. Once the whole thing was revealed to me, I got incredibly agitated. Did everything really come down to us five? There's no other explanation for why we were called. I was blown away. That's why none of you has seen me."

She shot Frank a significant look.

He glared back with hostility. "I'm sorry, but if it's your revelation against theirs, you can keep 'em both."

He jumped to his feet and made for the door. On the threshold he turned back, hoping to get a sign from Mare. Did she want him to go or stay? But she gave no sign. Her eyes glistened with the secret knowledge that wanted to be told.

Frank shook his head in disgust. "If you want to call me, it's okay. Just don't expect me to come running."

His footsteps clattered angrily in the corridor before fading away.

"And then there were four," said Galen mockingly.

Mare turned on him. "You want to be next?" She spat out the question.

He was abashed. "No. Who said I did?"

She didn't relent. "Stop sniping. It's either go or stay."

"Okay, okay." Galen took a breath. "If I hear you out, can I still leave?"

Mare nodded.

"Okay, then," he said, starting to feel secure again. "Shoot."

The air was vibrating with suspense now. Quietly Mare said, "It all revolved around Meg. I was the last one to see her. All of you deserve to know what happened."

She told them the story of Meg's last day, including the journey they took together and the ominous scene as Jerusalem was about to be torn apart. No one interrupted. When Mare was finished, though, each person had a different interpretation.

"You can't prove Meg is the disciple," Galen objected. "The house was empty when you came to. She might just be a spinster aunt who couldn't stay in one place."

"Maybe she was a spirit," said Jimmy.

"Or a saint," Lilith added.

Mare didn't try to convince them otherwise. For two days she had been agitated—she hadn't lied when she told the others that—but it wasn't the agitation of grief. When she found herself alone in the dark mansion, she went from room to room turning on the lights. She didn't call out Meg's name or expect to find her hiding under a bed. Her vanishing act, Mare knew, was final this time. Throwing open the curtains, snatching off the sheets that covered the furniture and pictures, Mare felt driven. The house needed to be filled with light, because she was.

The light inside her didn't burn, but it was incredibly intense and impossible to sustain for more than a few minutes. When she got to the main bedroom, Mare's energy was spent. She collapsed on the bed and immediately fell asleep even though the curtains were pulled open and the sun shone directly in. When she woke up, night had fallen. Normal reactions started to set in. Doubt about what had really happened. Anxiety about Meg and her strange fate. Disbelief that she would leave the house and a great sum of money to Mare. But when Mare rushed back to the kitchen, the legal papers were lying there on the butcher-block table, just where Meg had left them.

Now Mare looked at each face in the group. All the secrets had flown out of the cupboard, and she felt calm. "I'm not going to try and prove anything. We've shared the same journeys. You've formed your own version of events. Every version could be the truth, if it's true for you."

"No, it couldn't," Galen protested. "There are facts, and there are fantasies."

"You're forgetting faith," Jimmy said.

Lilith had nothing to say. She was the one whose dream had set everything in motion. Facts, fantasies, faith—who knows how they're woven into the tapestry of reality? In the end, she had no idea.

With a loud smack, Lilith slammed her hands on the table and stood up. "Meeting adjourned. I'm sure we all have places to go." No one could deny it. They made motions to leave.

"You're all welcome to come to Meg's house anytime you want," Mare said. "Even if the school is over, we need to keep in touch."

"Why?" Galen asked.

She smiled. "Because we're the same now."

"How can you say that? We argued all the time. We're still arguing."

"I know. But do you think anyone out there in the real world would believe a word of it? We're the only ones who understand."

"For now," said Jimmy, ever the optimist.

Somehow a group hug wasn't in the cards. They straggled out separately into the hospital parking lot, lit by yellowish halos from sodium streetlamps. Standing under one made a person's skin look zombified. Mare waited by the lamp closest to her car. She knew that Lilith would want to talk to her.

It took ten minutes before she appeared. She must have been turning everything over in her mind.

"So it was going to be you all the time. Who could have guessed?" she said.

"I'm sorry Meg didn't tell you good-bye," Mare replied.

Lilith shrugged. "It's just like her. It's her way of making me find her again. And I will, no matter how long it takes. You see, I get it now."

"You get what?"

"What Meg discovered years ago. Everything happens in the mind of God. The world, you and me, the march of history. It's all in the mind of God. Once you know that, nothing can stop you. It never stopped her."

A wave of emotion swept over them, and for the first time since her aunt disappeared, Mare began to cry. She brushed away the tears with the back of her hand.

"Doesn't this light make us look horrible?"

"Ghastly," Lilith said, managing to laugh. She turned away to go back to her car, and Mare got into hers.

The ride home was lonesome. In her mind's eye, Mare went around the table, singling out each one in turn. The light had turned them into something they could never have imagined, the souls they really were. Galen was a mental wizard. He could shut his eyes, make a wish, and reality obeyed his desire. Jimmy was a healer who could conquer death. Lilith became all-knowing, seeing through people's defenses like through glass. And Frank? He was a truth-teller, although his view was more obscured than the others. The light could only show them who they were; it couldn't force them to accept it.

It would take a while before any of them knocked on the thick oak door of Father Aloysius's mansion. Frank would be the last. Mare couldn't see where their relationship would go, but she knew his parting shot was wrong. He wanted to come running back. His wounded pride wouldn't let him. It was all right. Frank was more than his pride.

The empty mansion was just as it was the day Meg left. All the lights were on and the curtains wide open. Mare had stopped off at the supermarket. A person has to eat, as Meg reminded her.

"Quite right," Mare said to no one in particular.

She finished putting the groceries away. She'd bought roses— red ones this time—which had to be put in water. She climbed the stairs to the maids' quarters at the top of the house. She preferred sleeping there to the huge main bedroom and its ticking French clock smothered in gilded cherubs. Once the clock ran down, she wasn't going to wind it up again.

Father Aloysius had kept one maid in the house for the long periods he wasn't there. She'd left behind a neat, clean bedchamber under the dormer roof. Mare went inside and began to undress. When she pulled back the sheets, she saw a small envelope. *No package this time,* she thought.

She wasn't surprised, but her hands still trembled slightly as she opened the envelope and unfolded the note inside.

Dear Mare,

Don't waver. Be strong. There is only one thing to live by, and now you know it. "I am the way and the light and the life." Remember me.

Yours in Christ,
Meg

As Mare nodded off, the wind picked up outside, and the leaves of an ancient sycamore brushed lightly across the windowpane. It sounded soft and gentle, like the angel of mercy passing over the face of the earth.

Afterword:
The Mystery and You

If I've created any magic around the mystery school in this story, I hope readers are thinking, "Can I join?" Before writing the book, I had heard about mystery schools that still exist. Rumors floated around with the following contour: a friend of a friend (usually unnamed) was walking down the street of a major city (Los Angeles, New York, San Francisco), when a total stranger came up and said, "You are meant to be in a mystery school. I can tell by your aura. Accept now, or I walk away."

This snippet of a rumor became the starting point for a tale about ordinary people who become inducted into life-changing spiritual mysteries. I thought this was a perfect symbol of our time. We live in a secular society where mystery has been pushed to the fringes. It's not part of the official culture. Even the term "spiritual mystery" will annoy a wide spectrum of people—skeptics, rationalists, scientists, and many regular churchgoers. Yet their disapproval only makes the mystery more enticing.

My tale is fiction, but mystery schools are anything but. Whether they existed in ancient Greece or the Christian Middle Ages, mystery schools shared the same purpose: to enter the reality of God. God's reality, being invisible, isn't easy to enter.

What does it take? Here most, if not all, religions agree. It takes obedience to the rules of that particular religion. Do what you're told and a higher, divine reality will open up its gates. You will see God. Don't do what you're told, and access to God will be closed to you. (If your faith includes a vengeful God, you can also expect harsh punishment for your disobedience.)

The decline of faith in our time indicates that obedience is out of fashion. But spiritual yearning isn't. Let's imagine, then, that you are that friend of a friend who is approached by a perfect stranger and invited to join a mystery school. What happens next? How do you get from a street corner in Los Angeles or New York to God's reality? Clearly a path is implied, which means a process. Once you begin the process, there are obstacles and challenges. Some people will refuse to go forward—as the New Testament says, many are called, but few are chosen (Matt. 22:14). Those who survive the challenges and overcome the obstacles reach the goal. They are with God; they live in his light.

I can't tap you on the shoulder and invite you to join the school of the thirteenth disciple, but the path followed by Meg, Mare, Lilith, Galen, Frank, and Jimmy in the novel is open to you in reality. The process they undergo transformed them, and that process has been thoroughly mapped out in the world's wisdom traditions. In outline it's quite simple, in fact. The path from here to God looks like a "reality sandwich," as shown in the diagram below.

God's Reality = the Light

Transition Zone

Ordinary Reality = the Illusion

The bottom layer of the sandwich is the everyday reality we all inhabit, the world of the five senses, physical objects, and daily events. Being invisible, God doesn't appear in this reality (miracles, if they exist, are the exception). The top layer is God's reality, the realm of light, where "light" implies many things: truth, beauty, freedom from the darkness of pain and ignorance, and perfect love.

In between is some kind of transition zone. What is it like? The characters in our story find themselves in transition once they enter the mystery school and touch the golden shrine. They feel confused, but also enticed and intrigued. Galen, the rationalist, is awakened by love. Frank, the cynic, finds something of higher value to believe in. Jimmy, one of the socially downtrodden, finds in himself the spark of a healer. They each, in their own way, get a glimpse of the light, yet they also feel the pull to return to their normal lives. This push-pull motion is what the transition zone always feels like; spiritual growth comes with bewilderment.

Sri Aurobindo was one of the most educated twentieth-century gurus in India. He said that enlightenment would be easy if all it took was for people to be inspired. Truth isn't a hard sell. Children hearing about Jesus in Sunday school are inspired by a vision of heaven and the good shepherd gathering his flock. Even though the stories differ from culture to culture, with Krishna, Buddha, or Muhammad replacing Jesus as the spiritual ideal, there's a universal yearning to believe in a higher reality, which is what spiritual truth is about.

Where the problems arise, as Aurobindo also pointed out, is at the lower levels of life, where hard realities clash with inspiration. Peace is inspiring; violence is not. Gazing heavenward is inspiring; slogging through the mud isn't. Because the world is a place where we must confront violence, where slogging through the mud occupies far too much of daily existence, the transition zone between here and God is troublesome. Having entered it, our fictional characters encounter fear, anxiety, anger, confusion, sex, ambition, ego—the same things everyone in real life regularly encounters.

Joining a mystery school, then, is only a first step, a knock at the door. In the distance is the goal, which Meg states in her parting note to Mare: "I am the way and the light and the life." This is an intentional conflation of two of Jesus's most enduring statements—"I am the way and the truth and the life" (John 14:6), and "I am the light of the world" (8:12). In other words, the goal is a way of life that exists in the light of God.

Translating these words into a process, we can break it down into three components:

1. The way

2. The light

3. The life

With the way, you find a path that leads to God.

With the light, you begin to see the light of God.

With the life, you merge your present life with the life of God.

All three steps can be accomplished, and since "the way, the light, and the life" are familiar Christian terms in the West, we can stay with them while bringing in a few explanatory terms from other wisdom traditions.

THE WAY

Today finding the way to God is a do-it-yourself project. This is a radical change from the past, when the way to heaven was much more organized and collective, and yet a tiny band of outsiders—savants, saints, mystics, and visionaries—followed their own path. Today, the situation is reversed. Millions of people—modern-day seekers—crave spiritual growth on their own terms, which causes them to turn in many directions. This can't help but be bewildering, but all paths are about one thing: experience. Experiencing yourself getting closer to the goal is the only measure of success.

I can imagine a cooking school set up for people who, lacking taste buds, cannot taste anything, but I doubt it would stay in business very long. Having faith that your cooking is delicious is no substitute for actually tasting it yourself. What does it mean to taste God's reality? Such an experience is actually extremely common. God is defined as infinite joy, love, compassion, and peace. Everyone has experienced these things. But no one told us that these very experiences could be the first steps on the path to God.

The problem with any single experience, however beautiful, is that it fades away and is lost. It's as if Jesus said, "Knock and the door will be opened—for a few minutes." The reason people seek unconditional love, eternal peace, or lasting bliss is rooted in frustration with how fickle and temporary love, peace, and bliss seem. The reason even the most beautiful experiences last only a short while—maybe moments, maybe days or months—isn't mysterious. We move on. We are pulled down to earth by everyday realities: families to raise, jobs to pursue, groceries to buy. Someone once said, "Ecstasy is great, but I wouldn't want it around the house." The practicalities of life aren't compatible with higher reality.

That's why a path is necessary, to get from here to there. Trying to pencil in God when you have a spare moment doesn't work. Remembering the last time you felt love, peace, and bliss doesn't work either. The experience of God must happen in the present moment, and then, like pearls, the moments can be strung together into a necklace. Eventually, to continue the metaphor, the pearls turn into a continuous strand that has no end. Instead of God here and there, God is everywhere.

What makes this process, which is true spiritual growth, possible? To begin with, your brain. No experience exists without a brain to process it. A saint who sees God in every grain of sand exists on the same playing field as you or me when it comes to the brain. The difference is like an exquisitely fine-tuned radio that picks up the faintest signals and a radio filled with static that receives only the crudest signals. The better the receiver, the clearer the music.

When the Old Testament says, "Be still, and know that I am God" (Ps. 46:10), it is referring to a brain state. A brain that's restless, excited, distracted by the outside world, preoccupied with work, and so on—which pretty well describes the brain as you and I use it in everyday life—cannot be still. No matter how much faith you have that an FM station is broadcasting Mozart's beautiful music, if your radio can't pick up the signal, faith will be of little use.

What this means, in practical terms, is that the spiritual path is a positive lifestyle choice. The kind of lifestyle that fine-tunes the brain is far from mystical. It has five basic elements, which we can call the five pillars:

Sleep

Meditation

Movement

Food, air, and water

Emotions

These five pillars are basic for a balanced state of mind and body; therefore, they are basic for spiritual experience. Spiritual seekers, it turns out, must first pay attention to their well-being, and especially the well-being of the brain:

Good sleep keeps the brain alert and allows it to balance the entire mind-body system.

Meditation quiets the mind and trains the brain to operate at a very subtle level.

Movement keeps the system flexible and dynamic.

Pure food, air, and water nourish the system without impurities and toxins.

Emotions register joy, love, and bliss as personal experiences.

As you improve in each of these areas, your brain will shift, because you are giving it better input to work with. Your quality of experience, including spiritual experience, will improve. The five pillars work together to create a state of well-being, and it's this state that allows you to perceive finer signals from the source, which is God.

Kabir, a medieval mystical poet of India, who is beloved by people of all faiths, worked as a weaver. His view of spirituality rings with common sense, something I've appreciated since childhood. Here are two of his aphorisms:

Why run around sprinkling holy water?
There's an ocean inside you, and when you're ready
You'll drink.

A drop melting into the ocean—
That you can see.
The ocean melting into a drop—
Who sees that?

Linking the everyday with the sacred is critical. Kabir does just that through poetry. In another verse he says that he traveled to the sacred temples, bathed in the holy pools, and read the scriptures, but he found God in none of them. Only after he looked within did the divine reveal itself.

No great spiritual teacher has ever disagreed with him. What's been added in our day is that we now understand that "looking within" requires the use of a brain that's tuned to the subtle levels of experience where God is woven into the everyday. It isn't necessary to set aside holy places that work magic on the worshipper or to bathe in sacred waters or even to read scripture, although sacred writings do have their place—they offer inspiration, which is itself a subtle experience, the kind that points the way to the divine. These forces become amplified, so to speak, when your brain is trained to notice them.

THE LIGHT

No word is more important in the New Testament than "light." Even "love," the word that instantly comes to mind when thinking about Jesus, comes second. Once you realize that the light is a synonym for awareness, you understand that nothing is real unless we are aware of it. I'm sure you've heard someone say, "My father never told me that he loved me," which feels like a great loss. Silent love is love that creates doubt. You don't know if you can rely on it. You fear that it might not even be there. We're only human, and it takes hearing the words "I love you" to know for sure that we're actually loved.

Similarly, God has to enter your awareness in order to be real. Once the brain is attuned, the first step taken, the second step is focusing on the light. This is the only way to see past the illusion. In a movie theater, the romance, thrills, danger, and adventure on the screen are the illusion. The light that projects them is the reality. When Jesus tells his disciples, "You are the light of the world" (Matt. 5:14), we can accept him at his literal word. This is not a metaphor. Each of us is the light that projects the world.

You and I were born at the wrong time for this truth to sink in. Materialism rules. When I was twenty-something, I read Plato's famous "Allegory of the Cave," where he compares ordinary life to people huddled in a cave watching shadows play on the wall. They mistake the shadows for reality and can only awaken if they turn around to see the light that's projecting them. I knew what the image meant, but it made no difference to me. I firmly believed in the physical world and knew no one who didn't. The allegory can be updated. Instead of a cave, the audience can be seated in a Cineplex entranced by Hollywood glamour on the screen, unaware that a projector sits behind them, casting the illusion through incandescent white light.

It's still a huge leap to believe that the entire world is a projection, and an even bigger leap to realize that you are watching the movie and projecting it at the same time. Magicians don't believe in their illusions, after all. Apparently we do. We are gullible magicians. When you can separate the two roles, everything changes. Instead of loving the illusion, you become fascinated by the creator, which is yourself. Only a creator has enough freedom to alter creation.

We pay a high price for being gullible magicians. We feel imprisoned in daily life by anxiety, fear, limited opportunities, financial strain, and unfulfilling relationships, and since we don't accept these as our own creation, our immediate response is to struggle with the outer picture. We try to upgrade the illusion, which is possible to do, of course. You can see a doctor for your anxiety, find a better paying job, and walk away from an unloving relationship.

No matter how successful you are in upgrading the illusion, however, you will never be free of it. The rich buy into their movie as much as the poor. The well-loved feel as bereft as the unloved when the person who loves them goes away. The illusion is the level of the problem. The light is the level of the solution, in fact of all solutions, which is why Jesus said, "Seek first the kingdom of God, which is within you" (Matt. 6:33; Luke 17:21).

But going within is exactly what most people dislike and even fear, because it is "in here" where anxiety, insecurity, past traumas, and old conditioning reside. So the mind is called on to heal the mind. How is that accomplished? The answer is obvious, though it is too often overlooked. If you want to escape the illusion, stop creating it.

How? Refuse the story told by false consciousness. False consciousness says, "Get with the program. The world is a hard place. The universe is vast. The forces of nature are fixed. You are a speck in this infinitely huge scene." When all of society is based on such a story, as our age certainly is, dismantling it means shifting into a completely new worldview.

The world's wisdom traditions tell a different story, which I've encapsulated in Jesus's statement: "You are the light of the world." Identify with the light, and you will never again fear the enticing images on the movie screen, even when they are projected eighty feet high.

False consciousness is a net woven from many strands, the most critical being your core beliefs. Among the most destructive of these beliefs are the following:

I'm alone and isolated, disconnected from the universe.

I'm weak and powerless compared with the huge forces arrayed against me.

My life is bounded by this package of skin and bones called the body.

I exist in linear time, which squeezes my being into the short span between birth and death.

I'm not in control of my life.

My choices are limited by my circumstances.

I will experience love in very temporary, imperfect ways that can't be counted on.

Life is unfair and events are random—these are the hard realities.

The best way to deal with my insecurity and anxiety is to push them down out of sight.

If people knew the real me, they'd be repelled.

I have a right to blame others as much as or more than I blame myself.

God may be real, but he's not paying any attention to me.

This is quite a long list, because illusion affects every aspect of life. If you had to overcome every belief on the list, a lifetime wouldn't be enough, and in the end there would be no guarantee of success. I'm only underlining the point that the level of the problem isn't the level of the solution.

The level of the solution is awareness, the "light." Much of Jesus's teaching can be interpreted as pointing to this solution. That's what the characters learn in this book. The golden shrine literally gives off celestial light. Jesus sees the Shekinah, the light of the soul, when the thirteenth disciple approaches down a dark alley. When Galen makes a wish and Malcolm hasn't lost his job, he is manipulating a movie that everyone else accepts as reality. The magic sunglasses are symbolic of the new vision that alters their view of reality. I've magnified the effect by using magical realism. A brilliant show is nice, but the spiritual path has only one aim: to realize who you really are.

If you could see your true self, the more obscure parts of the New Testament would become clear, even self-evident. This especially applies to the portions of the Sermon on the Mount where Jesus tells his audience to do the following (Matt. 6:25–33; 5:5):

Rely on Providence for everything.

Don't plan for the future.

Don't worry about tomorrow. Let every day's problems take care of themselves.

Don't store up treasure, not even food.

Be assured that the meek will one day have all the power.

None of this advice, though, is realistic as a way to conduct daily life, and therefore Christianity has joined other idealistic faiths that hold out the impossible as a promise from God. There is a schism between the ideal and the real, succinctly captured in the Arabic proverb (which might be someone's clever invention), "Trust in God, but tie up your camel."

Many of Jesus's other teachings are impossible, from loving your neighbor as yourself to turning the other cheek. What makes them impossible isn't a flaw in Jesus's wisdom—it's in our own level of awareness. When we don't see ourselves as pure light, the creators and authors of our own existence, we can't access any of the ideals of the world's wisdom traditions. Buddha's pure detachment, the cure for pain and suffering, for instance, is just as removed from real life as Jesus's teaching of universal love. Islam's ideal of divine peace descending to earth, which is embedded in its very name, is unattainable in a violent world.

Nothing short of complete transformation will make the ideal a living reality. So confronting the illusion of false consciousness is the key to every problem, if what we want is a permanent, lasting solution. The true self isn't something you create, work toward, or have faith in. It's a reality that hides in plain sight.

In a movie theater, the projector is hiding in plain sight too; the pictures it creates are an enticing distraction that prevents us from turning around. I deliberately describe Meg's vision of the Crucifixion as feeling like a movie, to set the stage for her ten-year journey into the light. She's as bewildered as the rest of us, but she comes through.

Let's assume that you are leading the kind of life that gives your brain a chance to absorb new input at a subtler level, which I've called "the way." What is your brain supposed to notice? At first, it will notice occasional glimpses of the true self, and when that happens, there will be moments when the illusion falls away. These are unpredictable, because every life is unique, but we can say that in such moments a piece of false belief is exposed. Returning to the long list above, we can—and do—experience the reverse of each false belief. True belief rests on personal experience. So how does it feel to be in this light? The experience is profoundly different from everyday existence:

You feel connected to everything around you.

The forces of nature support you.

Your body extends beyond its visible boundaries, as if it is seamlessly connected to everything.

You experience the timeless, which removes the fear of death.

You feel in control, without effort or struggle.

You feel free. Your choices expand, despite the limitations of your present circumstances.

You experience love as an innate part of life, not something to be won or lost.

Events that once seemed random or unfair now begin to fit into a pattern that makes sense and contains meaning.

You feel secure in yourself, and this allows you to confront negative emotions, past hurts, and outworn conditioning.

There is increasing harmony with other people.

You feel a sense of acceptance that makes blame and guilt pointless.

God feels real and close by.

The characters in the story experience these shifts, and I'd like to emphasize that this part isn't fantasy—quite the opposite. Shorn of imagery, what happens to the characters has happened to me personally. I mean both sides, dark and light. My first moment of despair occurred when I spent a joyous day at the movies with my grandfather, only to have him die that very night. My deepest cynicism occurred in medical school, where nothing seemed more real than suffering and death—God was an illusion to be mocked. My experiences in the light were moments of awakened awareness in meditation, and these began to illuminate the most ordinary experiences—looking out a train window on the Northeast corridor and feeling that the drab industrial landscape stretched to infinity, catching the glance of a passing stranger and seeing in it the salute of another soul.

Every life contains moments when a person sees beyond the illusion. The secret is to pay attention, because once the moment is gone, so is its power to change you. You must be open and alert to signals from your true self.

What this takes is a kind of second attention. First attention, which we're all familiar with, deals with the events in daily life.

You eat breakfast, go to work, pick up groceries, watch TV. None of this has intrinsic meaning. It can be good, bad, or neutral. When second attention enters, you keep doing the same things you always did, but you are aware of them in a new way. Eating breakfast, you might be aware of your inner contentment, or of the food's subtle tastes, or of gratitude for nature's abundance. Going to work, you may feel inner satisfaction, excitement about new possibilities, or empowerment. There is often no neat match between what first attention is noticing and what second attention is realizing.

But there is a common thread to everything in second attention. You are glimpsing the truth of who you are. You are an unbounded field of infinite possibilities. You are infinite consciousness manifesting in space-time. You are the play of light as it shapes itself into forms. There is no arena for realizing these things except normal everyday life. Like a moviegoer turned halfway to the screen and halfway to the projector, you can appreciate the movie (first attention) while knowing all the while that it's a projection of light (second attention).

You can go on the Internet and find countless first-person accounts of experiences that derive from second attention. These stories narrate what happens when the illusion, the mask of materialism, falls away. Some of these stories appear to be exotic, as when people go out of body, view remote events, have foreknowledge of the future, or pop into enlightenment. But the focus shouldn't be on the supernatural, because second attention is completely natural, and "going into the light" happens here and now, not just in near-death experiences.

The more often you notice what's happening to you through second attention, the more you train your brain to go toward this direction. "Light" is a metaphor; awareness is how we exist—nothing is more real. Research into higher states of consciousness keeps growing, although most of the focus has been on disproving the skeptics by showing with solid data that the paranormal is real. It will be far more useful to have research on how consciousness expands, because as it does, there's a natural progression:

Physical: Your body feels less bounded and limited. There's a sense of lightness, along with the pleasant sensation of simple physical presence. Almost without noticing it, you experience your body as merged with everything around you.

Mental: Your thoughts become fewer as your mind quiets down of its own accord. The mind is no longer restless or scattered. It becomes easy to focus your attention; distractions don't affect you as much. The past doesn't intrude on the present. Old conditioning, which makes you stuck in unwanted habits, loosens its grip.

Psychological: You feel less constricted. Negative emotions like anxiety and hostility start to lessen. The whole emotional landscape is less dramatic—mood swings and depression, for example, are less likely. Your sense of who you are is no longer a source of doubt and insecurity. You find it possible to live in the present moment.

Spiritual: Whatever your spiritual beliefs happen to be, they start to become validated. You experience whatever your conception of God is, or isn't. There doesn't have to be a personal God whose presence is felt. You may experience unbounded inner freedom instead, or unconditional love, or compassion for all living things. The common element, however, is expanded awareness, which allows for experiences of transcendence. This "going beyond" opens up levels of reality that first attention cannot attain.

THE LIFE

Since we are approaching this in stages, let's say that you have taken the first two steps. You've found a way to live that makes your brain capable of subtle experience, and you've learned to apply second attention, which reveals the light as the essence of everything. If these two steps are in place, an inner transformation begins. You are being ushered into "the life." For countless people, life is the opposite of death, but here life means eternal unbounded existence. Jesus promises eternal life, and he is continually taken literally by the Christian faithful. Fundamentalists, for instance, believe heaven is a physical destination; on Judgment Day, their bodies will rise from the grave and join Christ somewhere above the clouds.

When I consulted the *Catholic Encyclopedia* online, the entry under "heaven" explicitly states that it isn't a physical place, but a state of being attained through grace. A picture of green meadows with blue skies, baby animals, and children at play is the most common image of heaven that people bring back from near-death experiences, and so we must face the fact that heaven as a nonplace isn't easy to accept. How do we go about it?

One opening comes from Erwin Schrödinger, one of the most brilliant pioneers in quantum physics, who turned his attention later in life to consciousness and its possibilities. Schrödinger said something very revealing about time: "For eternally and always there is only now, one and the same now; the present is the only thing that has no end."

This is a new definition of eternal life, which exists in the present moment. What makes the new eternal is that it is endlessly renewing itself. We can go farther and say that God (or the soul or grace) can only be encountered in the present moment. Finding eternal life in the present moment is the ultimate challenge. Looking at your own life, what happens from moment to moment? A great many things, which we can arrange vertically, one on top of the other, like layers in an archaeological dig or noodles in a pan of lasagna. Every present moment contains seven layers. The first three are visible; those below the dividing line are buried out of sight:

An event "out there" in the physical world
The sights and sounds of the event
A mental reaction

The opening of a new possibility
A level of quiet untouched by the outer event
Pure awareness
Pure Being

It's quite astonishing that you can answer the phone, decide to take a vacation, or catch a chance remark in an elevator, and far beneath the surface of this experience a hidden world is waiting to be revealed. In our story, Galen and Frank don't want to lift the rug, so to speak, to see what lies beneath. Lilith and Meg are the opposite. They were born to dive deep into their own consciousness. But all the characters are eventually pulled deeper and deeper.

You can take a knife and slice through all the layers of a chocolate cake at once, but most people experience the present moment only in the top two or three layers of their awareness. The deeper layers are unconscious.

They are the province of second attention. This is where Jesus was pointing when he said that the kingdom of heaven is within. The reason that we go within but don't find heaven is that our awareness is confined to the upper layers of experience. This can—and does—change as awareness expands.

Some examples will help. Imagine that you see a child starting to cross the street as you are driving. You stop to let the child go across, and then you move on. The event is superficial. If it is your own child you see, there's a deeper response. You care more about the child's welfare. There are moments when the sight of your child brings a wave of love—now your experience is starting to dip below the line. Something more profound, love, has entered. Can you go deeper? There may be a moment when you experience love for all children and compassion for all those in need. This may lead to a sense that you are connected to all of humanity. By going deeper and deeper, the same simple experience—the sight of a child—acquires new meaning.

Now comes the crucial challenge. Can you catch a glimpse of yourself in the mirror and see your true self? This is the challenge Jesus posed. He wanted his followers to see themselves in the light of love and compassion and then of all of humanity. Such an experience dives far under the line that divides everyday experience from what we call spiritual experience. If you can take a look at yourself as Jesus asked, you are seeing with the eyes of the soul.

One can also call it a journey into pure Being. For me, the greatest spiritual mystery is that existence *is* God. Every other secret springs from this one. If you allow your mind to find its source in silence, simply resting into existence, the simple state of being here is enough. The voice of the soul is silent. Yet as you attune yourself, you find that there is enormous power at the source, because silent awareness is the womb of love, creativity, intelligence, and organizing power. Invisible forces uphold your life. All of creation, including everything in the universe, is projected from the Godhead, which is found inside you.

As mystical as this may sound, it is grounded in ancient wisdom and modern science. In their teachings on higher consciousness, the world's wisdom traditions draw a flowchart of creation that's very different from the one in the book of Genesis and yet still compatible with it. In Genesis, God is the uncreated. He exists outside time and space, with no need for anyone to create him, because he is eternal.

In this precreated state, there is nothing but emptiness, a formless void. What emerges in the metaphorical seven days are time, space, physical objects, worlds, and life. Living things take on the qualities of their Creator, who is alive, sentient, and—by definition—creative. This flowchart, which moves from nothing to something, from a state of possibilities into a state of manifestation, fits the scheme of quantum physics very neatly. Before the big bang, according to physicists, the precreated state was outside space-time, but contained the potential for everything that has emerged since the big bang. It's rather like pointing out that Einstein's mind contained the potential for great thoughts before they were expressed.

What's astonishing is that the entire flowchart of creation exists in the present moment. In the world "out there," every physical object consists of atoms that are made of subatomic particles. These, in turn, are formed from energy states, and energy states are constantly bubbling up in the quantum foam, as it's called.

Similarly, the flowchart "in here" produces thoughts, sensations, images, and feelings: from the potential of silent mind, faint stirrings of consciousness move upward, then take shape as they emerge into the active mind. Note that the flow moves from the bottom up. Being comes first (the ground state, with no apparent activity). Then the mind becomes aware of itself as silence. Self-awareness is alert; it wants to engage with life. So it creates a new possibility, and from there comes the constant activity we call the stream of consciousness.

Can a person live in the eternal now? Yes, but only when awareness is expanded enough to embrace all the layers of the mind, right down to its source. All the beautiful truths expressed by the great spiritual teachers have gotten obscured by hoping and wishing that they are real, when what's needed is actually simple and natural: the expansion of consciousness. For me, that's the secret to the New Testament. It's a manual for higher consciousness, and Jesus, in his clarity of mind, knew precisely what it means to live in the highest state of consciousness where "I and the Father are one" (John 10:30). I have opened the New Testament at random, spotted a famous passage, and immediately felt a wave of Being emanate from the page.

What is happening is an experience of the eternal now, because an ordinary moment in my day is suddenly filled with light. If only people didn't place spirituality into a compartment marked "mystical." The only portal to God is the door opened by the present moment. That's why Mare learns a profound truth when she realizes that either nothing is a miracle or everything is a miracle. Actually, both are true. Nothing is a miracle when you see the world through first attention; everything is a miracle when you see it through second attention. You are in a position to make your life miraculous, then, simply by the kind of attention you pay to it.

In the end, this book comes down to something simple. It's an invitation to make the right choice, just as the characters in the story were invited to. In a moment of choosing, the process of transformation can begin, and once it does, you have taken the first and most important step into God's reality.

It would be fitting to give the last word to a poet. Kabir takes us to the place where God has always been:

> He is the tree, the fruit, and the shade
> He is the sun, the light, and the dream
> The word and its meaning
> A point in the All
> Form in the formless
> Infinity in a void.

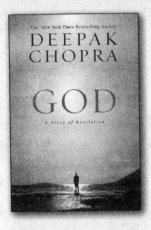
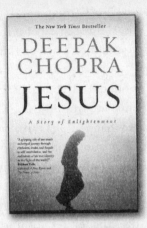
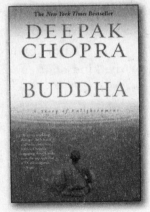
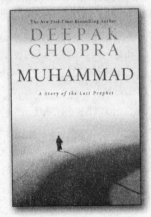